Prose That Works

Prose That Works

Suzanne S. Webb

Texas Woman's University

Harcourt Brace Jovanovich, Inc.

New York   San Diego   Chicago   San Francisco   Atlanta
London   Sydney   Toronto

ISBN: 0-15-597882-9
Library of Congress Catalog Card Number: 81-85548

Printed in the United States of America

Copyrights and Acknowledgments
For permission to use the selections reprinted in this book, the author is grateful to
the following publishers and copyright holders.

(continued on page 275)

PREFACE

Prose That Works offers the student a new way of looking at writing. Traditionally, students have viewed writing as a task they will perform only in an academic setting. Perhaps they have come to this conclusion because instructors have required them to read and write essays that primarily recount personal experience, express the writer's opinions or feelings, or take argumentative stands on controversial public issues. But students today—and some of their instructors—are also concerned with acquiring knowledge and skills that will serve them outside the English classroom—in courses in other disciplines and, eventually, on the job. What is needed, therefore, is a book that presents the kinds of writing students are likely to do not only in college but later in their careers—a book that shows them that writing is important in the world of work as well as in the English classroom.

This book contains thirty-nine selections, half drawn from the world of belles-lettres and half from the world of work. The selections from the working world come from two sources: about half of them are from professional or trade publications; the remainder are previously unpublished examples of writing actually done on the job. These on-the-job pieces should be particularly valuable in demonstrating to students the rhetorical similarities between writing done in the classroom and writing done at work. And because the unpublished examples represent a variety of writing styles, ranging from the utilitarian to the relatively polished, they can help motivate students to develop sound rhetorical techniques for presenting their own ideas clearly and convincingly.

The essays taken from trade and professional publications show how workaday writing often exhibits the rhetorical and stylistic characteristics we usually expect from more literary essays. Students can observe in these selections the writers' attention to rhetorical forms, clear and economical use of language, and choice of diction appropriate to their audience. Finally, in teaching the more traditional essays, the instructor can offer examples of the truly excellent and encourage students to emulate the work not only of a professional writer like E. B. White but of writers like Richard Selzer, a physician, or Raymond Wittcoff, an urban planner. In short, the diversity of the selections is meant to give students a more realistic picture of writing than they are usually exposed to.

Prose That Works is traditional in organization, presenting the rhetorical modes of development commonly included in anthologies intended for writing courses and arranging the selections according to these modes. Short introductory sections describe each mode and discuss the techniques ordinarily used in employing it. The introductory material also offers specific suggestions for student writing and points out potential problems. Selections that illustrate each mode follow the introductions. Both literary and workaday examples are provided for each mode of development.

Each selection is preceded by a brief headnote that explains how the rhetorical technique is used in the work and provides guidelines for students to keep in mind as they read the selection. Following each selection are short questions that help students analyze the ways in which the writer has applied the rhetorical technique. From time to time these questions include suggestions that students revise the selection, or compose a similar piece of their own. Unfamiliar terms and concepts in the selections are explained in footnotes. Although occasional correspondences in content are pointed out, it has not been the purpose of this book to present a group of selections on a single topic.

The labor of compiling this anthology has been considerably lessened by the cooperation and support of a number of people. I particularly appreciate the help I received from three members of Harcourt Brace Jovanovich: the unflagging encouragement and dry wit of Matt Milan, Carolyn Johnson's wise and energetic blue pencil, and Tom Hall's expertise with rubber cement. Arthur Pfeffer, formerly of the Police Management Writing Project of the New York City Police Department, John Blodgett of the Congressional Research Service, and Joe Dillingham and Bonnie Dauphine of Communication Support Services all spent time and effort helping me locate examples of writing; my colleagues Vivian Casper and Dean Bishop cheerfully criticized the manuscript for me; and Laurie Hammett typed it with her usual speed and accuracy. But most of all, my appreciation goes to Dick and Aaron for their tolerance and forbearance.

Suzanne S. Webb

CONTENTS

Preface   v

Part 1 Narration

An Evolution for Ocean Basins *by John McPhee*   5
Once Upon a Time *by Jean Stafford*   11
Are Children People? *by Phyllis McGinley*   17
Crocodile Rock *by Craig Horowitz*   25
Monthly Activity Report—March, April, May *by Keith Morgan*   31

Part 2 Process Analysis

How Waves Are Formed *by Rachel Carson*   41
The Future of Cities *by Raymond H. Wittcoff*   45
Sun to Breathe New Life into Old Reservoir *by W. B. Bleakley*   57
Shopping Center Survey: Dallas Metroplex 1980 *by Herbert D.
    Weitzman, Sam G. Kartalis, and Kenneth H. Orr*   63
Perspective on McDonnell Douglas Programs in Energy Systems
    by K. P. Johnson   77

Part 3 Cause and Effect

Recipe for an Ocean *by Isaac Asimov*   87
Three Mile Island and the Failure of the Nuclear Power Industry
    by Barry Commoner   93
Illuminating Some Obfuscation About Pesticide Safety
    by Keith C. Barrons   99
Right to Counsel *by William Calhoun*   105

Part 4 Description

The Praying Mantis *by Annie Dillard*   111
On Going Home *by Joan Didion*   117
How to Get Your Money's Worth from Your Doctor
    by Mike Oppenheim   121
Fluid Inclusion Research: An Informal Proposal
    by Roger Kolvoord   129

Part 5 Definition

Work, Labor, and Play *by W. H. Auden*   139
Why I Want a Wife *by Judy Syfers*   143
The Third Most Powerful Man in the World *by Norman Cousins*   147
Shipboard Electrical Safety Program *by Don C. LaForce*   151

Part 6 Classification

Can People Be Judged by Their Appearance? *by Eric Berne*   161
The Roots of Serendipity *by James Austin*   163
Artistic Research Tools for Scientific Minds *by George W. Ladd*   171
Fiber Facts *by Marvin Segal*   187

Part 7 Comparison

Dallas *by Larry McMurtry*   195
Computers *by Lewis Thomas*   199
Education—March 1939 *by E. B. White*   203

The Japanese Brain *by Atuhiro Sibatani*   207
Real Cops, Not "Reel" Cops *by Joseph Wilson*   213

Part 8 Argument

Capital Punishment *by William F. Buckley*   221
Smoking *by Richard Selzer*   225
Two Aspects of Scientific Responsibility *by John T. Edsall*   229
Pollution Control Strategies: Regulatory Problems?
   by John E. Blodgett   239

Part 9 Exemplification

The Peter Principle *by Raymond Hull*   249
Truth and Consequences *by Nora Ephron*   255
Complexity and Pomposity—Mostly Complexity *by John O'Hayre*   261
Nursing Communication: Nurse's Notes and Accurate Diagnosis
   by Carolyn M. Bell   269

NARRATION

Used constantly in daily conversation and in ordinary and extraordinary acts of writing, *narration* is a rhetorical form that most people recognize. However, much of this recognition is unconscious; many people do not fully understand what narrative is, who uses it, why they use it, or where it works best. A rhetorician might define narration as one of the four forms of discourse, or as one of the *topoi* of classical rhetoric described by Aristotle, but people who are neither professional writers nor rhetoricians usually want a more pragmatic explanation.

In practical terms, narration is simply an efficient and effective way of organizing the telling of events. Usually, it presents events as nearly as possible in the order in which they occurred or might occur. It also presents each event so that it appears to develop out of the event preceding it. Narration is, therefore, cumulative and, to a certain extent, suspenseful. Along with these qualities, many narratives contain conflict. The narrator in conflict with himself may narrate events to express personal feelings; the narrator in conflict with someone else may narrate events to explain his own position.

As the selections in this section will show, writers of fiction, essayists, and journalists all use narration. John McPhee uses narration in an essay on geology; Phyllis McGinley uses narration in an essay on the raising of children; Jean Stafford uses it in an account of her battles with a utility company; and Craig Horowitz, a journalist, uses narration to explain the origin of a fashion symbol. Moreover, as the selection by the engineer Keith Morgan illustrates, people who are not professional writers also use narration, often in the course of their jobs—for example, in reports to supervisors or to customers. Indeed, most of us use narration every day in letting other people know what has happened and what we are doing or are about to do. If you write letters to your friends and family, you undoubtedly make use of narration.

Four main purposes are associated with the use of narrative form: to explain something, to illustrate a point, to provide evidence, and to report events. The explanatory, or expository, use of narration and the illustrative use of narration both lead to a more detailed understanding of a situation; they are primarily analytical. Narration used to provide evidence or to report events is mainly cumulative. These purposes often interrelate and overlap. For example, the main purpose of a newspaper article may be to report certain events, but at the same time the journalist may want the reader to understand the importance of these events and perhaps be persuaded to adopt certain attitudes or take certain actions.

Before any type of narration is begun, a writer must decide which of the four purposes is his goal, and he must determine who he wants to communicate with—that is, who the desired audience is. An engineer who reports to his supervisor about events that led to the failure of an intricate machine must analyze not only who the immediate audience is—his supervisor—but also who his ultimate audience may be—perhaps a division manager or a regulatory agency. Once he has determined his audience, the writer of the report must analyze his purpose in presenting the events. Is he attempting to place responsibility, or is he attempting to show that the failure was unavoidable? His selection of narrative details will be dictated by both his analysis of audience and his determination of purpose. If he does not do both of these properly, misunderstanding and waste of effort could result. Several months before the nuclear accident at Three Mile Island, an engineer at the installation wrote a memo that narrated the ominous sequence of events that was possible if a particular part of the system happened to fail. However, the memo was not addressed to the person who had direct responsibility for that part of the system. Further, although correctly analyzed in regard to nuclear technology, the events the engineer predicted were presented in such a way that his main purpose, to warn the management of a possible accident, was not clear. As a result, the information did not get the attention it deserved. That bright engineer who discovered the potential problem might have been more successful in averting a nuclear accident had he known more about audience evaluation and the achievement of purpose in writing.

To use narrative effectively, then, we must put events in a logical sequence that reveals the main reason for telling them. In doing so, we can choose among several organizational strategies. The most common of these is the chronological approach, the presentation of significant events in the order in which they did or could occur. A second approach, the flashback, focuses directly on a single event but takes a look back at events which preceded it. However, if we choose to use the flashback technique, we need to have good reasons for doing so. The overriding importance of a single event in a sequence might be a good justification for using flashbacks. We could also use a psychological ordering of ideas that is a variation of the flashback technique. This is what the engineer at Three Mile Island might have done: describe the failure potential of the valve first, and then present the scenario that would end in such a failure. In any case, we must be careful to select only those events that are directly related to our purpose; those that are not relevant should be excluded, no matter how interesting they are in themselves.

Finally, in structuring your narratives, you will want to ask yourself five questions: Who is involved in the event (agent)? When did the event occur (time)? Where did the event happen (place)? What happened (action)? And why did it happen (cause and effect)? Elements one, two, and three all belong in the introduction. Element four forms the body of the narrative, and the fifth element works well in the conclusion if you are using a strict chronological progression. In a flashback the fifth element might come first, accompanied by a single important event; the others would follow.

An Evolution for Ocean Basins

John McPhee

John McPhee, a professional writer educated at Princeton and Cambridge universities, is the author of over a dozen books on a variety of subjects, including geology, botany, nuclear regulation, and tennis. He has also written for television and taught a course in the literature of fact at Princeton. McPhee is currently a staff writer for The New Yorker.

The following selection is a chapter from Basin and Range *in which McPhee treats a complex scientific subject in an unusual way. Rather than trying to explain the mechanics of the sea floor as a process, he makes the main focus of the chapter an account of how a particular theory on the subject was developed. Demonstrating that the main rhetorical technique used is narration, the chronologically organized tale relates the events that led to the discovery of the theory. Our understanding of the process develops out of the details that McPhee uses to support his narrative.*

Notice that the essay begins with an account of scientist Harry Hess's activities during the Second World War. McPhee explains that the technology provided by the government and the opportunity provided by the war set in motion a vital sequence of events that extended into the 1960s. Linking subsequent events in the development of the theory to Hess's initial work, McPhee shows us what happens on the sea floor by relating how each new discovery was made and integrated with existing knowledge. He concludes the chapter with a dramatic anecdote about how even the skeptical Russian geologists were eventually convinced of the validity of Hess's theory.

The level of diction and the avoidance of jargon in McPhee's chapter indicate that it is directed at an audience with little or no understanding of structural geology. The average college-educated person can understand the essay with little difficulty, but even the specialist can read it with interest and without finding gross oversimplifications. McPhee has accomplished the very difficult feat of making technical information clear to the reader who lacks specialized training, while managing to keep the interest of the specialist. He has written clearly and simply about a specialized and complex subject.

It was on the mechanics of the seafloor that geology's revolutionary inquiries were primarily focussed in the early days. Harry Hess, a mineralogist who taught at Princeton, was the skipper of an attack transport during the Second World War, and he carried troops to landings—against the furious defenses of Iwo Jima, for example, and through rockets off the beaches of Lingayen Gulf. Loud noises above the surface scarcely distracted him. He had brought along a new kind of instrument called Fathometer, and, battle or no battle, he never turned it off. Its stylus was drawing pictures of the floor of the sea. Among the many things he discerned there were dead volcanoes, spread out around the Pacific bottom like Hershey's Kisses on a tray. They had the arresting feature that their tops had been cut off, evidently the work of waves. Most of them were covered with thousands of feet of water. He did not know what to make of them. He named them guyots, for a nineteenth-century geologist at Princeton, and sailed on.

The Second World War was a technological Piñata, and, with their new Fathometers and proton-precession magnetometers, oceanographers of the nineteen-fifties—most notably Bruce Heezen and Marie Tharp at Columbia University—mapped the seafloor in such extraordinary detail that in a sense they were seeing it for the first time. (Today, the very best maps are classified, because they reveal the places where submarines hide.) What stood out even more prominently than the deep trenches were mountain ranges that rose some six thousand feet above the general seafloor and ran like seams through every ocean and all around the globe. They became known as rises, or ridges—the Mid-Atlantic Ridge, the Southeast Indian Ocean Ridge, the East Pacific Rise. They fell away gently from their central ridgelines, and the slopes extended outward hundreds of miles, to the edges of abyssal plains—the Hatteras Abyssal Plain, the Demerara Abyssal Plain, the Tasman Abyssal Plain. Right down the spines of the most of the submarine cordilleras ran high axial valleys, grooves that marked the summit line. These eventually came to be regarded as rift valleys, for they proved to be the boundaries between separating plates. As early as 1956, oceanographers at Columbia had assembled seismological data suggesting that a remarkable percentage of all earthquakes were occurring in the mid-ocean rifts—a finding that was supported, and then some, after a worldwide system of more than a hundred seismological monitoring stations was established in anticipation of the nuclear-test-ban treaty of 1963. If there was to be underground testing, one had to be able to detect someone else's tests, so a by-product of the Cold War was seismological data on a scale unapproached before. The whole of plate tectonics, a story of steady-state violence along boundaries, was being brought to light largely as a result of the development of instruments of war. Earthquakes "focus" where earth begins to move, and along transform faults like the San

abyssal plains the plains in the deepest parts of an ocean
cordillera the principal range, or chain, of a series of mountain ranges
rift valley a long, narrow valley formed when land sinks between roughly parallel faults
seismology the science of earthquakes and the mechanical properties of the earth
transform fault a fault occurring at plate boundaries

Narration

Andreas the focusses were shallow. At the ocean trenches they could be very deep. The facts accrued. Global maps of the new seismological data showed earthquakes not only clustered like stitchings all along the ridges of the seafloor mountains but also in the trenches and transform faults, with the result that the seismology was sketching the earth's crustal plates.

To Rear Admiral Hess, as he had become in the U.S. Naval Reserve, it now seemed apparent that the seafloors were spreading away from mid-ocean ridges, where new seafloor was continuously being created in deep cracks, and, thinking through as many related phenomena as he was able to discern at the time, he marshalled his own research and the published work of others up to 1960 and wrote in that year his "History of Ocean Basins." In the nineteen-forties, a professor at Delft had written a book called *The Pulse of the Earth,* in which he asserted with mild cynicism that where gaps exist among the facts of geology the space between is often filled with things "geopoetical," and now Hess, with good-humored candor, adopted the term and announced in his first paragraph that while he meant "not to travel any further into the realm of fantasy than is absolutely necessary," he nonetheless looked upon what he was about to present as "an essay in geopoetry." He could not be sure which of his suppositions might be empty conjecture and which might in retrospect be regarded as precocious insights. His criterion could only have been that they seemed compelling to him. His guyots, he had by now decided, were volcanoes that grew at spreading centers, where they protruded above the ocean surface and were attacked by waves. With the moving ocean floor they travelled slowly down to the abyssal plains and went on eventually to "ride down into the jaw crusher" of the deep trenches, where they were consumed. "The earth is a dynamic body with its surface constantly changing," he wrote, and he agreed with others that the force driving it all must be heat from deep in the mantle, moving in huge revolving cells (an idea that had been around in one form or another since 1839 and is still the prevailing guess in answer to the unresolved question: What is the engine of plate tectonics?). Hess reasoned also that the heat involved in the making of new seafloor is what keeps the ocean rises high, and that moving outward the new material gradually cools and subsides. The rises seemed to be impermanent features, the seafloor altogether "ephemeral." "The whole ocean is virtually swept clean (replaced by the new mantle material) every three hundred to four hundred million years," he wrote. "This accounts for the relatively thin veneer of sediments on the ocean floor, the relatively small number of volcanic seamounts, and the present absence of evidence of rocks older than Cretaceous in the oceans." In ending, he said, "The writer has attempted to invent an evolution for ocean basins. It is hardly likely that all of the numerous assumptions made are correct. Nevertheless it appears to be a useful framework for testing various and sundry groups of hypotheses relating to the oceans. It is hoped that the framework with necessary patching

fault a fracture in a rock formation that causes displacement of previously adjacent surfaces and disturbs continuity
mantle the layer of the earth between the core and the crust

An Evolution for Ocean Basins   7

and repair may eventually form the basis for a new and sounder structure."

In 1963, Drummond Matthews and Fred Vine, of Cambridge University, published an extraordinary piece of science that gave to Hess's structure much added strength. Magnetometers dragged back and forth across the seas had recorded magnetism of two quite different intensities. Plotted on a map, these magnetic differences ran in stripes that were parallel to the mid-ocean ridges. The magnetism over the centers of the ridges themselves was uniformly strong. Moving away from the ridges, the strong and weak stripes varied in width from a few kilometres to as many as eighty. Vine and Matthews, chatting over tea in Cambridge, thought of using this data to connect Harry Hess's spreading seafloor to the time scale of paleomagnetic reversals. The match would turn out to be exact. The weaker stripes matched times when the earth's magnetic field had been reversed, and the strong ones matched times when the magnetic pole was in the north. Moreover, the two sets of stripes—calendars, in effect, moving away from the ridge—seemed to be symmetrical. The seafloor was not only spreading. It was documenting its age. L. W. Morley, a Canadian, independently had reached the same conclusions. Vine and Matthews' paper was published in the British journal *Nature* in September, 1963, and became salient in the development of plate tectonics. In January of the same year, Morley had submitted almost identical ideas to the editors of *Nature*, but they were not yet prepared to accept them, so Morley then submitted the paper in the United States to the *Journal of Geophysical Research*, which rejected it summarily. Morley's paper came back with a note telling him that his ideas were suitable for a cocktail party but not for a serious publication.

Data confirming the Vine-Matthews hypothesis began to accumulate, nowhere more emphatically than in a magnetic profile of the seafloor made by the National Science Foundation's ship Eltanin crossing the East Pacific Rise. The Eltanin's data showed that the seafloor became older and older with distance from the spreading center, and with perfect symmetry for two thousand kilometres on either side. All through the nineteen-sixties, ships continued to cruise the oceans dragging magnetometers behind, and eventually computers were programmed to correlate the benthic data with the surface wanderings of the ships. Potassium-argon dating had timed the earth's magnetic reversals to apparent perfection for the last three and a half million years. Geologists at Columbia calculated the rate of seafloor spreading for those years and then assumed the rate to have been constant through earlier time. On that assumption, they extrapolated a much more extensive paleomagnetic time scale. (Improved radiometric dating later endorsed the accuracy of the method.) And with that scale they swiftly mapped the history of ocean basins. Compared with a geologic map of a continent, it was a picture handsome and spare. As the paleomagnetist Allan Cox, of Stanford Univer-

paleomagnetic reversals ancient reversals of the earth's magnetic poles
salient striking, conspicuous
benthic pertaining to the bottom of the sea, especially at the deeper levels
radiometric dating dating by means of measurement of radiation

8   *Narration*

sity, would describe it in a book called *Plate Tectonics and Geomagnetic Reversals,* "The structure of the seafloor is as simple as a set of tree rings, and like a modern bank check it carries an easily decipherable magnetic signature."

Meanwhile, geophysicists at Toronto, Columbia, Princeton, and the Scripps Institution of Oceanography were filling in the last major components of the plate-tectonics paradigm. They figured out the geometry of moving segments on a sphere, showed that deformation happens only at the margins of plates, charted the relative motions of the plates, and mapped for the first time the plate boundaries of the world.

If it was altogether true, as Hess had claimed, that with relative frequency "the whole ocean is virtually swept clean," then old rock should be absent from deep ocean floors. Since 1968, the drill ship Glomar Challenger has travelled the world looking for, among other things, the oldest ocean rocks. The oldest ever found is Jurassic. In a world that is 4.6 billion years old, with continental-shield rock that has been dated to 3.8, it is indeed astonishing that the oldest rock that human beings have ever removed from a seafloor has an age of a hundred and fifty million years—that the earth is thirty times as old as the oldest rock of the oceans. In 1969, it seemed likely that the oldest ocean floor would be found in the Northwest Pacific. The Glomar Challenger went there to see. Two Russians were aboard who believed that rock older than Jurassic—rock of the Paleozoic, in all likelihood—would be discovered. They took vodka with them to toast the first trilobite to appear on deck. Trilobites, index fossils of the Paleozoic, came into the world at the base of the Cambrian and went out forever in the Permian Extinction—eighty million years before the age of the oldest rock ever found in modern oceans. As expected, the oceanic basement became older and older as the ship drilled westward from Hawaii. But even at the edge of the Marianas Trench, the Russians were disappointed. No vodka. Ah, but there might be older rock on the other side of the trench, in the floor of the Philippine Sea. The ship pulled up its drill pipe and moved across the trench. This time the rock was Miocene, more or less a tenth as old as the Jurassic floor. The Russians broke out the vodka. A toast! Neil Armstrong and Edwin Aldrin were walking around on the moon.

---

paradigm an example or model
Jurassic the second period of the Mesozoic era, the time of dinosaurs and the earliest mammals and birds
continental shield the relatively stable inland portion of continents
Paleozoic the era of geologic time preceding the Mesozoic in which marine invertebrates, primitive reptiles, and land plants appeared
Cambrian the earliest period of the Paleozoic era, a period of warm seas and the development of marine invertebrates
Permian the final period of the Paleozoic era
Miocene the fourth epoch of the Tertiary period of the Cenozoic era, the epoch in which large apes and grazing animals appeared

An Evolution for Ocean Basins   9

Questions

1 Which of the four uses of narrative is illustrated in McPhee's essay?
2 Analyze McPhee's organizational strategy. How does the chronological organization aid the writer's purpose?
3 There are several indications of conflict in McPhee's account. The main conflict is between the old perceptions of geological mechanisms and the development of new ones. What other examples of conflict can you find?
4 How does McPhee incorporate an element of suspense into his narrative?
5 What is accomplished by the reference to Armstrong and Aldrin at the end of the essay?

Once Upon a Time

Jean Stafford

Jean Stafford (1915–1979), a professional writer of essays and short stories, was awarded a Pulitzer Prize in 1970.

In her account of a disagreement with Consolidated Edison, you will find a very straightforward use of narrative technique. Stafford begins by explaining her previous dealings with the utility company, which serve as background for the sequence of events she will describe. She then presents these later events chronologically. The reader's interest is heightened by her deliberate use of non sequitur *to express a sense of the absurd and feelings of frustration.*

If we realize that this essay appeared originally in The New York Times, *we have a clue as to the audience Stafford is anticipating. She is writing for the general public, but particularly for those people who have had similar problems with a large corporation. Humorous details and a clever use of absurdity suggest to us that her purpose is primarily to entertain. We should also be aware that there is a corollary purpose: to allow the reader to vent his or her own frustration through vicarious identification with Stafford's successful campaign against the idiosyncracies of computer billing.*

On quitting New York City in 1957 where I had been living under the name Jean Stafford, I asked Consolidated Edison to send my final bill. Instead of a bill, I received a check for six cents, which represented, I supposed, what was left of my deposit. I kept it, partly as a curio, partly in the hope that in a wee way I could bollix up the company books, and partly because I thought it might come in handy some day in one way or another. Eleven years later, thanks to my mean-spirited foresight, I was able to use it as a tactical diversion in a battle I fought with and won from Con Ed.

In the spring of 1968, having spent a miserable ten months in a stygian sublet in the East 80's, calling myself Mrs. A. J. Liebling, I once again asked to settle my account with the Diggers Who Must. When the bill came, I read it with interest and in detail; I read it in artificial light and I took it outdoors and read it in the sun; I read it with and without a magnifying glass; each time I saw the same incontrovertible figures.

Over a period of 27 days I had, according to the computers in Charles F. Luce's busy concern, used up $6.32 worth of electricity and $409.28 of cooking gas, but, because I had a credit of $8.03 from the month before, the total came only to $407.57 instead of $415.60.

I had the bill and the old check of six cents Xeroxed and then I sat down to write Chief Luce a seventeen-page letter. I began:

"The originals of these unusual documents are at the frame shop. They will hang, well lit by LILCO, in some conspicuous part of my house in Suffolk County on Long Island. Let me explain that while I am Mrs. A. J. Liebling, in debt to you for your clean energy to the tune of $407.57, I am also, professionally, Jean Stafford (I am a writer and am not to be confused with Jo Stafford, the popular singer) to whom you owe six cents. Perhaps I could apply the latter to the former.

"I am a widow and I live alone. My breakfast consists of coffee, made in an electric percolator, and fruit. I do not eat lunch. In the city I seldom dine in but when I do, I cook something simple on top of the stove or I have 'finger-food,' as my mother would have called it, sent in from a delicatessen.

"I have a very long history (I was born in 1915) of somnambulism and it could be argued that between April 29 and May 25, I used up $401.25 of cooking gas running a short-order house and snack bar in my sleep for the operators of your pneumatic drills. The facts, however, cannot support this proposition. For example, my grocery bill for that period came to $41.77— that may seem steep, considering how little I eat, but what I do eat is always of prime quality. No matter where I live, my butcher who is also my cat's meat man is listed in my personal telephone book simply as 'Tiffany.'

"There, is of course, the possibility that there might have been a leak in my two-burner stove, but in that event, don't you imagine I would be dead?"

stygian gloomy or dark, pertaining to the river Styx, the principal river of the underworld in Greek mythology

Narration

Chairman Luce and his subalterns had no way of knowing that the only entries I made in my engagement book are appointments with my dentist, my C.P.A., the doctors in charge of my giblets, of my eyes and my bones and my skin; and the hours of the departure of planes taking me away from my gas stove, my light bulbs and my electric blanket. So I felt free to describe, with a wealth of needless detail, where and with whom I had been each evening but two during the time in question.

My companions had all been illustrious in the world of *belle lettres*, architecture, painting, music, the natural and the physical sciences, jurisprudence, medicine and high finance. We had eaten ambrosia and drunk nectar in the smartest possible restaurants or in the dining rooms of splendidly appointed houses or apartments where Cézannes and Corots hung, where Aubussons and Sarouks lay and Chippendale and Queen Anne stood. These interiors reminded me of others I had seen or read about and I was happy to share my memories with my interlocutor—not, of course, that he was getting a word in edgewise.

I had in truth spent one weekend in Boston and another at my own house in the country, and in the course of one of those weeks, I had been in Nashville for two days and two nights. My weekend in Boston led me to nostalgic reminiscences of people I had known there and in all other parts of New England during the forties; the trip to Nashville caused me to discourse at length on the Southern Fugitive group and my association with them.

Relevant to nothing at all, I said:

"While I am writing to you, let me say a few words about a building you rent to Columbia University. It is known as Myles Cooper and is situated at 440 West 110th Street and it houses The School of the Arts where, while I was living in the city, I held a seminar. Myles Cooper is the most appalling place I have ever worked in and I have worked in some mighty appalling places. You should have seen my office at "The Southern Review" at Louisiana State University where I was my secretary . . ."

I named the distinguished editors, the distinguished contributors and described the parties held when the distinguished contributors came to call on the distinguished editors in Baton Rouge. I went into the pesky vermin of Louisiana, the tragic beauty of the antebellum houses, Spanish moss and the Long family.

Eventually I got back to Myles Cooper but then digressed, with many cross-references to colleagues, to talk of my offices on other campuses. Then back to Myles Cooper and to The Troubles at Columbia in April of 1968 when I was cooking up a storm at East 80th Street. I went into the woeful

subaltern a subordinate
Cézanne and Corot Paul Cézanne (1839–1906) and Jean Corot (1796–1875), French Impressionist painters
Aubusson and Sarouk valuable carpets, tapestries
Chippendale and Queen Anne types of antique furniture
interlocutor a partner in a dialogue

state of higher education. I concluded by wishing many years of health and prosperity for Mr. Luce and his.

My several verbose postscripts were followed by brief biographies of all the notables, in addition to those I had mentioned in the letter, to whom I was sending copies.

Ten days later I got a bill from Consolidated Edison for $407.57.

Now I was impatient. I wrote brusquely; "In my earlier letter, I told you to get your computers overhauled. Do as I say and do so instantly."

Two weeks went by and then one morning, a trembly-voiced Mr. Poltroon telephoned me from New York City and said that there had been a mistake in my Con Ed bill, that the figures had been based on an estimate.

"An estimate of what?" I demanded so loudly that my cat who had been spot-cleaning his gloves at my feet scuttered upstairs. "An estimate for Nedick's?"

The poor bloke tried to explain how the estimates were made, but the procedure is so tortuous, so idiosyncratically imaginative, that, at my suggestion, Mr. Poltroon gave up and went on to say that, in fact, Con Ed owed me 23 cents. I would not get the check, he was sorry to say, for ten days or two weeks and he sincerely hoped I would not be inconvenienced.

Two days later, Mr. P. was back on the hooter asking me to return the 1957 check for six cents. I refused. Testily. I said I thought I was to get a check for 23 cents; he said yes, but the company would like to combine the two so that I would get 29 cents. I told him nothing doing.

All through the summer Mr. Poltroon called me long distance every four or five days: If I got a bill for $3.67, I was to ignore it—it was a mistake. Had I got my check for 23 cents? Wouldn't I please turn loose my check for six cents? Each time he identified himself, I said, "Oh, Mr. Poltroon, could you hang on a sec? There's somebody at my back door."

Then I'd go out to the kitchen and make myself a bacon-and-tomato sandwich, work the daily crossword puzzle, comb the cat and sterilize a few Mason jars for canning watermelon pickles. He was always waiting for me when I moseyed back to the telephone; and before he could say a word, I'd tell him that I'd been in conversation with the plumber (I talked about sump-pumps, cesspools, elbows, Stillson wrenches, hard water, the high incidence of silverfish in the bathrooms of Monteagle, Tenn.) or the tree men (had Mr. Poltroon ever had trouble with fire-blight on his Japanese quince or powdery mildew on his mimosa?).

Toward the end of August, the calls stopped, but on the Tuesday after Labor Day, Mr. Poltroon rang up to apologize for not having been in touch for so long—he'd been away, he'd needed a rest.

Before I could compassionately inquire about his present condition, there was a knock at the back door and I had to leave him to confer with the cablevision man, to run up a batch of vichyssoise and to rearrange the spice shelf. Faithful Poltroon was still at the other end of the wire. His respiration

Nedick's a restaurant chain specializing in frankfurters

was shallow; I didn't like the sound of it at all. Had I got my money from Con Ed yet? I hadn't? That was the limit! His voice belied the indignation of his words: It was wanting the timbre of a healthy man.

I never heard that voice again. But late in September a Mr. Bandersnatch S. Pecksniff wrote:

"Mr. C. E. Poltroon informed me of his telephone conversation in which he explained the circumstances resulting in the issuance of our inaccurate billing. We have special programing and instructions to prevent such situations. I am sorry that these instructions were not followed in this instance.

"Enclosed are the two checks which Mr. Poltroon spoke to you about. I do hope you will cash them promptly and enable us to balance your account."

There was an imploring note, I felt, in that last sentence. Although the letter was dated Sept. 24, the new check for six cents (payable to Mrs. A. J. Liebling. Why? Con Ed had owed and had paid Miss Stafford six cents in 1957 but they didn't owe Mrs. L. six cents in 1968) was dated Aug. 8 and the one for 23 cents had been made out on Sept. 6. My case had clearly consumed far more clerical time than I had consumed gas.

The three checks and the amazing bill are framed and hang in my downstairs bathroom. I'm not sure yet, but I have a hunch that by and by I'll have to make room for another set of similar testaments under glass. For I have discovered that the Long Island Lighting Company, far from being Con Ed's easy-going country cousin, is his blood brother, foxy, avaricious and, not to put too fine a point on it, uppity. If he gets too far out of line—and he seems aimed in that direction—I may have to read *him* the riot act, in no uncertain terms.

Questions

1 Examine the phrases Stafford uses to indicate time sequences in her first two paragraphs. How do they prepare the reader for the tale that is to follow?

2 Notice that the letter Stafford describes is a narrative within a narrative. What is her reason for using this technique?

3 Examine the pace of the last half of the essay by looking carefully at the details given. Compare it with the pace of the first half. What purpose is served by changing the speed of the narrative?

4 Identify the tone of the essay. How does Stafford use detail to achieve that tone?

Are Children People?

Phyllis McGinley

Phyllis McGinley (1905–1978), on record as considering herself first a homemaker and only secondarily a professional writer, was, nonetheless, extraordinarily successful in her second career. She wrote a great many books of verse, essays, and children's books. The recipient of many literary awards, she was the winner of the Pulitzer Prize for poetry in 1961.

As you read McGinley's account of childhood, keep in mind the techniques of narration. You will undoubtedly notice that many of the anecdotes have a chronological order. Notice also that some of the experiences are presented as actual and others as hypothetical. As you finish reading the essay, think back to the beginning. Notice that McGinley has moved chronologically throughout the essay; she begins with toddlers and ends with adolescents. It is important to realize that although it has a narrative focus, the essay might be classified equally well as an example of comparison; this mixing of rhetorical techniques is not unusual.

Much of what makes this essay readable and enjoyable results from the writer's choice of tone. McGinley uses humor to reach the audience she has in mind, namely parents. She hopes to entertain by getting the reader to identify with her and, by extension, with all other parents.

The problem of how to live with children isn't as new as you might think. Centuries before the advent of Dr. Spock or the PTA, philosophers debated the juvenile question, not always with compassion. There's a quotation from one of the antique sages floating around in what passes for my mind which, for pure cynicism, could set a Montaigne or a Mort Sahl back on his heels.

"Why," asks a disciple, "are we so devoted to our grandchildren?"

And the graybeard answers, "Because it is easy to love the enemies of one's enemies."

Philosopher he may have been but I doubt his parental certification. Any parent with a spark of natural feeling knows that children aren't our enemies. On the other hand, if we're sensible we are aware that they aren't really our friends, either. How can they be, when they belong to a totally different race?

Children admittedly are human beings, equipped with such human paraphernalia as appetites, whims, intelligence, and even hearts, but any resemblance between them and people is purely coincidental. The two nations, child and grown-up, don't behave alike or think alike or even see with the same eyes.

Take that matter of seeing, for example. An adult looks in the mirror and notices what? A familiar face, a figure currently overweight, maybe, but well-known and resignedly accepted; two arms, two legs, an entity. A child can stare into the looking glass for minutes at a time and see only the bone buttons on a snowsuit or a pair of red shoes.

Shoes, in fact, are the first personal belongings a child really looks at in an objective sense. There they are to adore—visible, shiny, round-toed ornamental extensions of himself. He can observe them in that mirror or he can look down from his small height to admire them. They are real to him, unlike his eyes or his elbows. That is why, for a child, getting a pair of new shoes is like having a birthday. When my daughters were little they invariably took just-acquired slippers to bed with them for a few nights, the way they'd take a cuddle toy or smuggle in a puppy.

Do people sleep with their shoes? Of course not. Nor do they lift them up reverently to be fondled, a gesture children offer even to perfect strangers in department stores. I used to think that a child's life was lived from new shoe to new shoe, as an adult lives for love or payday or a vacation.

Children, though, aren't consistent about their fetish. By the time they have learned to tie their own laces, they have lapsed into an opposite phase. They start to discard shoes entirely. Boys, being natural reactionaries, cling longer than girls to their first loves, but girls begin the discalced stage at twelve or thirteen—and it goes on interminably. Their closets may bulge with footwear, with everything from dubious sneakers to wisps of silver kid, while most of the time the girls themselves go unshod. I am in error, too, when I speak of shoes as reposing in closets. They don't. They lie abandoned under sofas, upside down beside the television set, rain-drenched on verandas. Guests

---

discalced barefooted; unshod

in formal drawing rooms are confronted by them and climbers on stairways imperiled. When the phase ends, I can't tell you, but I think only with premature senescence.

My younger daughter, then a withered crone of almost twenty, once held the odd distinction of being the only girl on record to get her foot stabbed by a rusty nail at a Yale prom. She was, of course, doing the Twist barefoot, but even so the accident seems unlikely. You can't convince me it could happen to an adult.

No, children don't look at things in the same light as people. Nor do they hear with our ears, either. Ask a child a question and he has an invariable answer: "What?" (Though now and then he alters it to "Why?")

Or send one on a household errand and you will know that he—or she— is incapable of taking in a simple adult remark. I once asked an otherwise normal little girl to bring me the scissors from the kitchen drawer, and she returned, after a mysterious absence of fifteen minutes, lugging the extension hose out of the garage. Yet the young can hear brownies baking in the oven two blocks away from home or the faintest whisper of parents attempting to tell each other secrets behind closed doors.

They can also understand the language of babies, the most esoteric on earth. Our younger child babbled steadily from the age of nine months on, although not for a long while in an intelligible tongue. Yet her sister, two years older, could translate for us every time.

"That lady's bracelet—Patsy wishes she could have it," the interpreter would tell me; and I had the wit hastily to lift my visitor's arm out of danger.

Or I would be instructed, "She'd like to pat the kitten now."

We used occasionally to regret their sibling fluency of communication. Once we entertained at Sunday dinner a portrait painter known rather widely for his frequent and publicized love affairs. He quite looked the part, too, being so tall and lean and rakish, with such a predatory moustache and so formidable a smile, that my husband suggested it was a case of art imitating nature.

The two small girls had never met him, and when the baby saw him for the first time she turned tail and fled upstairs.

The older, a gracious four, came back into the living room after a short consultation, to apologize for her sister's behavior. "You see," she told him winningly, "Pasty thinks you're a wolf."

It was impossible to explain that they had somehow confused the moustache and the smile with a description of Little Red Riding Hood's arch foe and were not referring to his private life. We let it pass. I often thought, however, that it was a pity the older girl's pentecostal gifts did not outlast kindergarten. She would have been a great help to the United Nations.

Young mothers have to study such talents and revise their methods of child rearing accordingly. To attempt to treat the young like grown-ups is always a mistake.

senescence old age

Are Children People?   **19**

Do people, at least those outside of institutions, drop lighted matches into wastebaskets just to see what will happen? Do they tramp through puddles on purpose? Or prefer hot dogs or jelly-and-mashed-banana sandwiches to lobster Thermidor? Or, far from gagging on the abysmal inanities of *Raggedy Ann*, beg to have it read to them every evening for three months?

Indeed, the reading habits alone of the younger generation mark them off from their betters. What does an adult do when he feels like having a go at a detective story or the evening paper? Why, he picks out a convenient chair or props himself up on his pillows, arranges the light correctly for good vision, turns down the radio, and reaches for a cigarette or a piece of chocolate fudge.

Children, however, when the literary urge seizes them, take their comic books to the darkest corner of the room or else put their heads under the bedcovers. Nor do they sit *down* to read. They wander. They lie on the floor with their legs draped over the coffee table, or, alternatively, they sit on the coffee table and put the book on the floor. Or else they lean against the refrigerator, usually with the refrigerator door wide open. Sometimes I have seen them retire to closets.

Children in comfortable positions are uncomfortable—just as they are miserable if they can't also have the phonograph, the radio, the television and sometimes the telephone awake and lively while they pore on *The Monster of Kalliwan* or *The Jungle Book*.

But then, children don't walk like people, either—sensibly, staidly, in a definite direction. I am not sure they ever acquire our grown-up gaits. They canter, they bounce, they slither, slide, crawl, leap into the air, saunter, stand on their heads, swing from branch to branch, limp like cripples, or trot like ostriches. But I seldom recall seeing a child just plain walk. They can, however, dawdle. The longest period of recorded time is that interval between telling children to undress for bed and the ultimate moment when they have brushed their teeth, said their prayers, eaten a piece of bread and catsup, brushed their teeth all over again, asked four times for another glass of milk, checked the safety of their water pistols or their tropical fish, remembered there was something vital they had to confide to you, which they have forgotten by the time you reach their side, switched from a panda to a giraffe and back to the panda for the night's sleeping companion, begged to have the light left on in the hall, and finally, being satisfied that your screaming voice is in working order, fallen angelically into slumber.

Apprentice parents are warned to disregard at least nine-tenths of all such requests as pure subterfuge but to remember that maybe one of the ten is right and reasonable, like the night-light or the value of a panda when one is in a panda mood.

Not that reason weighs much with children. It is the great mistake we make with a child, to think progeny operate by our logic. The reasoning of children, although it is often subtle, differs from an adult's. At base there is usually a core of sanity, but one must disentangle what the lispers mean from what they say.

"I believe in Santa Claus," a daughter told me years ago, when she was

Narration

five or six. "And I believe in the Easter Rabbit, too. But I just can't believe in Shirley Temple."

Until I worked out a solution for this enigmatic statement, I feared for the girl's mind. Then I realized that she had been watching the twenty-one-inch screen. After all, if you are six years old and see a grown-up Shirley Temple acting as mistress of ceremonies for a TV special one evening and the next day observe her, dimpled and brief-skirted, in an old movie, you are apt to find the transformation hard to credit.

I managed to unravel that utterance, but I never did pierce through to the heart of a gnomic pronouncement made by a young friend of hers. He meandered into the backyard one summer day when the whole family was preparing for a funeral. Our garden is thickly clustered with memorials to defunct wildlife, and on this particular afternoon we were intent on burying another robin.

John looked at the hole.

"What are you doing?" he asked, as if it weren't perfectly apparent to the most uninformed.

"Why, John," said my husband, "I'm digging a grave."

John considered the matter a while. Then he inquired again, with all the solemnity of David Susskind querying a senator, "Why don't you make it a double-decker?"

Not even Echo answered that one, but I kept my sense of proportion and went on with the ceremonies. You need a sense of proportion when dealing with children, as you also need a sense of humor. Yet you must never expect the very young to have a sense of humor of their own. Children are acutely risible, stirred to laughter by dozens of human mishaps, preferably fatal. They can understand the points of jokes, too, so long as the joke is not on them. Their egos are too new, they have not existed long enough in the world to have learned to laugh at themselves. What they love most in the way of humor are riddles, elementary puns, nonsense, and catastrophe. An elderly fat lady slipping on the ice in real life or a man in a movie falling from a fifteen-foot ladder equally transports them. They laugh at fistfights, clowns, people kissing each other, and buildings blowing up. They don't, however, enjoy seeing their parents in difficulties. Parents, they feel, were put on earth solely for their protection, and they cannot bear to have the fortress endangered.

Their peace of mind, their safety, rests on grown-up authority; and it is that childish reliance which invalidates the worth of reasoning too much with them. The longer I lived in a house with children, the less importance I put on cooperatively threshing out matters of conduct or explaining to them our theories of discipline. If I had it to do over again I wouldn't reason with them at all until they arrived at an *age* of reason—approximately twenty-one. I would give them rules to follow. I would try to be just, and I would try even harder to be strict. I would do no arguing. Children, in their hearts, like laws. Authority implies an ordered world, which is what they—and, in the long

David Susskind motion picture producer and television talk show host

Are Children People?

run, most of the human race—yearn to inhabit. In law there is freedom. Be too permissive and they feel lost and alone. Children are forced to live very rapidly in order to live at all. They are given only a few years in which to learn hundreds of thousands of things about life and the planet and themselves. They haven't time to spend analyzing the logic behind every command or taboo, and they resent being pulled away by it from their proper business of discovery.

When our younger and more conversational daughter turned twelve, we found she was monopolizing the family telephone. She would reach home after school at 3:14 and at 3:15 the instrument would begin to shrill, its peal endless till bedtime. For once we had the good sense neither to scold nor to expostulate. We merely told her she could make and receive calls only between five and six o'clock in the afternoon. For the rest of the day, the telephone was ours. We expected tears. We were braced for hysterics. What we got was a calm acceptance of a Rule. Indeed, we found out later, she boasted about the prohibition—it made her feel both sheltered and popular.

But, then, children are seldom resentful, which is another difference between them and people. They hold grudges no better than a lapdog. They are too inexperienced to expect favors from the world. What happens to them happens to them, like an illness; and if it is not too extravagantly unfair, they forget about it. Parents learn that a child's angry glare or floods of tears after a punishment or a scolding may send the grown-up away feeling like a despotic brute; but that half an hour later, with adult feelings still in tatters, the child is likely as not to come flying into the room, fling both carefree arms about the beastly grown-up's neck, and shout, "I love you," into her ear.

The ability to forget a sorrow is childhood's most enchanting feature. It can also be exasperating to the pitch of frenzy. Little girls return from school with their hearts broken in two by a friend's treachery or a teacher's injustice. They sob through the afternoon, refuse dinner, and go to sleep on tear-soaked pillows. Novice mothers do not sleep at all, only lie awake with the shared burden for a nightlong companion. Experienced ones know better. They realize that if you come down in the morning to renew your solacing, you will meet—what? Refreshed, wholehearted offspring who can't under*stand* what you're talking about. Beware of making childhood's griefs your own. They are no more lasting than soap bubbles.

I find myself hoaxed to this day by the recuperative powers of the young, even when they top me by an inch and know all about modern art. More than once I have been called long distance from a college in New England to hear news of impending disaster.

"It's exam time and I'm down with this horrible cold," croaks the sufferer, coughing dramatically. "Can you rush me that prescription of Dr. Murphy's? I don't trust our infirmary."

Envisioning flu, pneumonia, wasting fever, and a lily maid dead before her time, I harry the doctor into scribbling his famous remedy and send it by wire. Then after worrying myself into dyspepsia, I call two days later to find out the worst. An unfogged voice answers me blithely.

"What cold?" it inquires.

Ephemeral tragedies, crises that evaporate overnight are almost certain to coincide with adolescence. Gird yourselves for them. Adolescence is a disease more virulent than measles and difficult to outgrow as an allergy. At its onset parents are bewildered like the victim. They can only stand by with patience, flexibility, and plenty of food in the larder. It's amazing how consoling is a batch of cookies in an emergency. If it doesn't comfort the child, at least it helps the baker. I stopped in at a neighbor's house the other day and found her busily putting the frosting on a coconut cake.

"It's for Steven," she told me. "His pet skunk just died, and I didn't know what else to do for him."

Food helps more than understanding. Adolescence doesn't really want to be understood. It prefers to live privately in some stone tower of its own building, lonely and unassailable. To understand is to violate. This is the age—at least for girls—of hidden diaries, locked drawers, unshared secrets. It's a trying time for all concerned. The only solace is that they do outgrow it. But the flaw there is that eventually they outgrow being children too, becoming expatriates of their own tribe.

For, impossible as it seems when one first contemplates diapers and croup, then tantrums, homework, scouting, dancing class, and finally the terrible dilemmas of the teens, childhood does come inexorably to an end. Children turn into people. They speak rationally if aloofly, lecture you on manners, condescend to teach you about eclectic criticism, and incline to get married. And there you are, left with all that learning you have so painfully accumulated in twenty-odd years and with no more progeny on whom to lavish it.

Small wonder we love our grandchildren. The old sage recognized the effect but not the cause. Enemies of our enemies indeed! They are our immortality. It is they who will inherit our wisdom, our experience, our ingenuity.

Except, of course, that the grandchildren's parents will listen benevolently (are they not courteous adults?) and not profit by a word we tell them. They must learn for themselves how to speak in another language and with an alien race.

Questions

1 What do you think is the purpose of McGinley's anecdote about being devoted to one's grandchildren? How is it integrated into the essay?

2 Examine each of the narrative examples used in the essay. Explain the types of detail each uses and how those details are effectively organized.

3 Organize the stages of childhood being discussed in each paragraph. Do you see a general progression from infancy to adolescence? Is the progression, if any, direct, or does it contain minor sweeps forward and backward in time? Evaluate McGinley's use of chronological sequence as a rhetorical device.

Crocodile Rock

Craig Horowitz

Craig Horowitz, a feature editor for the magazine Men's Wear, *believes that good writing can and should exist in any environment, even a fashion magazine. As you read his account of the great fashion success of the Lacoste shirt, pay particular attention to the way in which chronological episodes are incorporated into a basically psychological organization. Horowitz begins with a description of a typical beach party in an upper-class suburb of New York City, an episode that can be assumed to have taken place close to the writing of the essay; he then sets up the psychological organization by introducing an element of suspense: How did the shirt achieve its extraordinary popularity? He answers that question by first recounting the "simple beginning" of the shirt and its low sales throughout its first thirty years. He then heightens the suspense by reporting the surprising reluctance of those involved in making and selling the shirt to talk about its tremendous appeal. The information Horowitz does extract supports the contention that the history of the shirt as a hallmark of the privileged class is in large part responsible for its current success. After describing the shirt's present awesome impact upon the clothing market, the essay concludes with a discussion of the manufacturer's plans to increase distribution and thwart counterfeiting.*

Although much of the essay is narrative, Horowitz, like most writers, supports his account by using several other modes of development. He describes the party at Westhampton, and he also describes the shirt; he defines the appeal of the shirt; he analyzes its marketing history and gives examples of its marketing success; and he compares the Lacoste shirt with its imitators. These are legitimate and interesting ways to provide the specific details that make the narrative entertaining.

Horowitz wrote this article for people involved in fashion merchandising. However, since it is written in a style the average reader can easily understand, the article should also appeal to members of the general public who are interested in fashion. The accessible, informal style of the essay is evident in its use of fragmentary sentences and very brief paragraphs; these set a rapid pace for the narrative and suggest a strategy most often employed in journalistic writing.

Horowitz's purpose is mainly to provide information, but he also attempts to show the reader the importance of that information. His essay helps us understand not only a particular clothing phenomenon but also the ephemeral nature of most fashion.

It begins like most Westhampton evenings during the season, with city dwellers celebrating the rites of summer at a beach party on Long Island, N.Y.

For most people at the party it is a pleasant but uneventful evening, forgotten as quickly as the tide goes out in the morning. Nothing extraordinary, nothing unexpected and no guests who make the society columns. Just a driveway crammed with cars and a contemporary beach house crammed with alligators.

A breeze off the ocean cools the sunburned faces of lawyers, teachers, brokers and bankers who are dressed in remarkably similar fashion—Lacoste shirts, chinos and boat shoes.

Still, nothing unusual to the casual observer. But a closer inspection reveals the stuff that manufacturers' dreams are made of. Many of the men are wearing not one but *two* Lacoste shirts.

One worn on top of the other for a contrasting collar effect: red and yellow, pink and white, and green and beige. The ubiquitous alligator swimming in a sea of two-tone.

It is not the preppy look stretched to its most ridiculous limits, but rather a display of devotion. "So many people now wear the shirts that we have to be a little creative to maintain our individuality," offered one two-shirted guest. "Simply switching to a different shirt would be unthinkable."

It is not an allegiance to be taken lightly. It is responsible for entrenching the Lacoste shirt in American life. Like Levi's, MacDonalds and Coca Cola its appeal transcends the limits of economic, geographic and ethnic boundaries.

The Lacoste shirt has become the quintessential sportswear item in men's apparel. Worn by old and young, rich and poor, and men and women, the shirt has become a classic. It has gained uniform status on the streets of America.

Marketed and sold in more than 80 countries, the shirt is the cornerstone of a $350 million a year French business that manufactures apparel for men, women and children as well as leather goods, tennis rackets and cologne.

Today's overwhelming success enjoyed by the company belies its simple beginning more than 50 years ago in a small London tailoring shop.

Forsaking the custom of his day, French tennis star Rene Lacoste substituted the polo shirt for the long-sleeved, starched white shirt worn by all tennis players in 1926.

A two-time winner of Wimbledon and the U.S. Open, Lacoste had the shirt adorned with a crocodile to represent his nickname "le crocodile." The sobriquet had been given to him several years earlier when he requested a crocodile suitcase as his reward for winning a tournament in Boston.

The tradition-busting, short-sleeved polo shirt attracted so much attention that Lacoste went into business when he retired from tennis. The first products were sold in 1933.

sobriquet nickname

Narration

Sales were slow at first, however, and the numbers really didn't begin to soar until 1963 when his son took over the business.

The three-button placket shirt with its club collar has been marketed and sold in the U.S. since 1953 under the Izod license. Izod is a division of David Crystal, a 75-year-old women's dress company that was sold to General Mills in 1969.

Though specific figures are elusive, industry sources estimate the Izod volume in the U.S. to be $200 million a year, with 20 percent of this done in shirts alone.

"MYSTERIOUS" APPEAL

Like Ernest Hemingway who refused to talk about his writing for fear that somehow talking about it would ruin it, nearly everyone connected with Izod is similarly tight-lipped.

As for the ancillary businesses—retailers, contractors and the like—their reluctance to talk is probably based on a fear of getting cut out.

But the reticence may be even more deep rooted. It may in fact be based on the difficulty in pinpointing the product's appeal. Everyone knows it's there, but no one is really sure why.

The first explanation to roll off everyone's tongue is snob appeal. But at $22 retail the shirt may be the cheapest slice of snobbery available anywhere.

More than anything else, the shirt represents old money. Unlike Pierre Cardin and Yves St. Laurent, the Lacoste shirt has a history that traces its appeal originally to society's privileged class. It is not a fad or an overnight sensation, but rather a standard of taste that has withstood the test of time.

"People shopping today are very concerned with quality assurance," said Carl Schott, the Izod buyer for Bloomingdale's. "It's more than just a name or a label like a designer jean. The shirt represents good taste as well as durability."

At its flagship store in Manhattan and its 13 other locations, Bloomingdale's does a multi-million dollar business in Izod products. It is reported that the shirt alone accounts for more than $1 million a year with the sale of more than 50,000 units.

"If we could get more we could sell a lot more," Schott said. "At this point there's no limit to the sales potential. It's like selling hot dogs at Yankee Stadium. Most days the people are three and four deep at the counter. If I had the stock I could sell at least 700 shirts a week in the Manhattan store alone."

Schott said the appeal of the basic shirt is like nothing else he has ever seen. "People will spend all day going from store to store just looking for the particular color they want."

Saks, which along with Bloomingdale's is one of the largest Izod retailers, has devoted 1,400 square feet to a separate Izod shop on the main floor of its Manhattan store.

"The appeal is broad based and represents classic good taste," said Sak's Senior V.P. Matt Serra. "Even Giorgio Armani wears them."

Understandably, the Lacoste shirt has had a major impact on the rest of the knit shirt business. Estimates are that Munsingwear does $10 million a year with its Penguin shirt and J. C. Penney, which clams to have a stitch-for-stitch copy with a fox instead of an alligator, does about the same. In addition, many other companies now list their own version of the basic knit shirt as a best seller.

Despite efforts to copy the Lacoste shirt, executives at Izod easily shrug off competitive strikes.

"Our business is tremendous," understates Izod's head Leonard Resnick. "You can copy the shirt but it can't be duplicated. As for the Penney's shirt, well our customers just don't shop in Penney's and don't want to be identified that way. They might have been better off not using their fox for identification."

Resnick said the company has a five-year plan that includes further expansion and possibly some movement into new areas.

"Our major problem right now is delivery. We just can't make the shirts fast enough to satisfy everyone who wants them. So, production is the big thing for us. It's hard but we're getting there."

Izod has not opened a new account in more than a year, according to Resnick, and even its advertising has become something of a liability. You can't advertise what you don't have to sell.

"Last year we couldn't run the shirt in our Christmas catalog because we didn't have the product," said Schott at Bloomingdale's.

And they are not alone. The ad agency that handles Izod is frustrated.

Executives at Grey Advertising get understandably testy when asked about Izod's advertising strategy. Repeatedly the ad agency has had to cancel projected advertising because of swelling demand for the product.

Although promotion and competition are worries best left to smaller, less successful companies, Izod does have one nagging problem—counterfeiting.

Counterfeit shirts with all manner of bastardized alligators appear everywhere from flea markets to discount stores to street peddlers, and a major effort is required to limit it.

"Frankly we are desperately serious about defending our trademark," said David Crystal's president Jack Holmes. "We will leap on someone who makes even one counterfeit shirt with all our barrels open and all of our legal might."

The legal might is impressive, having been exercised repeatedly over the years with relatively good success.

"It really isn't much of a problem in the U.S.," Holmes said, "certainly not when compared with the problem overseas."

"It is reported that worldwide, Lacoste spends fully 10 percent of its total income battling counterfeiters. In fact, the shirt is sold in Japan emblazoned with an alligator that includes the name of the company to curtail counterfeiting.

Holmes views the major problem, aside from delivery, as maintaining the alligator's well-respected reputation for quality and reliability.

The much fussed-over and touted alligator actually costs less than 10 cents to make, and this includes stitching it to the shirt.

Though rumors fly from every dark corner of the apparel world about all sorts of difficulties at David Crystal, Izod and General Mills, they appear to be little more than superficial mudslinging.

Stories that range from lack of quality control to financial difficulties to corporate difficulties at General Mills are bandied about but appear to have little substance. None are substantiated by anyone with intimate knowledge of the company, including those who have left.

If there are problems they appear to be related either to corporate difficulties at General Mills or to the failure of the rest of Izod's line to perform up to the standards set by the shirt.

The complete line for men now includes shirts, sweaters, velours, warm-up suits, athletic shorts, socks, pants, jeans and walking shorts.

NO END IN SIGHT

Where all of this will lead is anybody's guess, but at least for the present the shirt shows no signs of weakening popularity.

When Izod unveiled its new line in early August the New York showroom resembled the floor of the stock exchange. Wall-to-wall people desperately trying to get a piece of the action.

"We literally had one buyer in the bathroom sitting on the sink and writing orders on his attache case," recounted one of Izod's sales managers.

When Rene Lacoste was first dubbed "le crocodile," the Frenchman thought the term appropriate.

"When I play tennis on the court I am voracious and thick-skinned." A fair description of the shirt that bears his name.

Questions

1 How does Horowitz employ conflict in his essay? Cite at least two kinds of conflict in the work.
2 Explain how the reader is shown that the Lacoste shirt has a wide appeal. What specifics does Horowitz use to convince the reader that the shirt is popular?
3 Explain the interrelatedness of the expository and factual purposes of the article.
4 Do you think the informal style of the article is effective? Why, or why not? If not, what would improve the article? Are your suggestions consistent with the constraints of audience and purpose encountered by those writing for the fashion industry? Are such constraints legitimate considerations for a professional writer?

Monthly Activity Report— March, April, May

Keith Morgan

Keith Morgan is a senior staff engineer at the Southwest regional office of General Waterworks in Little Rock, Arkansas. His responsibilities there include the evaluation of designs for water systems, the development of new projects, and the approval of newly completed or repaired water systems.

The three monthly activity reports that follow are typical of the kinds of reports people in business and industry write to their supervisors. While the development in these reports is not precisely sequential, each report is basically narrative in that it presents a series of events. Many work reports are written in a style more formal than the one Morgan uses; some even follow a format prescribed by the writer's company. Whatever their degree of formality, though, it is essential that such reports be clear and concise, since a supervisor may receive many reports each reporting period. For example, the most important information should be near the beginning of the report. This means, of course, that the best organization is psychological rather than chronological. In Morgan's reports, the material the writer considers most significant appears in the paragraph immediately following the short introductory sentence, or else it takes the place of such a sentence.

The three reports also make economical mention of agent, time, place, action, and effect. The agent is Morgan, except in passages concerning the cooperation of other engineers. The time is always the month preceding the date of the report, with occasional references to a specific day. Generally, he reports the apportionment of his time rather than the specific chronology. Substantial emphasis is given to where an activity occurred, what it entailed, and occasionally why it occurred the way it did.

The audience the writer expects is clearly indicated at the top of each memorandum: C. L. Reynolds, vice president of engineering for General Waterworks, and R. A. Corbitt, regional engineer for the company's Southwest region. The typical monthly report is addressed to the final authority in a chain of responsibility, with copies to intermediary supervisors. The concerns of these reports are almost entirely factual. They give the company a good indication of what its employees have been doing. There is little use of expository or illustrative narrative here. For instance, Morgan tells what he did, but only occasionally evaluates his activity.

GENERAL WATERWORKS

TO	C. L. Reynolds
FROM	Keith Morgan
SUBJECT	Engineers' Monthly Activities Report—March
PROPERTY	Southwest Region
DATE	April 6, 1981

During the month of March my job has shifted from a training mode to an education and production mode.

The majority of the month was spent on the Warsaw Projection Study in Indiana. Four days were spent in Warsaw to gather information about the system and develop a feel for the area and the system. The 1980 data for the system became available, and this was incorporated with information Cary Gaw had gathered. The population and water consumption projections have been completed. Also, while at Warsaw, information pertaining to the telemetry system was obtained for Reggie.

A day was spent in Russellville to run pump tests on the Shiloh Booster Station. Unfortunately, everything did not go by "the book," and the test turned out to be a failure. However, now that we (Dave Smith and I) are more familiar with the equipment and procedures, I am confident the test will be successful next time.

Part of one day was spent working some problems for the operators at Russellville to show them how to do examples to help them pass an Arkansas Certification Test. (We will find out how successful this was when their test results are available.)

As an aside, I enjoyed the Engineers' Conference. It proved to be a great opportunity to meet the other engineers and exchange ideas.

Sincerely,

Keith Morgan
Senior Staff Engineer

KM : pld
cc: R. A. Corbitt

GENERAL WATERWORKS

TO	C. L. Reynolds
FROM	Keith Morgan
SUBJECT	Engineers' Monthly Activity Report—April
PROPERTY	Southwest Region
DATE	May 4, 1981

The first three days of April were spent at, and returning from, the Engineers' Conference in Harrisburg.

I attended a three-day seminar on "Technical Report Writing for Engineers" in Houston, Texas. The seminar was hosted by the Southern Methodist University Management Center. I appreciated the seminar and would recommend it to anyone who has a limited writing background such as mine.

To meet Missouri state requirements for Capital City finished well water, I obtained the needed information to set up three fluoride treatment systems. These will treat the effluent from three of the system's wells. The I.W.O. will be completed very shortly so the system can be installed and operational as soon as possible.

The remainder of the month was spent working on Warsaw, Indiana. One week was used writing an operation procedure for the telemetry system and plant operations. In order to complete the report, I became familiar with the basic LIQSS procedures. Other areas covered in Warsaw were: Unaccounted-for water (all three methods), completing the distribution map, drawing plant diagrams, computing storage requirements, and writing a short history of the Warsaw system.

Sincerely,

Keith Morgan
Senior Staff Engineer

KM : pld
cc: R. A. Corbitt

I.W.O. investment work order, a type of purchase order
LIQSS acronym for a computer program that provides a model of a water distribution system

GENERAL WATERWORKS

TO	C. L. Reynolds
FROM	Keith Morgan
SUBJECT	Engineers' Monthly Activity Report—May
PROPERTY	Southwest Region
DATE	June 8, 1981

The report for the operators at Warsaw, Indiana, on the purpose, procedure, and operations of the Bristol telemetry system was completed. In the process of researching and writing the report, some other deficiencies in the system were located. I am presently investigating the costs of some additional equipment (pressure and flow recorders) that will increase our knowledge of the system.

Also completed this month were the specifications and drawings for the fluoride treatment equipment for Capital City, Missouri. The specifications are in Jefferson City, Missouri, for the necessary approvals from the Missouri Department of Natural Resources. Costs and equipment details are in Capital City for the I.W.O. to be written up.

The company now has head vs. flow charts for the Russellville Shiloh Booster Station. The flow tests were completed on May 19, 1981.

The remainder of the month was spent on the Engineering Evaluation and Projection Study for Warsaw, Indiana. I concentrated on completion of the graphics for the report. Other written portions completed include the Telemetry System, Fire Flow Evaluation, the Population Projection, and the Customer Projection.

Sincerely,

Keith Morgan
Senior Staff Engineer

KM : pld

cc: R. A. Corbitt

head vs. flow test test of a water pump to see how efficiently it runs
fire flow the amount of water a system must be able to deliver to put out a fire of a specified size

Narration

Questions

1 What was the most significant activity Morgan engaged in during March, during April, and during May? How do you know?

2 What would happen if engineers reported day-by-day, diary-fashion, what they had been doing all month? What might be the physical characteristics of such a report? What would a supervisor who received 250 such reports each month be likely to do with them?

3 In what ways do the demands of audience and purpose dictate the form and the style of these reports?

4 How could the reports be improved? Remember that these reports are not examples of bad writing; nor are they examples of extremely good writing. How could Morgan be clearer? How could he be more concise?

PROCESS ANALYSIS

Process analysis in writing makes use of two closely related developmental patterns, either of which can also be used alone. The first pattern, usually called *process*, describes a series of steps or operations that bring about a particular result; it is concerned with "how" something is done rather than with "what" is done. The steps described are usually interlocking; that is, they follow each other, and one step leads directly to the next. The second developmental pattern is *analysis*, the systematic division of a subject into simple elements so that it may be fully understood. *Enumeration*, for example, is an informal kind of analysis in which we determine how many parts something has, what they are, and how they fit together logically. The writer using process and analysis together, usually divides a procedure into simple elements to determine what the steps are (analysis), then traces the sequence of steps from beginning to end, explaining the interrelationships of the steps and how each one contributes to the particular result (process).

Writers can use process analysis to describe not only how something happens but also the interrelationships between the steps. For example, in the selections reprinted here, Raymond Wittcoff uses analysis not only to present the problems that afflict cities today but also to explain how these problems arose; he also uses process analysis to suggest how the problems might be solved. Rachel Carson uses process to determine the parts of a wave and then to explain the dynamics that shape it. K. P. Johnson uses analysis to explain a large aircraft company's diversification into energy systems. A scientist will often use process analysis to explain the development of a procedure; engineers use these forms of development to explain how something works; business and industry use process to provide users of products with directions; the gas station attendant uses process to tell the tourist how to get to a motel. All of us use process, analysis, or process analysis when we need to give a set of directions or to explain principles involved in an action or set of procedures. Process and analysis make clear the various ways in which a collection of facts builds into a concept.

There are two types of process writing. The first type explains how to do something, and is thus labeled *directive*. Cookbooks are written as a set of directions, as are instructional manuals and, to a certain extent, textbooks. In each of these, the main reason for writing the process is to teach someone how to achieve a desired, specific result. A process can also explain how something works, in which case it is called *informative*. If it is not simply a set of directions, it is more likely to require an explanation of the principles involved in the procedure—in other words, show how something works. While it may present a step-by-step exposition of how a procedure occurs, it will do so from one of several perspectives—for example, science, mechanics, history, sociology, or art. A scientific analysis, for instance, might explain how ordinary household bleach and ammonia create toxic fumes; a mechanical process analysis might explain how an automobile's air conditioner works; a historical analysis might explain how government is responsible for the current economic crisis; a social analysis might demonstrate the changing attitudes toward marriage in modern society; and an analysis of the artistic process might explain how a painter works. Process analysis is used to help us understand the elements of things and how these elements work together. For that reason, its uses are limited only by its purpose.

Process papers, analyses, and process analyses require slightly differing kinds of organization. When we write a process paper, there are several things we must keep in mind. First, if the process is a set of directions, the introduction should include a list and description of those items needed to reach the objective—tools, materials, ingredients. If the process paper is intended to be informative, the writer will need to explain the principles by which the process occurs. For example, Carson explains the way wind pushes water into waves. Furthermore, any special terms that the writer needs to use must be defined in the introduction. Introductions also serve to organize the process to be presented. Steps may be grouped into naturally occurring categories (preliminary, final; right side, left side; cutting, seaming, pressing, trimming; and so on). Objectives for the operations should be clearly stated, and those steps or items that are most important should be specified in the introduction.

Second, since a process involves a sequence of events, and since a description of a process shows how something operates, the steps should be explained in strict chronological order and as clearly and as fully as possible. No step should be omitted, reversed, or slighted. In addition, there should be an explanation of the reasons each step is necessary and, if possible, of why it occurs at a certain point in the sequence.

Process Analysis

Third, a reader finds it much easier to understand a process or a step in a procedure if some kind of *example* is used. Examples may include a description of a variation on a step to show flexibility in a process, a comparison to explain how one process is similar to another, or an illustration to provide visual explanation. Finally, the conclusion should express ways to evaluate the process and be certain that it is complete. The conclusion might also reiterate ways in which the process can be applied.

In writing an analysis, as in writing a process, you will want to take into consideration its purpose and the audience to which it is directed. An analysis should be more or less detailed and specific depending upon the purpose and audience. An analysis aimed at teaching a ten-year-old child will make use of divisions and types of language very different from those appropriate in an analysis informing a group of pharmacists about a new medication. Further, physical analysis breaks objects into their components and separates the parts spatially, whereas conceptual analysis distinguishes the various ideas that make up a concept.

The combination of process and analysis is particularly useful when a writer must simplify a complex process so that it can be more readily understood or when he must show that a process which appears to be complex and difficult is really quite logical and systematic. In combining the two methods of development to produce a process analysis, the writer should be careful to interpret the function of each step and to explain how the steps are interrelated.

How Waves Are Formed[*]

Rachel Carson

Rachel Carson (1907–1964), a marine biologist and writer, is known for her graceful interpretations of scientific concepts for the general reader. Toward the end of her life she became a focus of public controversy, largely as the result of her powerful and prophetic study of environmental pollution, Silent Spring.

The following excerpt from another Carson book, The Sea Around Us, *begins with a generalization that sums up the mechanism by which waves are formed; it then provides a brief analysis of the physical characteristics of a wave. In its next section, Carson describes the mechanical action of wind upon water: how steady wind blowing across the plastic surface of the water creates waves and how, as the wind increases in velocity, the waves behave in certain predictable ways. She then explains what happens as the force of the wind decreases, and as the waves near shore. Her account of this natural process is mainly informative. We learn which elements are involved—wind, water, the physical properties of waves—as well as how those elements work together to create waves. Notice also that the events are arranged in chronological order—we move from calm to hurricane to calm again—as well as in spatial order—we begin far out at sea and move to the shore. Carson also describes what different kinds of waves look like and provides us with ways to evaluate the waves we observe.*

Carson is writing for a general audience, and she manages to describe a complex process in language that can be easily understood by the average reader. Her language is simple and direct and does not include highly technical terms.

The form of development she uses is also appropriate to her purpose. She wants to inform the reader about wave formation and to remove much of the folklore bound up in people's conceptions of waves.

[*] *Editor's title*

As long as there has been an earth, the moving masses of air that we call winds have swept back and forth across its surface. And as long as there has been an ocean, its waters have stirred to the passage of the winds. Most waves are the result of the action of wind on water. There are exceptions, such as the tidal waves sometimes produced by earthquakes under the sea. But the waves most of us know best are wind waves.

It is a confused pattern that the waves make in the open sea—a mixture of countless different wave trains, intermingling, overtaking, passing, or sometimes engulfing one another; each group differing from the others in the place and manner of its origin, in its speed, its direction of movement; some doomed never to reach any shore, others destined to roll across half an ocean before they dissolve in thunder on a distant beach.

Out of such seemingly hopeless confusion the patient study of many men over many years has brought a surprising amount of order. While there is still much to be learned about waves, and much to be done to apply what is known to man's advantage, there is a solid basis of fact on which to reconstruct the life history of a wave, predict its behavior under all the changing circumstances of its life, and foretell its effect on human affairs.

Before constructing an imaginary life history of a typical wave, we need to become familiar with some of its physical characteristics. A wave has height, from trough to crest. It has length, the distance from its crest to that of the following wave. The period of the wave refers to the time required for succeeding crests to pass a fixed point. None of these dimensions is static; all change, but bear definite relations to the wind, the depth of the water, and many other matters. Furthermore, the water that composes a wave does not advance with it across the sea; each water particle describes a circular or elliptical orbit with the passage of the wave form, but returns very nearly to its original position. And it is fortunate that this is so, for if the huge masses of water that comprise a wave actually moved across the sea, navigation would be impossible. Those who deal professionally in the lore of waves make frequent use of a picturesque expression—the "length of fetch." The "fetch" is the distance that the waves have run, under the drive of the wind blowing in a constant direction, without obstruction. The greater the fetch, the higher the waves. Really large waves cannot be generated within the confined space of a bay or a small sea. A fetch of perhaps 600 to 800 miles, with winds of gale velocity, is required to get up the largest ocean waves.

Now let us suppose that, after a period of calm, a storm develops far out in the Atlantic, perhaps a thousand miles from the New Jersey coast where we are spending a summer holiday. Its winds blow irregularly, with sudden gusts, shifting direction but in general blowing shoreward. The sheet of water under the wind responds to the changing pressures. It is no longer a level surface; it becomes furrowed with alternating troughs and ridges. The waves move toward the coast, and the wind that created them controls their destiny. As the storm continues and the waves move shoreward, they receive energy from the wind and increase in height. Up to a point they will continue to take to themselves the fierce energy of the wind, growing in height as the

Process Analysis

strength of the gale is absorbed, but when a wave becomes about a seventh as high from trough to crest as the distance to the next crest, it will begin to topple in foaming whitecaps. Winds of hurricane force often blow the tops off the waves by their sheer violence; in such a storm the highest waves may develop after the wind has begun to subside.

But to return to our typical wave, born of wind and water far out in the Atlantic, grown to its full height on the energy of the winds, with its fellow waves forming a confused, irregular pattern known as a "sea." As the waves gradually pass out of the storm area their height diminishes, the distance between successive crests increases, and the "sea" becomes a "swell," moving at an average speed of about 15 miles an hour. Near the coast a pattern of long, regular swells is substituted for the turbulence of open ocean. But as the swell enters shallow water a startling transformation takes place. For the first time in its existence, the wave feels the drag of shoaling bottom. Its speed slackens, crests of following waves crowd in toward it, abruptly its height increases and the wave form steepens. Then with a spilling, tumbling rush of water falling down into its trough, it dissolves in a seething confusion of foam.

An observer sitting on a beach can make at least an intelligent guess whether the surf spilling out onto the sand before him has been produced by a gale close offshore or by a distant storm. Young waves, only recently shaped by the wind, have a steep, peaked shape even well out at sea. From far out on the horizon you can see them forming whitecaps as they come in; bits of foam are spilling down their fronts and boiling and bubbling over the advancing face, and the final breaking of the wave is a prolonged and deliberate process. But if a wave, on coming into the surf zone, rears high as though gathering all its strength for the final act of its life, if the crest forms all along its advancing front and then begins to curl forward, if the whole mass of water plunges suddenly with a booming roar into its trough—then you may take it that these waves are visitors from some very distant part of the ocean, that they have traveled long and far before their final dissolution at your feet.

What is true of the Atlantic wave we have followed is true, in general, of wind waves the world over. The incidents in the life of a wave are many. How long it will live, how far it will travel, to what manner of end it will come are all determined, in large measure, by the conditions it meets in its progression across the face of the sea. For the one essential quality of a wave is that it moves; anything that retards or stops its motion dooms it to dissolution and death.

Questions

1 How does Carson tie her final paragraph to the opening paragraph?
2 Examine the fourth paragraph. How many terms are defined in it? Is the

shoaling becoming shallow

paragraph a good place for these definitions? What purpose is served by defining the terms here?

3 How does Carson apply chronology to the formation of a wave?

4 How does Carson help the reader evaluate wave formation?

The Future of Cities

Raymond H. Wittcoff

Raymond Wittcoff was chairman of the St. Louis branch of the federal government's Human Development Corporation during the mid 1960s: he later became president of the Transurban Investment Corporation. Wittcoff's essay is an analysis of the problems cities face today and the measures taken to solve urban problems in the past. Accompanying the analysis are suggested solutions to contemporary urban problems. The analysis begins with the assertion that major American cities are in danger and with a list of observations that led Wittcoff to this belief. Proceeding inductively, he discusses the contradictions implicit in the urban situation and then looks at past approaches to solving urban problems, approaches he considers simplistic. Next he describes what cities could be like if proper steps were taken. His explanation of those steps includes many details and examples. Wittcoff then considers how his vision can be implemented; this part constitutes a process analysis. The essay's final section consists mainly of questions that might be raised in evaluating his analysis of urban problems.

Wittcoff is writing for an educated, politically liberal audience. The indications of a liberal bias in his essay include the belief that government intervention is a more reasonable course than laissez-faire; the suggestion that defense budgets be cut; and the proposal that government spend billions in what is essentially a social program. Wittcoff does not present his liberal proposals naively, however. They are moderated somewhat by his recognition of the important role to be played by private investment.

The purpose of the essay is to provide information and to suggest alternative approaches to a serious dilemma. Wittcoff wants people to question the ways in which urban problems have been handled in the past and, in some cases, to change their views on how to solve present social problems.

The urban situation is riddled with contradictions.

ITEM: In a nation with abundant open spaces, three-quarters of the American people are crowded together on ten per cent of the land, causing a congestion as unnecessary as it is enervating.

ITEM: Most people are living in metropolitan areas wrapped in crazy quilts of conflicting jurisdictions which make no sense at all.

ITEM: A technology that can transport an astronaut to the moon is not applied to the problem of getting a workingman across town to his job.

ITEM: The poor are subsisting in squalor in the shadow of skyscrapers, and the skyscrapers are proliferating on a scale that makes our incapacity to produce enough decent housing widely incongruous.

ITEM: People who call themselves free are living in areas where they are afraid to take a long walk or a deep breath because of the levels which crime and pollution have reached.

ITEM: The affluent have built peaceful enclaves for themselves but when they get there they have to gulp tranquilizers in order to remain calm.

The problems are obvious, but their roots are elusive. I do not believe that we are suffering the inevitable consequences of technology, self-government, or defects in human nature. Our difficulties, on the contrary, stem from defects in our habits of thought and institutional arrangements.

I do not suggest that there are any easy answers. Actually we tend to think about our problems too simplistically; we tend to become preoccupied with one facet of a situation while paying lip service to the possibility that there may be other facets. Often we have a single unshakable conviction about the human condition in the light of which all difficulties can be either resolved or endured.

Let us review some of the conspicuous examples of the simplistic approaches to our urban problems. One is to justify inaction by proclaiming that the problem has already been solved. Thus President Nixon accompanied his withdrawal of federal funds from urban programs with the baseless proclamation that the crisis in the cities had ended. It would not have required any more daring a display of Presidential imagination for him to have accepted Senator Aiken's suggestion several years ago that we should claim we had won the war and withdraw our troops from Vietnam.

Another simplistic approach is to assume that everything will be all right if the economy is left alone, or to assume that the economy will grow if we will just resist the temptation to tamper with the free play of the market. In this view, technological advances (and occasional tax incentives) will sustain spectacular economic growth in the wake of which our problems will wash away. Statistics showing the number of Blacks who have entered the middle-income group during the past decade are frequently cited in support of this

enclave a distinct cultural or territorial unit lying entirely within a larger area

Process Analysis

position. But many other people have become victims rather than beneficiaries of technological and economic progress. When they were replaced by machines on farms, millions of them migrated to the cities in a vain search for jobs in the factories which had moved to the countryside. These people are still in the slums and off the job market, unneeded and unwanted.

A generation ago some reformers fervently believed that all social ills were caused by slums, and that the city could get rid of its problems by getting rid of its slums. Another simplism. The way to get rid of the slums, we were told, was to replace old houses with new houses. Even as staunch a defender of laissez-faire as the late Senator Robert Taft became a sponsor of public housing when he acknowledged that people with low incomes could not find housing in the market.

Later, one of the nation's most notable public housing projects, Pruitt-Igoe, was built in St. Louis, Missouri, where thirty-three high-rise apartment buildings were erected at a cost of fifty-seven million dollars on the edges of a vast inner-city slum. Ten thousand poor people were taken out of old slum houses and put in these new buildings. When Pruitt-Igoe was opened in the late nineteen-fifties, it was acclaimed as a symbol of the nation's new sense of social responsibility; the contrast with the wretched hovels in which people continued to live in the adjoining blocks was cited as the dramatic evidence of a great achievement. It soon became apparent, however, that the only advantage the new housing had over the old was its indoor plumbing. The old population density of seven units per acre without plumbing had been traded for forty-five units per acre with plumbing. The impact on onetime rural folk, who were more familiar with open space than with indoor plumbing, was catastrophic. Pruitt-Igoe became a seething center of social strife, and it was gradually abandoned. City authorities finally called for the demolition of the entire project. And so, a few months ago, dynamite was set to the first Pruitt-Igoe buildings. It also exploded one more simplistic approach.

Still another simplism was the reaction to the failure of high-rise housing when low-rise housing was proposed. This was not undertaken extensively because of the high cost of land in the inner city compared with the low cost of land in the suburbs where people with higher incomes were moving. So the next phase was to attempt the rehabilitation of the old housing, which usually meant new plumbing. The unspoken premise here was that the poor belonged in the inner city. The fact that slum clearance and the provision of new housing for the poor did not always go forward together created not only new opportunities for the central cities but new dilemmas. The hard-pressed cities encouraged private investors to develop the cleared slum sites for middle-income apartment dwellers, who were taxpayers, while the displaced poor were obliged to move their problems to nearby neighborhoods. The ghetto was enlarged.

In the nineteen-sixties the main thrust was to try to make the ghetto livable. There was a fresh awareness that saving the poor and the heart of the

laissez-faire the idea that government should not interfere with business or the economy

cities was not an easy matter. So a number of programs were launched. They added up to a piecemeal approach to the problems of jobs, schools, crime, housing, medical and legal services. Earnest specialists charged into the inner city but none of them succeeded in any truly collaborative effort; instead, their principal contact with one another consisted of collisions in their pursuit of funds.

An effort at coördination was finally made in the War on Poverty. As the first chairman of the Human Development Corporation, which coördinated the antipoverty operations in our metropolitan area, I was exposed to the thinking of sociologists who were guiding the program both locally and nationally. In their search for a unifying principle they came up with only one idea: the root of our problems was alienation and the antidote to alienation was participatory democracy (a term whose redundancy suggested the need for a precise definition which was never produced). Although none of us defended paternalism or opposed the involvement of people in matters affecting their own lives, the ardor of the sociologists who were advocating participatory democracy implied that they had just invented the idea of citizenship. In retrospect, it is not clear to me whether their preoccupation with this single concept reflected a paucity of ideas or was merely another example of the same old simplistic approach. Their answer to the problems of public education was to propose that the management of the schools be turned over to the parents in each neighborhood, thus averting a discussion of the substantive issues in education. The answer to the problem of public housing was to turn the management of these projects over to the residents. Of course, the new managements could only become new power structures, which would provoke even more alienation. After their disenchantment with the consequences of this approach, some of these early advocates began to call for the complete abolition of public schools and public housing.

It is now fashionable to deprecate the War on Poverty of the Johnson years; nevertheless many, many poor people were helped by it and some worthwhile programs were set in motion. The national commitment to combat poverty was itself heartening. Yet if there had to be a single guiding idea, it should have been the inescapable fact that poverty means lack of money if it means anything; a direct attack on poverty would be to see to it that everyone's income is maintained above the poverty level. But it is interesting that no proposal for income maintenance was made by the Administration that sponsored the antipoverty program, and that although such a proposal was made by the Administration that is now dismantling the program, it was later shelved.

If family incomes were not permitted to fall below the poverty level (which for a family of four is now said to be between four and five thousand dollars a year), a great deal of misery would be relieved; however, the most serious problems confronting the cities would remain, for the poverty-level figure is simply not enough income to enable a family to break out of the ghetto.

alienation the sense of being isolated, of being an outsider
paucity smallness of number; small amount
deprecate belittle, depreciate (in this context)

The ghetto has to be dispersed. In the nature of the case, efforts to make it livable as it is are doomed to failure. There is simply no rational basis for piling the poor on a tiny fragment of the nation's land in the central cities. They are not there through the workings of inevitable market forces. It is not their natural habitat. They came to the city in pursuit of jobs and jobs are not to be had. The government has subsidized housing where it is bad for the poor and bad for the cities. Whether one's starting point is a humane concern for the circumstances in which children are brought up or a more hard-headed concern about the stacking of social dynamite at the cities' vital centers where the more highly valued properties are found, one must conclude that the destruction of the ghetto is imperative. Open housing by itself will not solve the problem because even after legal barriers have been removed price barriers remain.

The distribution of subsidized housing for low-income groups in the established suburbs is being resisted by these communities. The United States Supreme Court has held, in *James v. Valtierra,* that a municipality can reject low-income public housing if the rejection is not based on racial discrimination. This was its finding in a California case where the community had expressed its will in a referendum.

It is a gross oversimplification, of course, to ascribe these difficulties entirely to racial prejudice. To be sure, racism exists. It is significant, however, that there are people who cheerfully accept open housing in their neighborhoods but vehemently oppose public housing. In doing so, they talk about the correlation between poverty on the one hand and the incidence of crime and other pathological conditions on the other. According to the Urban Land Institute: "No special hindrance exists to racial integration when families share the same economic status. However, it has been shown that economically disparate groups do not make congenial neighbors."

A solution to these problems may be found by seeing them as a whole. At this point it would be useful to project a vision of what our metropolitan areas could be like in the future.

The central cities could be transformed through the total clearance of the slums and blight. The opportunity for redevelopment is in proportion to the blight, and in the old cities the blight is very extensive. Early in the history of these cities, concentric circles consisting of factories, warehouses, and housing for industrial workers were formed around the downtown centers. With the increase of motor transport and the movement of many industries to outlying areas, their abandoned plants and the adjacent residential areas became slums. Total clearance of these slums and the acquisition of the land by public authorities could result in the creation of a chain of parks, large and small, surrounding the center of the city. (Actually, public authority is already becoming the owner of much of this land through defaults in the payment of taxes or government-guaranteed mortgages.) Persons living in blighted areas could be relocated in new towns built in both the outer parts of the metropolitan region and the central city.

disparate completely dissimilar

New parks at the center of the old city could create the feeling of a new city-in-a-park. The density problem created by skyscraper office buildings, apartments, and hotels could be relieved by these new open spaces surrounding them. The traditional role of the central city as the hub of the metropolitan area's civic and cultural life as well as its commercial life could be revitalized as the structures that house these activities are re-created in a new environment. Theaters, art galleries, concert halls, libraries, sports stadiums, specialty shops, and restaurants could interact with each other and together with the gardens and fountains in the surrounding open spaces create a magnetic field which could attract people from throughout the region and provide the metropolis with a sense of community.

The center of the city need not be cluttered with cars. Freeways and transit lines could stop at the perimeters. There could be new kinds of people-movers in the parks and among the buildings. We could even learn to enjoy walking again.

Some of the cleared areas within the old cities could become sites for new towns-in-town: garden apartments, town houses, shops, and schools could be situated around inviting town squares. Other cleared areas could be converted into new industrial parks. There could be an opening of the spaces around industries now cramped in the central cities.

Large sections of our cities are frozen in rigid grids consisting of block after block of closely spaced houses which still have years of useful life remaining. In these areas an occasional block—one out of every eight, say—could be cleared and converted into a mini-park which would enable every family in the area to live within short walking distance of pleasant open space.

The central cities could become more attractive sites for universities and primary medical centers, and these could be functionally related to centers for learning and secondary medical-care centers distributed among the new towns in the region.

Public-utility corridors could extend from the central city in all directions to the perimeters of the metropolitan region according to a comprehensive land-use plan promulgated by a regional planning authority. Rapid transit lines as well as roads, sewers, and other utilities could extend along these corridors. The congestion, pollution, and waste of energy now caused by automotive strangulation are due to the piecemeal way in which highway systems were built with no relation to rapid transit. These public-utility corridors could be related to the location of the new towns.

Recently Americans have shown increasing interest in the new-town idea, which has already made headway in Britain and the Scandinavian countries. The proposal calls for the building of communities with residential, commercial, recreational, educational, and cultural elements that are rationally related to one another according to a master plan. The idea is offered as an alternative to urban sprawl. It assumes that a more congenial human environment can be created through comprehensive planning than through the random splattering of housing and shopping centers across the countryside.

New towns where they already exist seem to have worked out well for the middle- and upper-income groups for whom they were conceived. Unfortunately, they have not provided a significant amount of low-income housing. It has been suggested, however, that, through various forms of public subsidy, new towns could be encouraged to include people with more modest incomes, and moreover that the movement of these people to new towns, creating a housing surplus, would result in a drop in housing prices in the central city, so that the ghetto could be gradually dispersed as the poor moved to vacated central-city houses. The idea is certainly appealing, but questions may be raised as to whether, as is true with other applications of the trickle-down theory, the trickle would ever really get all the way down. Wouldn't a hand-me-down approach to housing in old neighborhoods merely result in transplanting rather than eliminating the ghetto environment?

This problem should be met directly: with the demolition of the ghetto, subsidized low-income housing should be allocated sparsely among new towns in the outer areas of the region, especially those areas where job opportunities exist, and in the central city. Public housing should not be imposed on established communities. It should be understood that when new towns are started, subsidized housing, possibly a specified percentage, can be included in some of their neighborhoods. Moving to a new town should be voluntary. Some people with higher incomes may even find one of the attractions of such new towns would be that they included neighborhoods whose inhabitants were not exactly like themselves.

What are the chances that this vision of the metropolis can ever materialize? It depends, I believe, on whether we can clear away some of our obsolete thinking; which may be even more difficult than clearing away slums. Solutions to proximate problems such as housing, traffic, urban sprawl, and new-town building depend on our solving what I hold is the ultimate problem, namely, the distortion in our allocation of economic resources and political power.

Private capital is invested where prospects for profits and long-term stability are favorable. This means that investors tend to avoid inner-city areas where there is marked instability (which will never be corrected without capital investment). In recent years, life insurance companies made a joint commitment of two billion dollars for inner-city investments which did not have to satisfy the usual criteria. What is required is not so much a change of heart among investors as a change of character in the environment in which they are being asked to invest. And this should be a public responsibility. It is simply not realistic to try to compel or induce managers of private capital to invest in situations which compromise their obligation to use their clients' money prudently.

Private investors, with perhaps a few rare exceptions, cannot be expected to take on the entire burden of financing new towns because of the sheer

proximate closely related, nearest

magnitude of the investment that is needed to acquire the land and to install the infrastructure (roads, sewers, utilities, schools, parks, lakes, etc.) and the long wait before the investment can return a profit.

This suggests the need for a new approach to the building of new towns in outlying areas as well as to the clearance of central-city slums. Regional land trusts should be created with the power of eminent domain and the funds to acquire the land.

This, it must be emphasized, is not a proposal to substitute public investment for private investment. Through public investment the inner cities can be transformed into stable environments that will again attract private investment. Through public investment in the acquisition of the land and the installation of the infrastructure the stage can be set for the building of new towns with private capital.

Regional land trusts could help insure that private development is compatible with high standards of over-all design. They could eliminate much of the land speculation. Through leasing or sale of the land, they could recapture the increase in land values resulting from the developments which they had initiated. This involves a new concept of public capital gains, which could go into a revolving fund to start other new towns, some of them within the central cities. The increases in land values now are frequently drained off by speculators who hold land adjacent to publicly installed freeways, and these increased values are reflected in higher housing costs. Sometimes they become the just rewards for those innovative entrepreneurs who are ready to risk their own money in order to transform a depressed environment.

Regional land trusts could facilitate the arrangements for lower-income housing. The trusts might retain ownership of the land in some neighborhoods where it is necessary to hold rentals down as a form of subsidy. In some situations the trusts might even become developers of last resort.

It is important to note that the poor and the Blacks are not the only people who are having trouble finding a place to live (and, incidentally, most of the poor are not Black). The costs of land, money, and construction have risen to the point where a substantial part of the population who have incomes well above the poverty level cannot afford a new house. Consider the extraordinary demand for relatively low-cost mobile homes.

The idea of new towns on publicly acquired land opens up the possibility of a new approach to lowering the costs of housing. The intrinsic value of the house is reduced relative to the extrinsic values in the surrounding environment. There are rich people who find more enjoyment in their rustic country cabins than in their elegant town houses. A family of modest means might be content with somewhat less if its house was set down where there was abundant open space or a small lake nearby and where their children could

eminent domain government's right to take private property for public use
entrepreneur one who organizes and takes the risks for large business projects
intrinsic part of the essential nature of a thing
extrinsic not essential

52   *Process Analysis*

breathe fresh air. Extending rapid transit lines to the peripheries of the regions and the dispersing of industries make this concept feasible.

Public ownership of the land could be conceived as a transitional arrangement, with the residents eventually becoming owners in a twentieth-century counterpart of the Homestead Act.

Although regional land trusts might attract some private investment through the issue of bonds, the enormity of the requirements and the fact that some investments—such as those necessary for parks and open spaces—will yield little or no financial return suggests that massive federal appropriations are needed. And the money is there. America's cities could be saved with some of the billions now being thrown away on the defense budget.

The lead article in the July 13, 1973, issue of the *Wall Street Journal* reported on a growing frustration in Washington, which was summed up in a question raised by the chairman of the House Appropriations Committee: "Why does peace cost more than war?" According to the article: "Despite Washington's improving relations with Moscow and Peking, despite the U.S.–Soviet agreement to limit strategic arms, despite the Vietnam cease-fire agreements, despite the coming end to American bombing in Cambodia, and despite sharp cutbacks in U.S. military forces, the Pentagon budget threatens to continue rising inexorably. Defense spending for the fiscal year that began July 1st is projected at seventy-nine billion dollars, up 4.2 billion dollars from a year before, a shade above the Vietnam war peak." The account adds that a group of former national security officials issued a report asserting that a conservative analysis shows that some fourteen billion dollars can be safely trimmed from the Pentagon budget.

General James Gavin, who says our national resources must be assigned to different priorities, stated just a year ago that "the military budget could be reduced from around seventy-six to sixty billion dollars, as a start, without undue exposure." The general added: "What has always troubled me most—during my association with the Pentagon and the years after—is our inability to understand events around us."

A Brookings Institution study (*Setting National Priorities—the 1974 Budget*) outlined a series of alternative budgets with different priorities that could provide from forty-four to seventy-seven billion dollars in additional revenues for domestic purposes by fiscal 1978. These alternatives are based on the expected rise in federal revenues generated by an expanding economy in 1978, and on different sets of assumptions about tax changes and defense cuts ranging from moderate to sweeping.

Recent studies by the American Institute of Architects, based on earlier studies by Bernard Weissbourd, have proposed the acquisition by public authorities of one million acres of land in metropolitan areas for new community development, at an estimated cost of five billion dollars. The more far-

feasible possible, practicable, able to be done
inexorably unyieldingly, relentlessly

The Future of Cities   53

reaching proposals made here should require substantially more funds over the years. The prevailing tendency to build bridges that extend only part way across the river should be avoided.

If the necessary funds were made available, how could they be managed? The metropolitan communities at the present time are actually ungoverned. To cite one example: The St. Louis metropolitan region is divided between two states and includes seven counties, 178 municipalities, and more than two hundred special districts. In St. Louis County alone there are ninety-three municipalities, sixty-four police departments, and forty-five fire departments. A nation which at its birth demonstrated a genius for creating a political order built on rational grounds should in its maturity be able to work out some political arrangements for the metropolis that make more sense than that.

The issues, to be sure, are complex. How can governmental authorities be devised which will deal effectively with matters that are metropolitan in scope and at the same time preserve municipalities on a scale that makes citizen participation at the local community level effective? How can metropolitan regional planning agencies be established with authority to make enforceable plans in matters having a regional impact—e.g., land uses and zoning, all modes of transportation, waste disposal—while continuing to offer the wide range of private and local choices that are essential to the diversity of a free society? How should regional land trusts be set up for the creation of new towns and the renewing of old cities? Having powers of eminent domain and substantial funds, the regional land trusts should be insulated from partisan manipulation, but they should also be responsive to the needs of the people. The trustees of the public land, it goes without saying, must be independent, incorruptible, and imaginative.

How can state governments act creatively in metropolitan regions? Counties and municipalities are creatures of the states. New York State, with its Urban Development Corporation, has made a start.

How can the federal government encourage metropolitan regional plans? One way is to make such plans a condition for federal grants. There should be a national land-use plan and regional plans should be required to be compatible with the national plan.

How can we preserve the separation of powers, which the Federalists considered "the sacred maxim of free government," in ways which facilitate rather than frustrate creative collaboration among the agencies and levels of government and between the public and private sectors of the economy?

How can we keep our cities from being shaped by either the mindless mechanism of the market or the blandness and blunders of the bureaucracy?

Aristotle taught that politics was the architectonic science. These and other questions should be considered by men who have the wisdom to design a

maxim a concise expression of a principle or a rule
architectonic relating to the scientific design of a structure

model charter for metropolitan communities. A good model could inspire the discussion that ought to be taking place in communities all across the country. It could suggest a basis for uniting our fragmented communities.

What we need is a charter for the city of man.

Questions

1 Wittcoff begins the essay with a series of problems. Find his response to each problem in the essay. How does he integrate each response?

2 The essay ends with a large number of questions. What rhetorical purpose does this technique serve?

3 Wittcoff combines analysis with process analysis. Explain his use of each method of development.

4 The essay is divided into five sections. Determine what each section does and why Wittcoff created these divisions.

Sun to Breathe New Life into Old Reservoir

W. B. Bleakley

W. B. Bleakley is an editor of Petroleum Engineer International, *a professional journal. In the following article he divides his analysis of an engineering project into five sections: "What Happened," "Floods Tried," "What Sun Has Done," "Future Plans," and "Problems Faced." In the first section, Bleakley explains what went wrong, how forces in an oil reservoir that once caused oil to flow out of the rock diminished as a result of heavy drainage. Essentially, the reservoirs dried up without releasing all of the oil. The second section explains the first attempts to force the oil to flow again, mainly procedures that had worked in other locations.*

The third section begins the discussion of the Sun Production Company's attempts to recover the oil. Bleakley describes the problems involved in acquiring leases, making the project economically feasible, and learning more about the oil field's peculiar characteristics. After outlining Sun's future plans for drilling and injecting water to learn more about the field, Bleakley considers the problems Sun must still solve. Not only do several major engineering problems remain—including how to get the oil out of the wells once it starts to flow—but, for legal reasons, Sun must track down the countless heirs of all those who held rights to any portion of the 23,000-acre field when oil was discovered there over sixty years ago.

Clearly and carefully organized, this article uses the technique of analysis in a standard way. That it is aimed at a highly specialized audience is evident in its presentation of technical information in engineering terminology. While readily understood by those with training in petroleum engineering, the article would have to shed its heavy technical apparatus in order to appeal to the average reader. However, while we are not able to evaluate the engineering procedures Bleakley describes, we can understand the basics of what is being proposed and why. Written mainly to inform people in the petroleum engineering industry, the article can also help to meet a growing public interest in oil and other energy sources.

Sun Production Co. Plans to tackle an old oilfield that came in like gang busters, died 3 years later, and has eluded rejuvenation attempts ever since. The McCleskey sand reservoir, Ranger field, Eastland County, Texas, about 40 miles east of Abilene, had a short, frustrating early life and a disappointing maturity, but promises an exciting future.

Sun feels that application of new technologies in reservoir management, production techniques, and geologic interpretation will pave the way to recovery of a large portion of the 41° API oil remaining in place. Estimates indicate that the early productive life of the field, which yielded about 27 million bbl, accounted for as little as 15% of the original oil in place, and probably not more than 20%.

A pilot waterflood will get underway soon, and careful monitoring of that project should provide answers to remaining questions. All signs are favorable so far, and Sun is optimistic about final results.

WHAT HAPPENED

Oil was first discovered on the J. H. McCleskey lease in October 1917 at a depth of 3,431 ft. The well came in with a high potential and triggered a drilling splurge that saw more than 1,000 wells drilled in the field during the next 2 years. By July 1920, there were 850 oil wells, 35 gas wells, and 150 dry holes in the area, with 220 cable tool rigs running.

The field covered about 23,000 acres and produced from nine separate reservoirs, but the McCleskey sand contributed 75% of the total production.

Cumulative production by mid-1920 was about 27 million bbl and production had declined to 20,000 b/d from a peak of 80,000 b/d.

Reservoir energy was quickly exhausted and operators noted that one-third of their ultimate recovery from a given well came during the first months's production and that wells would cease to flow after 12 months. The first well on an average-size lease would capture about 75% of the ultimate recovery from that lease.

A property-line well would easily drain 25% of the reserves from the adjoining lease, and many leases were depleted before all wells could be drilled.

The field was abandoned almost as quickly as it was developed, as operators moved on to other active plays. Most of the wells that remained active in the field were completed in one or more of the other zones. The McCleskey was dead, for all practical purposes.

41° API oil oil of a particular viscosity as measured by the standards of the American Petroleum Institute
field a coherent geographic location in which the oil wells all produce out of the same rock formation
bbl barrel, barrels
lease 5100 acres
b/d barrels per day

FLOODS TRIED

The reservoir has been dormant for the last 60 years, except for a couple of attempts to bring it to life through waterflooding. These came after water injection was found effective in other U.S. fields and floods were started with little or no engineering preparation. While other reservoirs in West Texas and the Mid-Continent responded to water injection on almost any basis or pattern, the McCleskey refused to awaken to these transfusions.

The reasons are thought to be related to the high permeability of the McCleskey sand and the possible existence of directional characteristics. Injected water either channeled quickly to the nearest producer or was never seen again as it followed the line of least resistance away from the injection well. Operators who initiated these waterflood attempts failed to do so on a scale large enough to minimize the influence of directional properties.

WHAT SUN HAS DONE

Sun's interest in the field started in 1972 when the company was looking for old fields to exploit with newly developed technology. By 1973, there was some urgency to this overall project because of the Arab oil embargo. After many discussions on the pros and cons of tackling this field and that, Ranger field was given a high priority and work began.

Leases were picked up, more than 500 old driller's logs were studied, ancient production records were perused, and a massive data file was put together.

Unfortunately, there was little in that file that could be considered accurate, since good engineering reasons for maintaining records did not exist at the time the field was discovered. The leasing program was successful, however, and Sun assembled enough acreage to make the project look promising.

One of the factors that put the project over the top was Sun's acquisition of Texas Pacific Oil Co., to form the new Sun Texas Co. Texas Pacific was one of the early and large operators in Ranger field (it was Texas Pacific Coal and Oil Co. then) and had held on to its leases through the years. It controlled a good portion of Ranger field, including a 3,500-acre block known as the John York Survey.

With the formation of Sun Texas Co. in April 1980, Sun Production Co. had some 16,000 acres under lease, which represented about 90% of the total field.

Since then, Sun has drilled and cored five wells in different parts of the field . . . and run complete log suites in an effort to gain more reservoir knowledge and assess the residual saturation. But even the high permeability

directional characteristics or properties the behavior of a substance in a particular direction
cored drilled with a hollow bit to obtain a cylinder of rock
log suites sets of records of the rock units traversed in a well, and all other records connected with drilling

Sun to Breathe New Life into Old Reservoir   **59**

of the reservoir—measured in darcies in some areas—allowed drilling fluids to flush the cores to yield inaccurate data. The logs were helpful, however, and Sun has divided the field into eight major waterflood areas. . . .

FUTURE PLANS

The first water will be injected into an 80-acre inverted nine-spot pilot pattern using the Norwood No. 37 as the center producing well. Four injection wells will be drilled, and the first of these will use foam as a drilling fluid in an attempt to retrieve unflushed cores. Four additional wells will be drilled on the lines between the injection wells to serve as producers and observation wells. . . .

With this pattern, Sun hopes to learn more about directional permeability in the McCleskey sand, but already feels it trends southeast-northwest, following anticlinal features.

Water will be injected at 3,500 b/d to start, but the Possum Kingdom source will ultimately provide 150,000 b/d through a 27-in. pipeline extension of Sun Texas system located near the Veale Parks field.

This plan could change, depending on the outcome of the foam coring operation in the injection well to the east of Norwood No. 37. If the saturation is high, a well to the west of Butler No. 33 will be drilled the same way—using foam—to determine the saturation there.

The reason is that Butler No. 33 is one of the wells that showed lower-than-expected saturation when cored. Sun now thinks the saturation is lower in Butler No. 33 as a result of a gas injection program begun prior to 1960. It was planned as the center well of the pilot flood until coring results became known. The lower saturation made it a riskier choice for the pilot area, so Sun turned its attention to the Norwood area. Given a good reason to believe oil saturation is still high in the Butler area, Sun may reconsider that for the pilot location.

Details for future operations will depend largely on the outcome of the pilot's performance. Sun feels an analysis of the pilot operational data will provide many answers now lacking and that the new data will permit sound engineering to be applied to the proposed larger flood areas. Development will be on 80-acre five-spots or staggered line-drive patterns.

darcy a standard unit of permeability equivalent to the passage of 1 cc of fluid of 1 centipoise viscosity at 1 atmosphere during 1 second through a porous medium 1 cc in volume

inverted nine-spot pattern standardized drilling patterns used to produce maps of subsurface features

retrieve unflushed cores to recover oil from wells without using water action

directional permeability a degree to which a substance can be penetrated from a particular direction

anticlinal features folds with strata sloping downward on both sides from the apex

saturation the amount of oil left in the rock

five-spots standardized drilling pattern used to produce maps of subsurface features

staggered line-drive pattern standardized drilling pattern used to produce maps of subsurface features

PROBLEMS FACED

Since 1972, many problems have been faced and some have been solved, but others remain.

Leasing is no longer a major worry. Sun has control over enough acreage to permit operations on the large scale needed to make the project successful if the pilot indicates success is at all possible.

Another problem is the assembly of reservoir data. The solution is to move ahead with the drilling and logging of new wells; Sun will make giant strides with the recovery of an unflushed core and analysis of the pilot flood performance. Additional core data from the three remaining corner injection wells in the pilot will vastly increase reservoir knowledge.

Core tests show it is not difficult to flood to low oil saturation, but tell nothing about the behavior of water injected into the formation. Nothing is known about vertical properties with respect to injected water, and there is no way to predict areal sweep efficiency at this point.

Plans must be made to drill more than 400 total wells to develop all eight major flood areas. This doesn't sound like much of a problem for a reservoir only 3,400 ft deep, but there is a troublesome sand overlying the McCleskey, through which all wells must go. This is the Marble Falls zone, known to cause lost circulation problems. In previous wells, part of the trouble in obtaining decent cores in the McCleskey was blamed on the mud conditioning needed to get through the Marble Falls. In the first injection well to be drilled in the 80-acre pilot area, Sun plans to drill through the Marble Falls to the top of the McCleskey, then set 8⅝-in. casing. Mud will be replaced by foam and the McCleskey will be cored free of outside influences. At total depth, 5½-in. casing will be set and run back to the surface, and the well completed by using conventional perforation methods.

The mud conditioning needed to prevent lost circulation in the Marble Falls also appears as a potential threat to the McCleskey, other than in flooding the cores. Sun engineers fear formation damage could occur because of the low pressure remaining in the McCleskey—30 psi—along with its high permeability. Mud invasion could reduce the permeability to oil at the sand face, restricting normal flow.

The projected 400 wells will be needed to put flooding patterns in the eight areas selected so far, but these have been selected on the basis of reservoir size as it is known today. Additional drilling, followed by further geological studies, could redefine the reservoir and establish new productive limits.

A lift method remains to be selected. It is anticipated that the flood will create an oil bank and most production will be at low water-oil ratios to start. But all floods eventually perform with high water-oil ratios, and Ranger is not expected to be an exception. One of Sun's problems, then, is to antic-

casing tubing to support the sides of a well and seal off fluids
lost circulation problems any problem that stops the flow of oil
formation damage damage to the oil-bearing rocks
psi pounds per square inch
lift method a way to bring oil to the surface

Sun to Breathe New Life into Old Reservoir

ipate total fluid rates per well, and design a lift system accordingly. Beam pumping units will be used in the pilot area, but engineers are already thinking in terms of submersible electrical pumps.

Another problem Sun is facing is the need to look beyond waterflooding and consider enhanced recovery methods. If the straight waterflood is a success, there is the possibility that a water additive—polymer, for example— would be an even greater success. If the straight pilot waterflood fails, there is the possibility that some other recovery technique would work. Surfactants appear to be too expensive, even with decontrolled oil prices, and Sun engineers are not convinced carbon dioxide would be effective, but other possibilities exist.

Finally, the initiation of the eight proposed floods depends on Sun's ability to form the units needed to carry out the program. There are few other operators, and negotiations are already underway, but the number of royalty owners is in the thousands. Lots of work lies ahead in tracking down all the heirs of royalty owners of record in 1917.

Questions

1 Does Bleakley use technical terms unnecessarily? Using ordinary language, rewrite one or two of the paragraphs that do not seem to need their difficult terminology.
2 Find two passages in which Bleakley explains the principles involved in his analysis of Sun procedure.
3 What steps in the recovery operation appear to be most important? Do we have enough information to figure out which steps are most important?
4 Does Bleakley work inductively or deductively? Does he begin with a whole or with its parts? How does he then develop the essay?

beam pumping unit the standard above-ground oil well pump
surfactants wetting agents used to reduce surface tension

Shopping Center Survey: Dallas Metroplex 1980

Herbert D. Weitzman, Sam G. Kartalis, and Kenneth H. Orr

Herbert Weitzman is president of the Commercial/Retail Division of the Henry S. Miller Company; Sam G. Kartalis is an executive vice president; Kenneth H. Orr is a research analyst. The company that employs them is a large real estate firm with offices in five major Texas cities; Brussels, Belgium; and Frankfurt, West Germany.

The shopping center survey reprinted here is part of the company's analysis of one aspect of economic life in the Dallas area: retail trade. The survey includes data about occupancy and vacancy rates in several types of shopping centers in or near Dallas, as well as the authors' views on developmental trends in the area, particularly about the kinds of shopping centers being built and renovated. The authors also analyze the influence of the economy on the availability of capital for the development of more commercial centers. An especially interesting part of the survey is its analysis of demographic and economic trends: what kinds of people can be expected to shop in the centers; where they live now and will live in the near future; what kinds of housing they will want; and what changes in commercial and industrial construction, retail sales, and employment are likely to occur.

The language of the survey is more abstract than that of any other analysis in this section. This abstractness is consistent with the survey's subject matter; discussions of economic or sociological trends tend to use rather abstract language. The audience for this economic analysis is mainly the business and investment community. The survey gives general information and evaluations that people planning to invest in commercial properties might need. It might also prove useful to owners and managers of such properties. Although its appeal among members of the general public is limited, particularly in areas beyond the Southwest, some of the findings about shopping centers in Dallas can be applied to shopping centers in other towns or cities and may therefore interest a broader audience.

1980 SURVEY RESULTS INDICATE
STRONG RETAIL MARKET
AND DEMAND FOR SPACE,
DESPITE NATIONAL ECONOMIC DOWNTURN

The economy of the Dallas–Fort Worth area showed a remarkable resilience during the 1980 national recession. Long-term population and economic growth and short-term resistance to the severity of national recessions has buoyed the growth of commercial development in the Metroplex. The survey area for our Tenth Annual Shopping Center Survey includes cities, where retail growth is significant, that are located within Dallas, Collin, and Denton counties, as well as eastern Tarrant county. The Dallas survey area is continuing a pattern of significant growth. The total gross leasable area of retail space for 1980 was 54,140,824, over 7 percent above the 1979 inventory of 50.5 million square feet.

In 1980, 40 new centers (28 started and completed in 1980) officially opened their doors, providing 2,286,170 square feet of new space. There were 26 expansions of existing shopping centers, which accounted for 726,852 square feet of additional space to the marketplace, or about one-quarter of the new shopping center space. In addition, 10 new centers under construction with planned openings in 1981 have already begun to prelease retail space, and these centers contributed 609,325 square feet to the total growth in retail space. This represents a total of 3,622,347 square feet which was completed in 1980, a drop of 40 percent from the prior year. Neighborhood centers, the predominant type of new center, captured over a 60 percent share of the total space completed in 1980.

Although a sharp drop in the growth rate of retail space occurred during 1980, retailers are showing a strong demand for retail space. In 1980, the total inventory of vacant retail space sharply declined to 2,562,179 square feet, more than 20 percent below the 1979 total and about the same as the 1978 level. The overall vacancy rate in 1980 sharply dropped to 4.7 percent, more than 25 percent lower than in 1979 (6.4 percent). The overall absorption rate for the survey area was 62.5 percent in 1980, a healthy increase over the 61.8 percent absorption rate reported in 1979.

The strong demand for retail space and plans for future shopping center developments vividly demonstrate the endurance of the Dallas–Fort Worth area as a major retail center. Major trends that strengthen this dominance, other than those previously mentioned, included the following:

(1) An overall occupancy rate of 95.3 percent, the highest rate reported during the 1975–1980 period;
(2) Over 60 percent of the 21 sectors reported their highest occupancy rates for any year between 1975–1980;

Metroplex term coined to refer to the complex of metropolitan areas in and around Dallas and Fort Worth
absorption rate the rate at which vacant retail space is occupied

Process Analysis

(3) Over 75 percent of the sectors showed higher occupancy rates than in 1979; most of the other sectors had lower rates due to significant growth in retail space during the latter part of 1980;

(4) 46 centers planned for completion during the next two years report an additional 7,257,805 square feet of gross leasable area will be added to the existing total inventory of retail space.

Most of the sectors in the survey area reported a strong market for shopping center development. The twelve sectors that experienced the most significant growth (100,000 square feet or more of gross leaseable area) between 1979 and 1980 were: (1) the Northwest Quadrant of Dallas (723,506 square feet); (2) Arlington (442,850 square feet); (3) Carrollton (438,304 square feet); (4) Garland (350,168 square feet); (5) Plano (288,600 square feet); (6) Addison (325,415 square feet); (7) the Northeast Quadrant of Dallas (254,902 square feet); (8) DeSoto/Lancaster (181,219 square feet); (9) Richardson (174,065 square feet); (10) Duncanville (145,000 square feet); (11) the Dallas Central Business District (128,000 square feet); and, (12) Irving (119,396 square feet). Total new and expanded space in these twelve sectors accounted for 98 percent of the overall growth in the survey area.

Several growth sectors showed a rapid gain in the total space absorbed that was well above the total of new and expanded space. These sectors included: the Northeast Quadrant of Dallas (146 percent); Richardson (135 percent); Irving (65 percent); Plano (27 percent); and Garland (21 percent). The Northwest Quadrant of Dallas, Arlington, and Carrollton reported an absorption of new and vacant space that was almost as high as their respective growth in total new and expanded space. The highest growth rates in total gross leasable area occurred in Addison (168.0 percent) and Carrollton (88.5 percent).

Not only is the overall absorption rate high (62.5 percent) for the survey area, but 19 of the 21 sectors had occupancy rates greater than 90 percent. Of the two remaining sectors, Addison and Duncanville had occupancy rates above 84 percent, and absorption rates of greater than 53 percent. Absorption rates ran the highest among those sectors with the strongest growth in total retail space. The growth sectors with the highest absorption rates were: DeSoto/Lancaster (97.4 percent); Carrollton (89.2 percent); Richardson (78.3 percent); Garland (76.8 percent); and the Dallas Central Business District (76.0 percent). The largest increases in occupancy rates among the twelve growth sectors occurred in DeSoto/Lancaster (9.2 percentage points); the Northeast Quadrant of Dallas (8.2 percentage points); Richardson (6.9 percentage points); and, Garland (3.1 percentage points). In addition, Denton/The Colony showed a 3.7 percentage point gain.

Although the construction schedules for some of the planned centers may change or some centers may never be built, the proportion of centers which may not be constructed will probably, in all likelihood, be offset by planned centers not yet announced. A necessary influence that will spur the growth of retail space is the plans of major retailers to expand in the Dallas–Fort Worth area. It is anticipated that larger shares of these companies' investments will be expended to expand operations in the Metroplex.

INNOVATIONS IN
SHOPPING CENTER DEVELOPMENTS,
FINANCING INSTRUMENTS EXPECTED
TO ENHANCE FUTURE DEVELOPMENT
OPPORTUNITIES

Shopping Center Development Trends

The greatest growth opportunities for retail development exist in the Sunbelt states. While development and investment opportunities will occur in other areas of the U.S., the Dallas–Fort Worth area offers a higher appreciation in values and less difficulty in securing locations than most areas.

The diversification of shopping center development in the Metroplex is readily apparent as a growing number of centers with less than 100,000 square feet of gross leaseable area are appearing in a variety of forms. Neighborhood centers, regional centers, mixed-use developments, recycled centers, and specialty centers have maintained a competitive marketplace, where innovations in the design and tenant mix of shopping centers have become commonplace. The planning and development process has become much more complex. The planning stages of the development process now encompass a stronger emphasis on various business tools, which integrate comprehensive profiles on site selections, trade areas, and consumers with marketing, merchandising, and investment-yield strategies.

Shopping center development trends in the Dallas–Fort Worth area indicate a shift from an emphasis on super-regional and regional centers to neighborhood and community centers. However, the dominant influence of these mammoth centers on dvelopment patterns persists in the local marketplace.

Regional center developments have closely followed the tremendous population growth here during the last two decades. The diversification of shopping center development has greatly benefited from the extremely high customer draw that is attracted to these centers.

In the future, consumers will be making more destination-oriented trips to regional centers. Visits are more likely to be less frequent and longer. A stronger emphasis will be placed on amenities, such as eating and drinking places, recreation/leisure activities, more seating/rest areas, child-care, and a more socially and community-oriented environment. Although regional centers have begun to saturate the Dallas–Fort Worth area, they will continue to serve as boosters for future commercial and residential development, as well as the drawing card for large numbers of consumers.

The combination of increasing residential densities and higher energy costs has made mixed-use developments more attractive opportunities in both central cities and established suburbs. Mixed-use developments often are comprised of office/retail space and are more oriented toward recreational and

Process Analysis

entertainment amenities. Frequently, these developments are located in areas of high residential density or in areas where the potential for higher-density residential developments is greater than other areas. Regional centers are becoming the nucleus of many multiuse phase projects, helping to bring together the home, the workplace, and shopping activity into a closer, more immediate proximity.

Neighborhood and strip centers have evolved as the dominant retail development trend in the Metroplex. Less expensive construction and operational costs, changing lifestyles and demographic patterns, the concern for energy conservation, and recent economic trends have fostered a stronger tendency toward smaller and more "personalized" shopping centers. More attention is being given to the design and tenant mix of neighborhood centers and to drawing a large segment of the consuming public.

Most neighborhood centers being built are comprised of 100,000 or less square feet of gross leaseable area. Supermarket/drug stores serve as the backbone of neighborhood centers, providing the one-stop shopping experience to nearby residential areas and businesses.

Recycling old centers that are located in established markets will become more prevalent during the next decade. The rising land, material, and construction costs of new centers have lured developers and retailers toward considering attractive locations for potential redevelopment in the City of Dallas and older neighborhoods in the surrounding suburbs. The consumer market in these areas generally consists of either a high proportion of long-term residents, particularly in some areas of central cities, who closely identify with neighborhood centers or a high percentage of residents who annually move out of the trade area. Women shoppers are the predominant customers in most of these centers.

The emergence of specialty shops and specialty centers as a major segment of shopping center development has strengthened the diversity and general character of shopping centers. With its elaborate architectural and landscape design and extraordinary tenant mix, specialty centers can draw customers to areas that appear to be poor locations. Specialty stores generally provide the more affluent consumer with non-essential goods and services, offering a larger variety of soft lines, hard lines, personal services, craftware, and other specialty items than other types of retailers.

The tenant mix in specialty centers, which is often comprised of a high percentage of local merchants, ideally creates an environment of "sophistication" and personalized services. High density–high income areas, the close proximity to regional malls, and natural amenities with a strong geographical and amusement potential will continue to be the determining factors for site selection of specialty centers.

FINANCING SHOPPING CENTER DEVELOPMENTS

The nation's economy is showing surprising strength, even with the record high interest rates of recent weeks. Interest rates are beginning to show signs of creeping downward. Many business executives and economists are predicting a mild to moderate recovery from the 1980 recession by the second half of 1981. It is anticipated that federal and state government actions within the next few months will promote a more favorable business climate, allowing the market more flexibility to influence the pace of rate setting. Given this situation, a reasonable scenario for commercial development might include:

Economic Conditions

Modest decreases in interest rates.
U.S. dollar will strengthen.
Some degree of investment stabilization.
Variable rate mortgages will become more prevalent.

Dallas–Fort Worth

Strong backlog in housing demand will be relaxed.
Metroplex will become first among top five housing markets in U.S.
Home mortgage rates may drop to as low as 12–13 percent.
Variable interest rates, which are renegotiated at intervals, will become more prevalent.

Federal Government

Tax reforms favoring incentives for investments, including federal tax cuts and investment tax credits.

Texas Legislature

State ceiling on interest rates will soften.
Limits on commercial loans will be relaxed.

Financial commitments involving retail developments are rapidly changing from long-term to various forms of alternative debt instruments. A shift from an emphasis in debt financing toward equity financing, shorter terms and higher or variable interest rates, is beginning to take hold.

In an attempt to offset rapidly rising interest on rents, increasing construction costs, and high interest rates, developers and lenders are leaning toward a variety of different financial arrangements. The emergence of new forms of financing is expected to enhance development opportunities in the near future. A few alternative debt instruments include:

—Shorter-term loans for construction and interim loans
  Allow developers to delay permenant financing until long-term rates are more favorable and project is occupied by tenants

—Package deals integrating construction, permanent, and equity financing into one package

—Fixed rate shorter-term loans
  Allow lenders to renegotiate rate at frequent intervals—every 5 to 10 years

—Participation loans
  Lender makes permanent loan at fixed rate and takes percentage of income as additional interest

Process Analysis

—Indexed loans
    Renegotiated at certain intervals, interest rate tied to publicly known rate

In addition, other types of financing techniques have emerged, such as the broader use of investment trusts, revenue bonds, and the flow of funds from money market investments.

DEMOGRAPHIC AND ECONOMIC TRENDS, THE UNDERLYING STRENGTH BEHIND DALLAS' DOMINANCE AS A MAJOR RETAIL CENTER

Population and Income Growth

Population growth and a strong demand for residential and commercial real estate have been fostered by long-term economic growth and short-term resistance to the severity of national recessions. The Metroplex is still ripe for significant growth in retail trade and construction. Growth trends continue to be strongly influenced by the following:

(1) The perpetual, but slower, in-migration of people
(2) The rapid growth of per capita income
(3) The moderate strength of the housing market with its strong backlog in demand
(4) The diversification and interdependence of the regional economy
(5) The growing strength of the energy, high-technology and aerospace industries

Although high interest rates have recently slowed the growth of retail space, the Dallas–Fort Worth area is expected to enhance its role as a major retail center throughout this decade. In 1981, there is a strong possibility of greater growth in retail space; the earlier in the year that a prolonged drop in interest rates occurs, the better the chances are for a significant upswing.

Population in the Dallas–Fort Worth area increased by 28.5 percent during 1970–1980, surpassing the 3 million mark. Since 1978, net migration to the area has accounted for approximately two-thirds of the total population gain. Cities surveyed having the fastest population growth rates between 1970–1980 were Addison (1370.6 percent), Plano (319.1 percent), Carrollton (219.0 percent), Lewisville (168.2 percent), Bedford (142.3 percent), DeSoto (125.9 percent), and Duncanville (103.5 percent). (See table on p. 70 showing population trends.) The Metroplex population is projected to be over 3.4 million by 1985, largely impacted by migrants and job expansion.

The Dallas–Fort Worth area has a greater proportion of population between the ages of 25–34 (over 18 percent) than the vast majority of 25 major metropolitan areas and independent cities in Texas. Population trends show that major demographic changes, resulting from the post-World War II baby boom, as well as other factors, will be occurring in the 1980's. The most rapidly growing age group will be between 24–45 years old, the major segment of the consuming public.

With such a high proportion of younger adults entering the Metroplex marketplace (most migrants are among the 25–44 year old age group), the consuming public is expanding, and demographic trends are changing the population mix. Several national demographic patterns prevalent in the Metroplex include: (1) smaller household and family sizes due to lower birth rates, more one-parent families, and more people marrying later in life; (2) higher percentage of population in the employment age group and more women in the labor force; (3) an increasing number of two wage-earner households; and, (4) generally more affluent population with greater discretionary incomes. As a major center of population and economic growth, the Metroplex has reaped greater benefits from these demographic patterns than most major metropolitan areas in the U.S.

Population and Income Growth of Survey Area

	Jan. 1980 Population	Percent Change 1970–1980	Percent Change in Per Capita Money Income 1970–1977	
Addison	8,750	1370.6		95.2
Arlington	176,450	96.0		86.5
Balch Springs	13,650	30.4		82.5
Bedford	24,350	142.3		110.0
Carrollton	44,200	219.0		114.8
Dallas	914,100	8.3	(Collin Co.)	106.1
			(Dallas Co.)	85.6
			(Denton Co.)	85.6
Denton	53,300	33.7		94.6
DeSoto	14,950	125.9		104.4
Duncanville	28,700	103.5		104.7
Euless	28,500	47.5		88.3
Farmers Branch	28,650	4.2		82.6
Garland	144,100	76.9		92.4
Grand Prairie	71,800	41.1	(Dallas Co.)	75.3
			(Tarrant Co.)	92.1
Hurst	37,650	38.3		90.9
Irving	117,700	21.0		88.7
Lancaster	14,800	40.7		96.8
Lewisville	24,850	168.2		104.0
Mesquite	71,950	30.5		97.2
Plano	74,900	319.1		100.6
Richardson	78,050	60.7	(Collin Co.)	99.2
			(Dallas Co.)	99.2
The Colony	10,800	—		114.8
Dallas/Ft. Worth SMSA	3,054,950	28.5		N.A.

SMSA abbreviation for "Standard Metropolitan Statistical Area"

Process Analysis

Between 1975–1980, Dallas–Fort Worth per capita personal income, adjusted for inflation, rose 3 percentage points higher than U.S. per capita income. Per capita money income, which is estimated by the U.S. Bureau of the Census, showed significant gains between 1970–1977 for all cities in the shopping center survey area.

Several communities experienced per capita income gains of more than double their 1970 income levels. Cities with the largest increases in per capita money income included Carrollton (114.8 percent), The Colony (114.7 percent), Bedford (110.0 percent), Far-North Dallas–Collin County (106.1 percent), Duncanville (104.7 percent), DeSoto (104.4 percent), Lewisville (104.0 percent), and Plano (100.6 percent). Most of the other cities surveyed showed income gains in the range of 90 percent and above. (See table above for income trends.)

Though inflation contributes to a significant portion of these income gains, the rapid jump in per capita incomes during the 1970's is indicative of the strong economic well-being of a relatively large proportion of the population, many of whom are recent migrants. The Dallas–Fort Worth area is expected to experience significant advances in income growth throughout the 1980's.

RESIDENTIAL CONSTRUCTION TRENDS

The post-World War II baby boom population, now 25–35 years old, will be in its peak earning and spending period during the 1980's. The high proportion of 25–35-year-olds in the Metroplex and the strong backlog in housing demand will bolster the local housing industry when a prolonged drop in interest rates occurs, which is expected by the second half of 1981. Total residential building permits in Dallas–Fort Worth were down by one-quarter in 1980. However, between 39,000–46,000 new residential building permits are projected during 1981, which will rank Dallas–Fort Worth with the largest increase among metropolitan areas in the U.S.

While residential permits are expected to rise by 15–36 percent in 1981, the magnitude of the housing recovery, as mentioned above, will largely depend upon how early in 1981 interest rates begin and sustain a downward trend. Home mortgage interest rates are expected to drop to around 13 percent by year-end 1981. Variable-rate mortgages, which are renegotiated at intervals, will become more prevalent. The renegotiated-rate mortgage reduces the risk caused by future interest rates. In addition, it obviates the need for home purchasers and lenders to wait for rate changes.

A strong relationship exists between housing growth and the development of new retail space. In 1980, growth rates in housing permits and retail space decreased by less than one-quarter and 40 percent respectively from the prior year. Many new retail centers are being constructed near large clusters of new housing developments. Expansions and renovations of older centers are more frequently occurring in older, redeveloped, more stable neighborhoods. The anticipated strengthening of residential construction for 1981 may help to spawn a moderately healthy rise in new, expanded, and renovated retail space.

As the local housing market diversifies, higher density housing, such as townhouses, garden (low rise) condominiums, patio homes, and high rise condominiums are becoming more prevalent. The tendency toward later marriages, smaller family and household sizes, and a larger percentage of one-adult households will bring greater importance to the household as one unit of housing demand. The immigration of a higher proportion of home-buying population to the Metroplex (25–44 years old) will have a significant impact on the growth of retail space. In addition, the household formation of younger adults, who are moving from home or migrating here, will strengthen the demand for rental housing.

COMMERCIAL AND INDUSTRIAL CONSTRUCTION

The Dallas six-county area (Dallas, Collin, Denton, Ellis, Kaufman and Rockwall counties) surpassed the $1 billion mark in non-residential construction during 1980, an increase of 6 percent over 1979. A surprising number of major projects contributed to a record-breaking year for non-residential construction. This is partly due to the fact that many financial commitments were made prior to the rapid rise in interest rates. In 1980, the Dallas six-county area had over a 4 percent share of all non-residential construction in the U.S., about double the share experienced in 1976–1977.

While year-end figures are not available, the value of permits for retail construction is expected to be well over $100 million in 1980, and the total value may reach as high as $120 million. For three consecutive years the total value of retail building permits has hovered around $100 million mark, and retail construction for 1980 may be as high as four to five times the value of retail building permits accumulated in 1976.

Retail construction accounted for 10–12 percent of the total non-residential construction activity during 1979–1980, compared to a peak of 16 percent in 1978. Office space, an increasingly important consideration for site selection of retail centers with the recent onslaught of numerous mixed-use developments, accounted for one-third of the total value of permits during 1980. Industrial plants and office-warehouse developments contributed more than one-third of the value of permits in the Dallas six-county area. During 1976–1980, the Dallas–Fort Worth area benefited from over 200 new manufacturing plants or plant expansions, or about 20 percent of all expansion in Texas.

Major categories of retail construction completed in 1980 were restaurants, shopping strips near regional shopping centers and neighborhood centers. Over one-half of the total value of building permits for retail construction was related to restaurants and shopping strips.

Retail shopping center developments in 1981–1982 will be greatly influenced by interest rate levels, the direction of policies by the new federal administration, and the recovery from the 1980 recession. In 1981, a moderate to slow recovery from the 1980 recession is anticipated. Considering the continuation of a large influx of migrants to the Metroplex and the apparent, but slow, downward trend in interest rates, shopping center development may be above 1980 levels in terms of total square footage and the value of building permits. The strongest evidence for this trend is shown by the numerous projects that are planned, unannounced, and pending. Commercial construction, in general, should remain strong as an upswing is expected in the second half of 1981. However, developers' perceptions and decisions and consumer spending and borrowing patterns will not noticeably improve until lower interest rates take hold.

RETAIL SALES

Nationwide, consumers continue to buy more cautiously and conservatively. During the first three quarters of 1980, the growth rate in retail sales for the Dallas–Fort Worth area decreased by more than one-third to 5.4 percent. Retail sales are expected to approach or exceed $15.5 billion by year-end 1980. Department store sales rose by over 11 percent during the first three quarters of 1980. These are relatively modest increases, considering that population growth, a slowdown in the expansion of the housing market and overall economy, and growth in spendable incomes of consumers are moderately healthy here in comparison to most major metropolitan areas in the U.S.

The post-World War II baby boom has come of age, emerging as the major segment of the consuming public. Dallas–Fort Worth has been a beneficiary of the baby boom through the continual process of a heavy immigration of people and job expansion. Although population growth and job expansion slowed down in the Metroplex during 1980, the population is expected to grow by over 60,000 during 1981, and job expansion is expected to be over 50,000. In contrast, job expansion in the U.S. has recently been at the no growth level, while the annual population growth rate in the Metroplex has compared favorably with the U.S. rate.

Changing patterns in consumer spending are greatly affecting the nature and scope of shopping center development and fluctuations in the growth rates and retail sales. The growth rate of retail spending has recently slackened; however, retail spending as a percentage of disposable personal income has been growing at a reasonable rate of 3–4 percent a year. Since 1974, a larger portion of the consumer dollar has been spent on eating and drinking places, specialty items, furniture and related items, and building material-hardware-garden supplies. Smaller portions are being allocated to food stores, general merchandise stores, car dealers, and service stations. Recent retail construction trends indicate that commercial development in the Metroplex is closely following changing spending patterns.

During 1981–1982, business expansion and relocations and job expansion are expected to maintain an important role in fostering growth in retail sales and commercial development. Discount chains, groceries, and other major retailers are continuing to expand locally, as larger shares of their company investments enter the Dallas–Fort Worth market.

EMPLOYMENT

Total employment in the Metroplex reached 1.5 million in September, 1980, up 3.9 percent from a year ago. Retail trade employment rose to over 264,000 during September, 1979, to September, 1980, increasing by 6.4 percent. The trade industries (retail and wholesale trade) account for over 395,000 jobs in the Metroplex, or one-fifth of total employment. Retail trade employment rose by 15,800 between September, 1979, and September, 1980, accounting for almost 30 percent of the growth in total employment. In 1981, job gains should reach the 50,000–60,000 range for the Dallas–Fort Worth area, or one-half the job gain experienced during 1977–1978. In contrast, the job gain for the U.S. has recently been at a no growth level.

The Dallas–Fort Worth area, as well as the rest of the state, continues to outpace economic growth in most of the U.S. particularly more so than the northeastern and midwestern states and metropolitan areas. The Metroplex has been able to withstand the severity of national recessions because no industry or type of employment has been so predominant that the area would face a critical downturn if one industry faltered.

Local employment in the construction industry increased only slightly, less than one percent, between September, 1979, and September, 1980. Seasonal factors and a downturn in the construction industry have greatly affected the lack of employment expansion in this economic sector. Despite a sharp fall in residential construction during 1980, the unemployment rate in the area for September, 1980, was only 4.1 percent, well below the Texas (4.6 percent) and U.S. (7.6 percent) unemployment rates.

The manufacturing sector generates about 20 percent of the total personal income in the Dallas–Fort Worth area; the trade industries contribute approximately 19 percent, a higher proportion than any major SMSA in Texas. Business expansions and relocations of major retailers are shifting proportionally from many regions of the U.S. to the Metroplex and other retail centers and real estate hotbeds in the Sunbelt. This trend should bolster both retail trade employment and the trade industries as a major contributor to personal income in the Dallas–Fort Worth area.

CONCLUSION

While no one has a crystal ball to foresee what precisely will happen during the next decade, all indications are that the Dallas area will strengthen its role as a major U.S. retail center. Population migration, employment opportunities, the rapid growth of per capita incomes, the diversification of the regional economy, and the growth of high-technology industries will continue to attract both consumers and retailers to our area. More important, perhaps, is the enhancement of the quality of life which will occur as a result of these economic and demographic trends, and the business community and community of individuals whose concern for future growth and whose optimism about future planning will serve as the benchmark for the continued success of retail activity and growth in the Dallas area.

Questions

1 What clues are there in the survey to help you determine its probable audience?

2 How well is the survey's factual information evaluated? For example, does the survey explain the significance of the fact that 60 percent of the total space completed in 1980 was devoted to neighborhood centers? What facts of the survey need further explanation?

3 What relationship is implied between the growth figures in the first part of the survey and the discussion of demographic and economic trends in the latter part?

4 What rhetorical purpose is served by the survey's listing of certain kinds of factual data? Could this information have been presented more effectively in paragraph form? Why, or why not:

Perspective on McDonnell Douglas Programs in Energy Systems

K. P. Johnson

K. P. Johnson is director of Corporate Diversification—Technology for McDonnell Douglas Corporation, one of America's largest aerospace companies. His purpose in writing the following essay was to inform the people at McDonnell Douglas about the company's efforts to expand and become more profitable.

The writing style that Johnson uses is clear and concise. In the introduction he explains that McDonnell Douglas, wishing to spread out its production and investment beyond its traditional aerospace business, chose the development of new energy systems as one of three fields to enter. He then explains how the diversification into energy systems is being accomplished and what its objectives are. With this background information established, Johnson discusses five types of systems the company has been producing and then notes a recently acquired system. His analysis closes, properly, with an assessment of the success of the programs.

Despite the inclusion of some engineering terminology, Johnson's analysis is an excellent example of good rhetorical technique. Indeed, the specialized vocabulary is not inappropriate, since the report was intended for the engineers of McDonnell Douglas, who can be expected to be familiar with such terms. Furthermore, Johnson's analysis is not so technical that it frustrates the average reader. Even its complex concepts are presented very clearly.

The McDonnell Douglas Strategic Diversification Plan, initially for- mulated in 1976, selected energy systems along with two other indus- try groups, information systems and laboratory automation, as targets for diversification beyond our traditional aerospace business. The plan em- phasizes complementary acquisitions and internal development programs in these industries.

To accomplish our diversification objectives in energy systems, we want to acquire an established company providing equipment and/or services to energy suppliers in several important market sectors. Our strategy has been to emphasize electric power generation, but also to seek long-term participa- tion in synthetic-fuel programs, and we have evaluated several acquisition opportunities with these objectives in mind.

A parallel objective is to strengthen related internal programs so that we can add advanced technologies that could be important in the long term. Current internal energy system programs include cryogenic insulation, solar energy, fusion energy, wind energy, and heat-pipe applications. These pro- grams offer unique opportunities for our technology.

CRYOGENIC INSULATION PROGRAM

The cryogenic insulation program at Huntington Beach was our first com- mercial program in energy systems. The business involves two elements: pro- duction of a proprietary 3-D reinforced polyurethane foam insulation, and design and construction of complete cryogenic containment systems for li- quefied-natural-gas ships and land storage tanks. The cryogenic insulation technology was developed initially for liquid hydrogen tanks in the space program.

We received a contract for two ship containment systems from Sun Ship- building in 1976, which led to construction of an insulation production fa- cility at Huntington Beach. However, this project was delayed by government approval procedures, and then our ship contract was cancelled in December 1980 when Sun withdrew from the shipbuilding business. Meanwhile, the U.S. government disapproved three major gas-import projects, so emphasis has shifted to Japanese and European import projects. The next important ship contract opportunity during 1981 involves transport of liquefied gas from Nigeria to Europe.

Under license from McDonnell Douglas, Toyo Kanestsu, the leading builder of liquefied-natural-gas storage tanks outside the U.S., has built a prototype concrete tank near Tokyo that will complete cryogenic testing in mid-1981. We will have several opportunities to bid on land storage tanks for foreign terminals during 1981.

cryogenic insulation very-low-temperature insulation

Process Analysis

SOLAR ENERGY

The solar energy program at Huntington Beach is based on the central-receiver concept pioneered by McDonnell Douglas in 1973. This concept currently offers the most economical path to the generation of solar electric power and the production of large-scale industrial process heat. Our business objective is to be a prime contractor for central-receiver steam-supply systems. This involves two complementary activities: system engineering/project management and heliostat production. The solar energy program's most notable achievement is winning the system-integration contract for the 10MW solar electric pilot plant currently under construction near Barstow, California. This plant will be operational in early 1982.

We have also received important contracts for heliostat development and the definition of heliostat production concepts. Two second-generation heliostats, which are prototypes of a commercial product, have been developed during 1980 and will be tested by the Department of Energy during 1981.

Our business development plan emphasizes two near-term commercial markets: steam-generation systems for enhanced oil recovery (principally in California), and large-scale electric-power-generation systems for electric utilities located in the southwestern states. Several heliostat production concepts have been defined with increasing levels of automation, which could achieve solar-system costs that are favorable relative to projected oil prices. Planning studies underway with interested oil companies and electric utilities could lead to near-term design/construction contracts and then to significant commercial business during the 1980s.

FUSION ENERGY

The Magnetic Fusion Energy Engineering Act of 1980 establishes two important goals for the accelerated development of fusion technology. The first is operation by 1990 of a large fusion-reactor engineering test facility, designed for self-sustaining plasma ignition conditions. The second is operation by 2000 of an experimental fusion-power reactor that will generate electricity; our business objective in this program is to prepare to become a prime contractor and/or a supplier of major subsystems. The strategy of our fusion energy program in St. Louis is to develop expertise and hardware capabilities for the leading magnetic confinement concepts. Our current contracts on major subsystems include preliminary design of the nuclear subsystem (reactor first wall and breeding blanket) for the engineering test facility, and design and fabrication of plasma heating subsystems for several fusion experiments, including both neutral-beam injectors and radio-frequency heating devices. Our studies indicate that the projected cost for fusion power could be within the expected range for conventional coal-fired and nuclear electric power generation systems.

heliostat a device that moves a mirror to reflect sunlight in a constant direction

The fusion energy program's most notable achievement is winning the prime contract for design of the Elmo bumpy torus proof-of-principle experiment. We will build a fusion engineering laboratory at Oak Ridge to house the experiment. This program will accelerate development of this concept to the current more advanced status of the tokamak and mirror concepts.

WIND ENERGY

The wind energy program in St. Louis is based on the development of the Giromill, a unique vertical-axis wind-energy conversion concept. . . . A 40kW Giromill prototype was constructed and began tests near Denver during 1980. The technology has been licensed for the agricultural and remote-site market to Valley Industries. The next goal is to scale up the Giromill to the range of 0.5 to 1.5MW, suitable for the electric utility market, and to construct a large-scale demonstration unit with a host utility. A meaningful commercial market for wind-energy systems is expected during the 1980s.

HEAT PIPES

Techniques for fabricating low-cost ammonia-filled heat pipes were developed at Huntington Beach for space applications during the early 1960s. The first commercial application was the Cryoanchor®, used to stabilize permafrost for Arctic construction. Approximately 140,000 Cryoanchors were used for the Alyeska oil pipeline. Cryoanchor technology has been licensed to Mobile Augers, a Canadian construction company. The second heat-pipe application is an efficient dry-cooling-tower concept, developed jointly with Foster Wheeler. A prototype successfully condensed steam at a power plant at Wyodak, Wyoming, during 1978 and 1979. Foster Wheeler is now marketing this system for electric utilities and process plants.

VENTURES

We get many business-venture proposals in various fields and we constantly search for new opportunities. Recently McDonnell Douglas made an equity investment in CoaLiquid, an entrepreneurial company marketing a proprietary technique for producing stable coal/oil mixtures. This approach allows the use of coal in existing oil-fired facilities with minimum retrofit. CoaLiquid will both produce fuel in its own plants and license joint-venture partners.

Elmo bumpy torus new fusion technology still in the experimental stage
tokamak a nuclear fusion machine developed in Russia which uses a mechanical principle analogous to an electrical transformer to ignite and contain the fusion reaction
mirror concept the use of magnetic "mirrors" to confine plasma ions so that energy can be derived from a fusion reaction
retrofit the reworking of equipment to modify its use

Process Analysis

ASSESSMENT

During 1980 our energy system programs had revenues of $33.6 million, with favorable earnings and a year-end backlog of $121 million. Recent business planning indicates a sales potential exceeding $100 million per year during the 1980s. Therefore, it is conceivable that our current programs could spawn a major multi-program energy-system business. However, these are not yet stable enterprises with assured long-term growth or continuity. Government contracts have been an important factor in developing some of these new technologies, but commercialization can require substantial investment by McDonnell Douglas. Both thorough business planning and engineering excellence will be required if we are to realize the commercial potential of these programs.

Questions

1 What natural categories does Johnson use to organize his analysis?
2 What purpose is served by the essay's preliminary remarks?
3 Is Johnson's conclusion a good one? Why, or why not? What alternatives can you suggest?
4 Is Johnson's use of such "mysterious" terms as *Elmo bumpy torus* and *tokamak* unavoidable? Can you read the essay and find it interesting without knowing precisely what these terms mean?

CAUSE AND EFFECT

A *cause* is a force that makes things happen; that which happens is an *effect*. *Causal analysis,* or development by cause and effect, explains the relationships between them by answering the question "Why?" It is a useful and important tool for people in all walks of life. Human beings are constitutionally disposed to want to know why things happen as they do, and the very concept of responsibility to which our society is so devoted ensures that this disposition will be reinforced in our personal and professional lives as long as we live. A sales manager wants to know why sales are down; taxpayers want to know why taxes are up; geologists want to know why volcanoes erupt; police officers need to know why cases are thrown out of court; nuclear engineers need to know why a valve fails; farmers want to know why their crops return so little profit; the bank wants to know why your car payment is overdue; and prospective employers want to know why you left your last job. Causal analysis, properly used, can answer all of these questions, at least in part.

The terms *cause* and *effect* are complementary; one presupposes the other. A cause always produces one or more effects; an effect always has one or more causes. When we set about determining how these relationships exist, we are trying to find out the reasons things happen as they do. We have been taught by philosophers that systematic reasoning will bring us nearer the truth than emotional response or generalizing from a particular. In reasoning systematically, we need to recognize first that effects rarely result from single causes and that a cause is the sum of all the conditions that influence a result. Some of these relationships are simple; others are so complex that a complete analysis of them may be beyond the ability of the human mind to grasp. For example, do we fully understand why there is a literacy crisis? The causes are so many that we can scarcely recognize all of them. But we should not simplistically conclude that low literacy levels are the result of too much television-watching or of declining standards in the classroom. In any analysis, to ignore the caution against oversimplifying is to engage in simplistic thinking. For example, the assassination of Archduke Franz Ferdinand of Austria was not "the cause" of the First World War: many economic and political factors caused the war. However, the assassination of the archduke seems to stand out from the other factors, allowing us to call it the immediate (or direct) cause. Others causes in the complex are called the *necessary conditions*. If we mistake the necessary conditions, we are likely to find ourselves committing the logical fallacy known as *post hoc, ergo propter hoc* (Latin: "after this, therefore because of this"). For example, it is a statistical oddity that the birth rate in New York City fluctuates in inverse proportion to the sidewalk temperature in Nairobi, Kenya. However, the sidewalk temperature of Nairobi has no rational connection with the number of babies born in New York. The correlation is mere coincidence. We must always be cautious in seeing cause-and-effect relationships. Often, it is extremely difficult to prove a causal relationship even when it seems simple and obvious. When tempted to try, we are likely to find that the problem lies in showing not only the immediate cause, which may be fairly easy to determine, but also the usually numerous and complexly related necessary conditions. We also want to be careful not to overstate the case or to be guilty of a hasty generalization, one which is made without taking account of the necessary conditions.

Finally, we must remember to remain objective in assigning causes. Obviously, we cannot take the word of a five-year-old who says that a toy is broken because a dinosaur stepped on it. In the first place, his analysis is suspect because he is not objective; he has a vested interest in not being blamed. That is to say nothing of the violation of reality in his assignment of blame to a dinosaur. The case seems extreme, but equally fallacious arguments occur frequently in causal analysis. An example would be your saying that you failed a test because you stayed up to watch a late movie the night before. Staying up has nothing directly to do with failing the test; you failed because you did not answer the questions correctly. In writing a causal analysis, we must ask ourselves whether we have distorted the analysis by thinking we know the cause and making the evidence fit or by ignoring important evidence that would lead us to a conclusion we do not want to accept.

For most purposes the kind of complete causal analysis philosophers advocate is unnecessary. Unless we are seeking a level of accuracy approaching that required of scientific investigation, we can usually be satisfied with analyzing only the immediate event. Much will depend upon the abilities of our

Cause and Effect

expected audience. The analysis we use to explain why dinosaurs became extinct will vary enormously, in depth and language, depending upon whether we are addressing ten-year-olds or trained paleontologists. Even the analysis geared to the ten-year-old will be more or less complete depending upon its immediate purpose. If the purpose is to explain a science unit, we will take greater pains than if we are simply answering a young relative's casual question.

Recipe for an Ocean

Isaac Asimov

Isaac Asimov is the author of approximately two hundred books on scientific subjects, a large number of science-fiction novels, and many articles on science for the general reader. Primarily a discussion of causes, the following Asimov essay begins by exploring the physical and chemical conditions that must exist if an ocean is to be formed. Asimov contends that the key to the presence of these conditions—that is, to the actual causes of oceans—is to be found in the conditions under which a planet itself is formed. In order to possess an ocean, a planet must be of a certain size, temperature, gravitational intensity, and atmospheric pressure. Even those planets formed close enough to a central star are unable to develop large bodies of liquids if they are too small or too hot. After exploring the causes of oceans and the effects those causes have produced and might produce, Asimov summarizes his data and says that, given the combination of chemical and physical conditions (causes) necessary to form oceans (effects), there are probably only two ocean-possessing planetary bodies in this solar system—one is Earth and the other is Titan, a moon of Saturn.

In this reasoning from cause to effect, Asimov maintains a proper scientific objectivity; he has no particular stake in locating other oceanic planets or in not doing so. His essay is written to inform a well-educated general audience. Little technical training beyond high-school chemistry is needed in order to understand the details, but Asimov's tightly reasoned development obliges the reader to fully understand each cause as it is presented. Nonetheless, the style is informal, and the ideas are presented as simply and as clearly as possible.

Earth has an ocean. Its ball of solid material is covered by a film of moisture. At least it is a film by planetary standards, but it is up to 11 kilometers deep in some places, just the same. Land surface pokes up through the ocean in places, but the continents and islands make up only 30 percent of the Earth's surface.

Is this a common situation? May we expect any planet to have an ocean? Will it always be a water ocean as Earth's is?

Or is an ocean a rare thing?

To answer the question, let us consider what the requirements of an ocean are. First, it must be made of a substance that is liquid at the temperature and atmospheric pressure of the planet's surface. Second, it must be a substance that is cosmically common, so that enough of it will be found on a planet to form an ocean.

There are not many elements which are cosmically common. Only fifteen might be listed: hydrogen, helium, carbon, nitrogen, oxygen, neon, sodium, magnesium, aluminum, silicon, calcium, sulfur, argon, iron, and nickel. Any substance that is not either one of these fifteen elements, or a compound made up of two or more of these fifteen elements, cannot possibly be present on any planet in sufficient quantity to make up an ocean.

If we start with these fifteen elements, can we foretell what combinations will form?

To begin with, helium, neon, and argon will not enter into combinations with other elements, or among themselves, for that matter. They will remain uncombined elements.

Then, hydrogen is the predominant component of the cosmic mixture, making up an estimated 90 percent of all the atoms in the Universe. Hydrogen combines with other elements rather freely, but even if it did so with all the other material available, a great deal of it would be left over uncombined.

Of the other elements, carbon, nitrogen, oxygen, and sulfur will easily combine with the superabundant hydrogen to form, respectively, methane, ammonia, water, and hydrogen sulfide.

Oxygen would also tend to combine with silicon and the combination would itself tend to combine with the sodium, magnesium, aluminum, and calcium to form "silicates," the stuff of which the rocky crust of the Earth is made. Iron and nickel may also be found in the silicates, but the tendency for this is rather small, and an iron-nickel mixture (9 to 1 in proportion) is likely to remain uncombined.

We see, then, that the possible recipe for the manufacture of a planet will include the following as ingredients: hydrogen, helium, neon, argon, methane, ammonia, water, hydrogen sulfide, silicates, and iron-nickel.

We can divide these ten ingredients into three classes.

The first class includes hydrogen, helium, neon, and argon. These have boiling points below $-170°$ C. and are going to be gases under all but the most unusual conditions. They are not likely to be ocean-forming substances.

The second class includes silicates and iron-nickel. These have melting points above $1000°$ C. and are going to be solids under all but the most

Cause and Effect

unusual conditions. They, too, are not likely to be ocean-forming substances.

That leaves us with the third class: methane, ammonia, water, and hydrogen sulfide. These are the only substances that might be liquid under reasonable conditions and that can be present in quantities sufficient to form an ocean.

Next, let's consider the conditions under which a planet can form (and the word "planet" is meant here to include smaller bodies, too, such as satellites and asteroids).

The chief variable in the formation of a planet is its distance from the central star. The planet can be forming relatively close to the star, or relatively far from it.

If the planet is forming close to the star, its temperature is going to be comparatively high and all the atoms and molecules coming together to form it will be moving comparatively rapidly.

Under these conditions the small, and therefore particularly nimble, atoms of helium and neon cannot be held by the gravitational field of the forming planet. Neither can the small two-atom molecules of hydrogen be held. Since hydrogen, helium, and neon, together, make up some 99 percent of all the atoms or molecules in the original mix, the planet, forming out of the scraps that are left, *cannot* be large.

If the planet is sufficiently close to the central star, or if it is particularly small, it can't even hold the somewhat heavier molecules of the third-class substances—the so-called "volatiles" (because even when they are liquid they can easily volatilize, or turn to gases). All that is left are silicates and nickel-iron, the atoms and molecules of which hold to each other tightly by chemical forces and do not require a gravitational pull for the purpose.

That means that particularly hot bodies like Mercury, or particularly small bodies like the Moon, must be entirely solid and can have no oceans.

For an ocean to exist, a planet must be large enough and cool enough for the purpose, or warm enough. The requirements are rather stringent.

Thus, Mars is larger than Mercury and cooler, so that it can hold some volatiles—but not enough for an ocean. And Mars is sufficiently cool so that its volatiles are mostly in the frozen state. Venus, on the other hand, is even larger and has much more of the volatiles than Mars does—but it is so warm that all the volatiles are in the gaseous state. Under its thick atmosphere, Venus is a solid ball and has no oceans.

A planet as large as Venus or a trifle larger, one which is also considerably cooler, could retain ocean-sized quantities of volatiles and have much of it in the liquid form. But then, which volatile would form the ocean, or could the ocean be a mixture?

Suppose a planet is small enough to lose the hydrogen surplus, but is large enough to retain the volatiles. In that case, minus the hydrogen, there are chemical processes that tend to cause ammonia to become nitrogen (which

---

variable lacking a fixed or definite quantitative value

remains gaseous) and water. There is also a tendency for methane to become carbon dioxide (which remains gaseous) and water. There is, finally, a tendency for hydrogen sulfide to become sulfur (which is solid and combines with other solids in the crust) and water.

Such a planet is therefore left with only *one* volatile in ocean-sized quantities and that is water. —And that is why the Earth is as it is.

Now what about the objects that form far from the distant star?

There the small atoms and molecules of helium, neon, and hydrogen are sluggish enough to be captured and, in their overwhelming presence, the mass of the forming body can increase rapidly. With increasing mass, the gravitational field grows more intense and the small atoms and molecules can be held even more efficiently.

The result is a giant planet made up very largely of hydrogen. Solid components, if any, make up an inconsiderable fraction at the center, and we have what used to be called a "gas giant." To be sure, it is now thought that Jupiter, although mostly hydrogen, compresses that gas into a red-hot liquid and that the giant planet is an enormous liquid sphere. It might be considered *all* ocean, but that is not the ocean in our sense of a partial liquid cover of a solid planet with dry land emerging here and there. No giant planet can have an ocean in our sense.

The far reaches of a planetary system need not contain only giant planets, however. Minor bodies are formed also out of leftover materials, and these can be as small as or smaller than any of the bodies of the inner planetary system.

The small bodies that are distant from the central star are cold, but even so don't have gravitational fields capable of retaining hydrogen, helium, or neon. Since the giant planets have swept up most of those substances, the smaller bodies cannot grow to the point where their gravitational field passes the critical point and a snowballing effect begins. Nevertheless, the small bodies of the outer planetary system can hang on to the volatiles, but the temperatures are so low that ammonia, water, and hydrogen sulfide, if present, will be there only in solid form. In the particularly far reaches even argon and methane will be frozen.

The result is that the small bodies of an outer planetary system are generally a mixture of ordinary solids (silicates and iron-nickel) and of "ices" (frozen volatiles). This is true, in our own Solar system, for instance, of the satellites of Jupiter, and of the comets.

It would seem, then, that the small bodies of the outer planetary system cannot have an ocean either—unless here, too, there are stringent conditions which, if met in JUST the right way . . .

The possibility arises in connection with methane, which boils at a temperature of $-161.5°$ C. Bodies of the nearer portions of the outer planetary system would be warm enough to keep it a gas; bodies of the outermost portions would keep it a solid. What about the region in between?

Suppose we have a body at just the right distance from the star to keep methane in the liquid state. If it is large enough to hold methane and not large enough to hold hydrogen, it may gather enough methane to possess a fairly thick atmosphere of that substance—with some of it liquid at the body's surface.

In fact, there's something more than that. Unlike the case of the other volatiles, the molecules of methane can, under certain conditions, combine into larger molecules which could be liquid even while methane itself is gaseous. These larger molecules would be "hydrocarbons," rather like lighter-fluid in nature.

As it happens, there is a body in our own Solar system which just possibly may qualify in this respect. It is Titan, the largest satellite of Saturn, and, in point of volume, the largest in the Solar system. Titan has a fairly thick atmosphere (the only satellite known to have a sizable one) containing methane.

Has Titan, then, a hydrocarbon ocean covering much of its surface? We can't say, but it is, at least, conceivable.

To summarize, then, for an astronomical body to have an ocean on its surface, it must fulfill very stringent conditions in terms of size, temperature, and gravitational intensity, so that only a small proportion of the planetary bodies in the Universe may be expected to have one.

On the other hand, any astronomical body that happens to be just about Earth's size and temperature is almost sure to have an ocean, and that ocean is bound to be water.

Furthermore, there is a chance that an astronomical body that is Earth-size and somewhat smaller, and that is much colder than Earth, could have the only other variety of ocean that is even conceivable—one of hydrocarbon.

The source of our own Solar system is one water-ocean (Earth, or I wouldn't be here to write this article, or you to read it) and just possibly one hydrocarbon-ocean (Titan).

Questions

1 What methods of development does Asimov employ in addition to cause and effect?
2 Reread paragraphs 4 through 15 on ocean types; then describe the technique Asimov uses to reduce the almost infinite possibilities to only four.
3 Do you think the style of the essay is appropriate to its subject? Is the writing too chatty? Is the information clear enough regardless of the style?
4 Is Asimov's conclusion effective? Is the parenthetical material in the final paragraph necessary? Why, or why not?

Three Mile Island and the Failure of the Nuclear Power Industry

Barry Commoner

Barry Commoner, who studied biology at Columbia and Harvard universities, is currently University Professor of Environmental Science at Washington University in St. Louis. Long known as a critic of the nation's environmental and energy policies, Commoner advocates the use of solar energy and other renewable resources. He is the author of over two hundred articles and in 1970 was the recipient of the first International Humanist Award, presented by the International Humanist and Ethical Union.

Commoner's application of cause and effect in the following selection reflects several different patterns. Published originally as a section of a long essay, the selection begins by proposing a set of causes for a very wide-reaching effect—the possible economic collapse of the United States. The causes that Commoner suggests are the economic and political risks he considers inherent in any heavy development of nuclear energy. The selection's next treatment of cause and effect presents a cause in the midst of a discussion of effects: Commoner feels that the hazards of nuclear waste disposal (cause) will produce a better-organized and more official opposition to nuclear power plants (effect). These hazards have already led to the development of the Clamshell Alliance and similar groups and to the banning of nuclear-plant construction in several states until the problems surrounding the disposal of nuclear wastes are solved. Another effect attributed to this cause is the loss of popular support experienced by some foreign politicians who advocated nuclear power in their own countries. Commoner's main use of cause and effect, the detailed discussion of the accident at Three Mile Island, involves a chain of causes and effects. Here he cites a direct cause, the failure of a pump, and then presents a chain of conditions that made the effect worse; in one long paragraph he cites some seven causes and nine effects.

This discussion is followed by two additional linkages of cause and effect which are themselves tied to the direct cause he cited previously, the failure of the pump.

The selection's conclusion again places a cause in the midst of its effects: Commoner suggests that since uranium is a nonrenewable fuel (cause), nuclear power plants will be obsolete in about a quarter century (effect)—if technology remains the same. Only if breeder reactors are developed (cause), can nuclear power solve the long-term energy crisis (effect). But as the concluding sentence suggests, Commoner does not approve of breeder reactors.

Cause and effect is not the only rhetorical technique evident in this selection; there is a great deal of argument as well. Commoner has not tried to remain objective in this essay; he has a point to make. He believes that the true solution to the energy crisis lies in solar power and considers massive investment in the nuclear industry to be a dangerous waste of money and resources. Perhaps as a result, he is occasionally guilty of forcing the effects to fit the cause. But despite any disagreement with his positions, and despite his lack of objectivity, we should recognize that the rhetorical technique of cause and effect is expertly handled by Commoner in the service of his argument.

The essay is most likely to appeal to the well-educated, and Commoner probably assumed that its audience would be at least partly in sympathy with his views, and willing to be convinced. Such an assessment of audience is consistent with his purpose: to present evidence in support of a plea for redirecting our economic support of nuclear power.

Perhaps the most persuasive evidence of the failure of the nuclear power industry comes from the business community. Saunders Miller, a prominent utilities investment adviser who has thoroughly examined the business potential of the industry, analyzed the economic impact of the numerous risks that affect an investment in a nuclear power plant. These include their high capital costs, which always greatly exceed the initial estimates; their unreliability; the growing scarcity and rising price of uranium fuel; economic and operational risks in fuel reprocessing; security problems. Miller's final evaluation of the wisdom of investing in nuclear power plants is devastating:

> . . . the conclusion that must be reached is that, from an economic standpoint alone, to rely upon nuclear fission as the primary source of our stationary energy supplies will constitute economic lunacy on a scale unparalleled in recorded history, and may lead to the economic Waterloo of the United States.

One of the chief manufacturers of nuclear power plants, General Electric, has announced a reorganization of its nuclear division, which the *Wall Street Journal* interpreted as a preparatory step toward closing down its nuclear power plant section if profits failed to materialize.

Nevertheless, the Carter administration has made a strong effort to revive the dying industry by proposing legislation that would limit environmental

Waterloo the battle (1815) in which Napoleon was finally and irretrievably defeated

Cause and Effect

challenges to new plants. The administration's intense interest in expanding the role of nuclear power comes as a surprise to those citizens who remember Mr. Carter's declaration, during the [1976] election campaign, that nuclear power is a "last resort," a position he has reiterated in subsequent public statements. However, his more private statements have been different. In a meeting in April 1978 with executives of the nuclear industry and the building trade unions (to endorse a no-strike pledge in the construction of nuclear power plants), Mr. Carter announced his strong support for rapid construction of nuclear power plants—but only after he had asked reporters to leave the room. Dr. Schlesinger has been more forthright and has proclaimed that nuclear power "is enshrined in the President's program." It is. If the Plan is carried out, nuclear power would account for nearly one-fourth of the new energy produced between 1976 and 1985.

For many Americans the Plan's emphasis on nuclear power elicits the terrifying prospect of a nuclear catastrophe. The argument over the safety of nuclear power plants is not new, but in 1977 it broke out of the narrow precincts of environmentalism into the broad arena of public affairs. At Seabrook, New Hampshire, nearly two thousand people from all over New England, with the support of townspeople, occupied the site of a new nuclear power plant. Most of them were arrested. Nevertheless, the idea spread from the New England Clamshell Alliance in the East to the Great Plains Alliance in the Midwest and the Abalone Alliance in California. In August 1977 there were more than one hundred anti-nuclear demonstrations all across the country. In June 1978 twenty thousand people massed near the Seabrook site to protest its construction. That November, in a surprising political upset, the Governor of New Hampshire, Meldrim Thomson (who had made much over his support for the nuclear plant), was defeated in a bid for reelection.

A good deal of this opposition to nuclear power plants was based on concern over the hazards of their intensely radioactive wastes. In the absence of a "disposal" procedure that can isolate them from people and the environment over the 100,000-to-200,000-year period in which they will remain dangerous, the wastes have been stored in temporary places. The federal government's effort to find long-term storage sites has met considerable resistance from local populations and state governments. Several states, among them California, Iowa, Maine, Wisconsin, and Montana, have banned the construction of new nuclear power plants until this issue is resolved. Opposition to nuclear power has become a fact of political life in the United States, as it has in Sweden (where the Social Democrats lost power for the first time in forty-four years and the succeeding coalition broke up over the issue); in France (where an anti-nuclear "ecology party" got nearly 10 percent of the votes in the last election); in West Germany (where occupation of reactor sites literally brought the country's nuclear program to a standstill); in Spain (where 150,000 people came to protest the construction of a nuclear power plant near Bilbao); in Italy (where an intense political debate has forced a sharp reduction in the government's nuclear plans); in Austria (where despite the prime minister's opposition, a recent referendum forbade the operation of that country's first completed nuclear power plant, constructed at a cost of some $650 million); in Iran (where the Shah was forced, by his political opponents, to cancel all but two of twenty planned nuclear power plants).

The accident at the Three Mile Island Nuclear Power Plant in March 1979 is certain to intensify this opposition, and not only in the United States. (In direct response to the accident, the government of the city of Montalto di Castro, Italy—a coalition of the Communist, Socialist, and Republican parties—voted to demand that the construction of Italy's largest nuclear power plant, near that city, be stopped, and Sweden is preparing a referendum on the issue.) Even from the sketchy information that was available about the accident shortly after it happened, it was clear that the event confirmed the view that because of its very design nuclear power is an *inherently* dangerous technology. The high and growing cost of nuclear power plants is due not so much to the difficulties associated with the technology that it has in common with non-nuclear plants—that is, the conversion of energy of steam into electricity—but rather to its unique feature, the use of fission to supply the heat needed to produce steam. The accident at Harrisburg showed that a failure in the steam-to-electricity section of the plant that would have caused very little trouble in a conventional power plant came close to producing a catastrophic disaster in the nuclear one and has shut down the plant for a long time, and possibly permanently.

The Three Mile Island Nuclear Power Plant produced the steam needed to drive its electric turbines in a pressurized-water reactor. In such a reactor, water is circulated through the reactor's fuel core, where—because it is under pressure–it is heated far above its normal boiling point by the heat generated by the fission reaction. The superheated water flows through the reactor's "primary loop" into a heat exchanger, where it brings water, which circulates in a "secondary loop," to the boiling point, and the resulting steam flows into the turbine to generate electricity. The spent steam is recondensed and pumped back to the heat exchanger, where it is again converted to steam, and so on. A third loop of cooling water is used to condense the steam, carrying off the excess heat to a cooling tower, where it is finally released into the air. This arrangement is much more complex than the design of a conventional power system, where the steam generated in the boiler passes directly into the turbine. In this type of nuclear plant the water that circulates through the reactor (which is equivalent to the boiler in a conventonal plant) becomes intensely radioactive, and the complex successive circulation loops are essential to keep that radioactivity from leaving the reactor.

On March 28, 1979, at 3:53 a.m., a pump at the Harrisburg plant failed. Because the pump failed, the reactor's heat was not drawn off in the heat exchanger and the very hot water in the primary loop overheated. The pressure in the loop increased, opening a release valve that was supposed to counteract such an event. But the valve stuck open and the primary loop system lost so much water (which ended up as a highly radioactive pool, six feet deep, on the floor of the reactor building) that it was unable to carry off all the heat generated within the reactor core. Under these circumstances, the intense heat held within the reactor could, in theory, melt its fuel rods, and the resulting "meltdown" could then carry a hugely radioactive mass through the floor of the reactor. The reactor's emergency cooling system, which is designed to prevent this disaster, was then automatically activated; but when it was, apparently, turned off too soon, some of the fuel rods overheated. This produced a bubble of hydrogen gas at the top of the reactor. (The hydrogen is dissolved in the water in order to react with oxygen that is produced when the intense reactor radiation splits water molecules into their atomic constituents. When heated, the dissolved hydrogen bubbles out of the solution.) This bubble blocked the flow of cooling water so that despite the action of the emergency cooling system the reactor core was again in danger of melting down. Another danger was that the gas might contain enough oxygen to cause an explosion that could rupture the huge containers that surround the reactor and release a deadly cloud of radioactive material into the surrounding countryside. Working desperately, technicians were able to gradually reduce the size of the gas bubble using a special apparatus brought in from the atomic laboratory at Oak Ridge, Tennessee, and the danger of a catastrophic release of radioactive materials subsided. But the sealed-off plant was now so radioactive that no one could enter it for many months—or, according to some observers, for years—without being exposed to a lethal dose of radiation.

Some radioactive gases did escape from the plant, prompting the Governor of Pennsylvania, Richard Thornburgh, to ask that pregnant women and children leave the area five miles around the plant. Many other people decided to leave as well, and within a week 60,000 or more residents had left the area, drawing money from their banks and leaving state offices and a local hospital shorthanded.

Like the horseshoe nail that lost a kingdom, the failure of a pump at the Three Mile Island Nuclear Power Plant may have lost the entire industry. It dramatized the vulnerability of the complex system that is embodied in the elaborate technology of nuclear power. In that design, the normally benign and easily controlled process of producing steam to drive an electric generator turned into a trigger for a radioactive catastrophe.

Even if it is ever possible to resolve these troubles, the nuclear power industry, in its present configuration, cannot support the transition to a renewable energy system. Present (light-water) reactors are fueled with natural uranium, and can operate only as long as this fuel is available at some reasonable cost. But natural uranium is a nonrenewable fuel and recent estimates indicate that if present plans for the development of nuclear power were carried out, useful uranium supplies would be exhausted, both in the U.S. and in the world, in about twenty-five to thirty years. Nuclear power can sustain a renewable energy system capable of solving the energy crisis only if it is based on breeder reactors, in which the nuclear reaction is so arranged as to produce new fuel as the reactor generates power. If the planned-for U.S. nuclear power system is based on breeders, the supply of fuel will be enough to support appreciable nuclear power production for perhaps 1,500 to 2,000 years. But before that can happen, nuclear power will need to survive the growing challenge to both its economic and its political viability.

Questions

1 Starting with the sentence that begins, "On March 28, 1979, at 3:53 a.m.," list all the events that Commoner mentions; label each event either "cause" or "effect" and group the effects under their causes. Can you see any relationship between the different groups? How does Commoner make these relationships clear?
2 Try to find examples of a lack of objectivity in the selection. Do you think that Commoner has a rhetorical justification for slanting the information he presents? Why, or why not?
3 Why is the failure of the pump a "direct cause"? What necessary conditions are related to its effects?
4 What in the selection suggests that Commoner is writing for a sympathetic audience? If he were writing for a hostile audience, how would he have to handle his information differently?

Illuminating Some Obfuscation About Pesticide Safety

Keith C. Barrons

Keith C. Barrons has been a faculty member at Auburn and Michigan State universities, and he has also worked for the Dow Chemical and Burpee Seed companies. He is co-developer of the Great Lakes variety of lettuce and the author of two books and over one hundred articles and patents.

In the following article on pesticide poisoning, Barrons uses cause and effect in two ways. First, he explores whether other *factors may have contributed substantially to many of the human deaths attributed to pesticides. As he evaluates the statistical material, his underlying question is, How many deaths are the result of actual pesticide poisoning? That is, How many are attributable to dangers inherent in the pesticide itself, rather than to dangers generated by its misuse? Second, Barrons uses cause and effect when he complains that some scientists have been careless in their use of the statistical information on pesticides and that they have thus drawn invalid conclusions about the general dangers. He suggests that many of the alarming scientific findings may come about either because scientists are not using accurate statistical data, or because they are using accurate data improperly. In this article, Barrons is questioning the basic assumption that pesticides are highly dangerous to human beings. His contention is that the mishandling of data (cause) is producing unreasonable fear about pesticide use (an undesirable effect).*

Barrons' article is aimed at a specialized and technically expert audience. A scientist himself, the writer is evaluating the ways in which his colleagues have used specialized information on pesticides, a subject of interest mainly to regulatory agencies, industry, and agricultural chemists like himself. His purpose is chiefly to clear up whatever mistaken views have developed through the improper handling of this information. His rhetorical purpose is both informative and argumentative.

Obfuscate—to confuse or perplex. So sayeth my dictionary. The word has not been a part of my vocabulary, but it seems to best describe the careless or purposeful way data of questionable validity is sometimes thrown around, even by university professors with presumed dedication to the truth. I hope to throw light on some recent obfuscation of the subject of pesticide safety.

Not long ago I had occasion to review data on the incidence of lethal episodes in the U.S. in the category "accidental poisonings by pesticides, fertilizers or plant foods," as recorded since 1968 by the National Center for Health Statistics. Their numbers reflect mainly accidental deaths and do not include deaths reported as suicides or homicides. The Center's tabulation of mortalities in this category as published in *Vital Statistics of the United States* is as follows:

1968—72	1973—32
1969—56	1974—35
1970—44	1975—30
1971—43	1976—31
1972—38	1977—34

The U.S. Environmental Protection Agency (EPA) has made estimates of the deaths associated with pesticide exposure (accidental plus intentional) by projection from data recorded by representative hospitals in different regions of the country. Relatively few of the observed episodes in this study were occupationally related. The estimated average number of mortalities attributable to pesticides for 1971 through 1976 (the years for which the statistical projections have been completed) is 53.

Considering that this number includes suicides and homicides while the average of 35 recorded by the Center for Health Statistics for the same years (1972–76) involves only accidents, the two sets of data appear in sufficient agreement to justify confidence in their validity.

Then I read on page 248 of Dr. Samuel Epstein's book, *The Politics of Cancer,*[1] ". . . approximately 200 people estimated by EPA die annually from pesticide poisoning. . . ." How come data sent me by EPA averaged 53 while Epstein attributed the number 200 to the same source? I will risk possible misuse of the term to say I was badly *obfuscated.*

Although Epstein did not document his data beyond attributing it to EPA, he appeared to be quoting David Pimentel. Then in a new book of which Pimentel is co-author[2] I found the statement, "The total estimated mortality from pesticides is about 200 per year (EPA 1976)." Turning to the book's page of references I found that the EPA publication cited was precisely the one I had used, along with subsequent data sent me by EPA, for the derivation of the average of 53 lethal incidents for the years 1974–1976. A further study of these EPA reports confirmed that neither the data nor the accompanying discussions said anything about 200 mortalities per year. I was still *obfuscated.*

validity the state of being logical, provable

Cause and Effect

Possibly the 200 figure of Pimentel (as apparently quoted by Epstein) came from Table 101 of the 1976 EPA document.[3] This table summarized the projected lethal incidents for the entire period covered by that report—a total of 200 over three years. This is an average of approximately 67 per year. The lower average of 53 for the total span of these EPA records as referred to in the above paragraph reflects a marked reduction for the last three years that data has been made available, 1974–1976.[4]

In the literature review on page 1 of the 1976 EPA publication, I did find the following statement: "It has been estimated that mortality resulting from pesticide intoxication approaches one death per million population annually." This carried a reference to a 1964 paper by Dr. Wayland J. Hayes, Jr.,[5] now of Vanderbilt University and author of the book *The Toxicology of Pesticides*.

The literature review in the EPA document was obviously intended to give a comparison of mortalities in earlier years with more recent experience as set forth by the data contained therein. Possibly the 200 figure of Pimentel and Epstein came from this estimate, considering that U.S. population had passed the 200 million mark when they did their writing. But note the 1964 date on the paper by Hayes in which this statement appeared.

Dr. Hayes and his colleagues have performed a valuable service by critically analyzing available information on mortalities, including a review of death certificates for certain years. In Table 11 of the latest report of their findings,[6] they present the number of deaths associated with pesticide poisoning for all those years in which they carried out detailed studies as follows:

1956—152
1961—111
1969— 87
1973— 61
1974— 52

As in the EPA study, they found most lethal episodes to be non-occupational in nature. Accidents included drinking a pesticide kept in unlabeled soft drink or liquor bottles; storages accessible to children or the incompetent; grossly careless use of fumigants or poison baits; allowing children to play around a loaded sprayer where valves could be opened. According to the death certificates reviewed, several victims were intoxicated with alcohol when the careless pesticide exposure occurred.

The reference to one mortality per million in Dr. Hayes' 1964 paper was a valid estimate for years prior to that writing. However, a review of his more recent data above, together with that from EPA and the National Center for Health Statistics, should convince anyone that Pimentel's and Epstein's 200 figure could grossly mislead the public as to recent experience.

It is inconceivable that neither of these authors had at hand the publica-

intoxication inducement of toxic reaction
fumigant a substance that kills vermin by smoke or fumes
poison bait poisoned food or other lure used to kill insects or vermin

tion by Hayes and Vaughan[6] which appeared in a respected journal. They surely must have had the entire 300-page 1976 EPA report[4] and not just the three pages devoted to a literature review or Table 101 which was misread. One wonders why they did not refer to data from the National Center for Health Statistics as published in *Vital Statistics of the United States,* a reference book found in every university library.

Attributing data to EPA that erred by a factor of three or passing off a 20-year-old estimate to the unsuspecting public while ignoring an abundance of more recent data that documents a marked reduction in mortalities is hardly the kind of scholarship expected of university professors.

A glance at the accompanying table, which presents U.S. lethal poisoning data for various classes of substances for the years 1975–1977, as collected by the Center for Health Statistics (the last three years for which figures have been published at this writing) will indicate their relative importance as causes of mortality.

Records of acute poisoning cases admitted to a hospital for treatment are believed by EPA[3] to "provide the best potential for a reliable data source." That agency's estimates of U.S. hospital admissions resulting from pesticide poisoning for the years 1974–1976, the last three years for which their statistical projections have been completed, are presented in the accompanying table.

Lethal Poisonings in U.S. (Various Substances)
Source: Center for Health Statistics

Type of Poisoning	Number of Deaths		
	1975	1976	1977
Total lethal poisonings	6271	5730	4970
Gases and vapors	1577	1569	1596
Drugs and medicaments	3132	2839	2214
Other solids and liquids (excluding agricultural chemicals)	1532	1291	1126
Pesticides and Plant Foods	30	31	34

Estimated Hospital Admissions from Pesticide Poisonings
Source: Environmental Protection Agency

Year	Occupational	Non-Occupational (including unclassified)	Intentional	Total
1974	686	1733	535	2954
1975	985	1830	499	3314
1976	685	1879	446	3010

Cause and Effect

All statistics on pesticide-related mortality and morbidity indicate that children account for a distressingly high proportion of victims. According to EPA estimates nearly 40% of hospital admissions in the non-occupational column in the accompanying table were under five years of age. Let us hope that future statistics will show a safety benefit from the elimination of the more toxic materials from home and garden use. Let us further hope that with our current drive toward safer application procedures, secure storage, more careful container disposal, and precautions regarding re-entry time, the occupational column will show a downward trend.

In recent years fear of cancer has dominated concerns for the safety of all classes of substances, including pesticides. The public needs reminding that:

1. No instance of human cancer associated with the approved use of any pesticide has even been documented.

2. For more than two decades all prospective new pesticides have been evaluated for carcinogenicity in laboratory animals, and only those found to be free from tumor-inducing effects (and otherwise safe from the toxicological standpoint) have been commercialized.

3. A number of older pesticidal chemicals found to have a carcinogenic potential when retested on laboratory animals have been removed from the market.

The public should also be reminded that older pesticides that have been banned or uses restricted because of carcinogenicity caused tumors in laboratory animals only at doses considerably exaggerated over likely human exposure. Even though one subscribes to the philosophy of the Delaney Clause and believes that response to relatively high doses in animals is evidence that traces of a substance may cause an occasional cancer in humans, he must recognize that the odds are very, very slight. Those who believe that the body's natural defense mechanisms prevent traces of substances from inducing cancer will have no true concern. With respect to non-carcinogenic risks, the public needs to be reminded of the very wide margin for safety that regulatory autorities provide when establishing tolerances in foods.

References Cited

1. *The Politics of Cancer.* By Samuel S. Epstein. Sierra Books, San Francisco. 1978

2. *Pest Control: Cultural and Environmental Aspects.* By David Pimentel and J. H. Perkins, eds. Westview Press, Boulder CO. 1980

3. National Study of Hospital Admitted Pesticide Poisonings (1971–1973). U.S. Environmental Protection Agency, Washington, D.C. 1976

4. The National Study of Hospital Admitted Pesticide Poisonings for 1974–1976. A yet unpublished document supplied by the Human Effects Monitoring Branch, Office of Pesticide Programs, U.S. Environmental Protection Agency, Washington, D.C.

morbidity the state of being diseased, the relative incidence of disease
carcinogenicity the ability to cause cancer

5. *Toxicological Problems Associated with the Use of Pesticides.* By Wayland J. Hayes, Jr. Industrial and Tropical Health:V. Published for the Industrial Council for Tropical Health by the Harvard School of Public Health. Boston. 1964.

6. "Mortality from Pesticides in the United States in 1973 and 1974." By Wayland J. Hayes Jr. and William K. Vaughn. *Toxicology and Applied Pharmacology* 42; 235–252. 1977

Questions

1 Review the article's use of the cause and effect technique. Does Barrons begin with effects and try to find the cause, or does he (like Asimov and Commoner) establish a cause and then project its effects? Support your answer by giving specific examples.

2 What rhetorical purpose is served by the essay's introduction? Beginning an essay with a dictionary definition is not usually effective. Is Barrons' use of this technique effective? Why, or why not?

3 Think about the audience and the purpose of this essay. Does Barrons' use of cause and effect here accomplish his purpose? Why, or why not?

4 Is the essay easy to read? Is its language simple and direct? Are the connections between the parts of the essay clear enough for you to understand Barrons' point? What is Barrons' point?

Cause and Effect

Right to Counsel

William Calhoun

William Calhoun is a sergeant in the Legal Division of the New York Police Department. In the following Legal Division bulletin, Calhoun uses two main rhetorical techniques, cause and effect and narration. The information that supports the major technique, cause and effect, is presented as reportorial narrative. The first section of the bulletin, "Facts," narrates a specific legal circumstance: a defendant in a robbery case incriminates himself, without his attorney being present, while he is being questioned about an unrelated case. The second section, "Decision," explores the effect of this circumstance or cause: the conviction of the defendant is overturned. After evaluating the importance of the unrelated crime as a catalyst producing the incriminating statement, the bulletin offers the additional information that an earlier legal decision had permitted not only questioning of a person not under arrest and statements freely offered but also questioning on unrelated charges.

This bulletin is directed at a specific and clearly defined audience, officers of the New York Police Department. It is not likely to interest anyone not involved in law enforcement. Its purpose is to inform the officers of legal decisions that will affect the way they do their jobs, and the bulletin is carefully written, clear, and to the point. Clarity and precision are particularly important considerations in police communication, since a mistake in law enforcement can have serious consequences. Therefore, if the bulletin seems to be repetitious, it is probably because it aims at a level of completeness not usually required in many other types of writing.

I. SUBJECT: RIGHT TO COUNSEL.

II. QUESTION: When a defendant is represented by a lawyer in a criminal matter, may the police question him about an <u>unrelated criminal matter</u> without the defendant's attorney being present?

III. ANSWER: No, according to the New York State Court of Appeals in <u>People v. Rogers</u>, 48 N.Y. 2d 167 (October 23, 1979).

IV. DISCUSSION:

A. Facts:

On February 7, 1975, two men committed an armed robbery in a liquor store located in Nassau County. During the course of the holdup, one of the robbers accidentally discharged a shot. Later on, one of the store employees identified a photograph of the defendant as being one of the holdup men.

On December 16, 1975, the police went to the defendant's home and placed him under arrest. The defendant was, at that time, informed he was being arrested and charged with the February 7th liquor store robbery. The arresting officers read him his *Miranda* warnings but did not question him at the time of arrest or during the ensuing trip to the station house.

Upon arriving at the station house, the defendant was re-advised of his rights. He informed the police he had an attorney, but said he was willing to talk without his attorney being present. After a two-hour period in which the defendant denied any participation in the liquor store robbery, his attorney called and instructed the police to discontinue any questioning of his client. The police did not ask him any more questions about the robbery, but did question him about other activities in which he had not participated and which were unrelated to the liquor store robbery. This interrogation continued for four hours after the attorney had called, and during the entire period, the defendant was manacled. When the paperwork was completed, the defendant was overheard saying, "That God damned gun would have to go off!" The police had done nothing to trigger this seemingly spontaneous outburst, and in view of the facts surrounding the crime for which the defendant had been arrested, the statement was highly inculpatory.

The defendant moved the court to suppress the incriminating statement regarding the gun, but that motion was denied on the ground that the statement had been spontaneous and unsolicited. The statement was subsequently introduced at the defendant's trial, at the conclusion of which he was found

Miranda warnings   the statement of rights that must be read to a person being arrested
manacled   handcuffed
inculpatory   incriminating

guilty. The Appellate Division affirmed, without opinion, the defendant's conviction.

B. Decision:

The Court of Appeals reversed the Appellate Division, vacated the conviction and ordered a new trial. The Court held that the statement in question should have been suppressed.

The Court found that the statement had been the product of an improper police interrogation and, therefore, could not properly be considered a "spontaneously volunteered statement." The questioning was deemed improper because it occurred after the police had been made aware the defendant was represented by an attorney. It made no difference that the questioning related to matters in which the defendant was not involved. The Court declared that once a defendant is represented by an attorney, the police are prohibited from extracting statements from him, with the exception of those "necessary for processing or his physical needs," unless the attorney is present or the defendant has waived, in the attorney's presence, his right to counsel.

This decision reaffirms the rule that:

"Once an attorney enters the proceeding, the police may *not* question the defendant *in the absence of counsel unless there is an affirmative waiver, in the presence of counsel,* of the defendant's right to counsel." (*People v. Arthur,* 22 N.Y. 2d 3251).

In the case of the *People v. Hobson,* 39 N.Y. 2d 479 (1976) (Legal Division Bulletin Vol. 6, No. 5) several exceptions to this rule were outlined:

1) *Non-custodial interrogation*—Where the person being questioned is not under arrest and is free to come or go;
2) *Spontaneously volunteered statements*—Statements which are freely offered by a person, and are not the result of any inducement, coercion or encouragement;
3) *Unrelated charge*—Where the defendant is represented by counsel, he may be questioned without counsel being present regarding matters unrelated to the charge on which the attorney has been retained.

In *Rogers,* the Court of Appeals has now overruled the exception permitting questioning of a defendant represented by an attorney on matters unrelated to the pending charges.

V. CONCLUSION:

When a police officer is aware of, or informed by a person in custody that he is represented by counsel, the officer may not question that person regard-

vacated annulled, made void

ing the charges for which he is currently in custody, or on *unrelated matters,* without that person's attorney being present. Additionally, a valid waiver of the defendant's right to counsel can only be made in the presence of the attorney.

> *NOTE:* The *Rogers* case does not prevent a defendant in custody from voluntarily furnishing information on matters he has merely witnessed or about which he had knowledge, even in the absence of his attorney. However, extreme caution must be exercised during the interrogation of an accused under such circumstances since any incriminating information disclosed concerning an unrelated crime will not be admissible against him.
>
> In the opinion of the Legal Bureau, the *Rogers* case does not prohibit the police from conducting a non-custodial interrogation of a suspect represented by a lawyer on some unrelated matter.

Legal Division Bulletin Vol. 6, No. 5, June 18, 1976, is *Revoked.*

Questions

1 Often organizations and agencies establish formats for particular kinds of communication. This police bulletin adheres to such a format. What advantages do you think result from having mandatory formats in writing? What disadvantages?

2 Calhoun's bulletin is written in a legalistic style that might be described as terse. The facts are presented with only as much elaboration as is necessary for clarity, and the discussion of their effect—the overturning of the decision—is equally free of excessive elaboration. In what kinds of writing situations might such economy of expression be especially desirable?

3 What was the precipitating event that set the direct cause in motion? How does the conclusion explain the relationship between that event and the cause of the decision's being overturned?

DESCRIPTION 4

Description is a way of communicating the details of an object or an abstraction so that another person can experience it concretely. As a form of discourse, it is also the means by which we arrange those details in an orderly manner. Most often applied to concrete objects, description tends to make use of sensory impressions and to define objects in terms of the senses.

Description is used by many different kinds of people from professional writers to scientists to ordinary people attempting to share an image with someone else. You have probably used description in telling someone about a new car, new clothing, your dormitory, a teacher, or a close friend. As the selections in this section will show, professional writers Annie Dillard and Joan Didion use a great deal of description in their works. Roger Kolvoord, a consulting geologist, uses it in discussing geological equipment and rock types, and Mike Oppenheim, a physician, uses description in explaining how patients should relate their symptoms to a doctor.

Description is sometimes used alone, conveying word-pictures for their own sake; at other times it is used in support of another form of writing, such as narrative or analysis. It can be used to give extremely precise factual information or to express attitude and intimate insight. The writer of objective description—that is, description used factually—does not allow his own feelings to intrude; he presents only the measurable facts about the object. The writer of subjective description is primarily trying to create an impression, and some of his own feelings and attitudes may be included. However, description is almost never wholly objective or wholly subjective. Most descriptive writing combines the two points of view.

If the description of an object or an abstraction is to be effective, the details offered must be presented in some kind of order. The three types of organization most often used are *spatial, point of view,* and *sensory.* Spatial organization describes the object by presenting details in a vertical or horizontal order, or in depth order, or in a radiating order from a fixed point. In describing a high rise building, for example, a writer might easily employ spatial organization—that is, might begin with the first floor or the top floor and work up or down accordingly. Similarly, in describing the main street of a small town, a writer might begin with the first building on the left side, and move along the street to the end, and then describe the right side. A description of the Grand Canyon would almost certainly move from the rim to the canyon floor, or vice versa. And a concertgoer's description of a grand music hall would most likely view the hall as radiating from a fixed point.

When using point-of-view organization, a writer describes details from a fixed perspective—along a direct line, from above or below, far or near, inside or outside, and so on. To describe what a character sees through a crack in a door, for instance, a writer would present the objects along a direct line. To describe how the world looks from the cockpit of an airplane, a writer would have to present details of the landscape as they appear from above and from a great distance.

Sensory organization presents details as they are perceived through the senses: sight, sound, touch, taste, and smell. To describe an object visually, one might refer to its shape and its color. Details of sound might include pitch, duration, and emotional content. The touch sensations most often noted are hardness and softness, temperature, sharpness, and pressure. Most descriptions of taste indicate whether something is sweet or sour, salty or bitter. These are often closely associated with descriptions of smell, which tend to note whether something is floral or musky, pungent, rank, sour, or tart.

Description

The Praying Mantis

Annie Dillard

Annie Dillard is the author of several books, including Pilgrim at Tinker Creek, *which earned her the Pulitzer Prize for nonfiction in 1974. She is also a contributor to the* Atlantic, Harper's, *and* Science 81 *magazines.*

At first glance, Annie Dillard's essay on the praying mantis appears rhetorically simple. It seems nothing more than a finely detailed and beautifully drawn description of the life cycle of a praying mantis. Only when we begin to analyze the essay do we become aware of its complex organization.

Dillard begins the essay with conventional descriptive techniques. The first paragraph contains both spatial organization—the description of the size and shape of the egg case and of the way it is attached to the twig—and sensory organization—the description of the color, texture, hardness, and weight of the egg case. As we soon realize, the description is mixed with narrative, which has become the vehicle for the description. Her tale of how she learned to see praying mantis egg cases provides an opportunity to describe those cases more fully, as Dillard teaches us to see the cases too. As she continues with her description, she also offers us some process analysis— in her account of the egg cases and of the mantises in the Mason jar—and there are brief uses of cause and effect as well.

What is important to note, however, is not simply the presence of these other rhetorical methods. We should realize that Dillard has included them in order to enhance the description, the essay's primary rhetorical mode, and that each of the techniques has the same purpose as the description: to enable us to recognize egg cases and understand what they imply about the life of a mantis. However, Dillard does not reveal this aim. The first impression we get is that she is simply sharing her own feelings and observations with us. When we ask ourselves why she is including some of the rather distasteful details, we begin to see more clearly what she wants us to understand.

Like Pilgrim at Tinker Creek *as a whole, this excerpt displays the meditative quality Dillard is noted for, a quality that appeals to a well-educated audience. The selection can also be admired for its interest in the unusual as well as the natural, particularly the ironies in nature itself.*

have just learned to see praying mantis egg cases. Suddenly I see them everywhere; a tan oval of light catches my eye, or I notice a blob of thickness in a patch of slender weeds. As I write I can see the one I tied to the mock orange hedge outside my study window. It is over an inch long and shaped like a bell, or like the northern hemisphere of an egg cut through its equator. The full length of one of its long sides is affixed to a twig; the side that catches the light is perfectly flat. It has a dead straw, deadweed color, and a curious brittle texture, hard as varnish, but pitted minutely, like frozen foam. I carried it home this afternoon, holding it carefully by the twig, along with several others—they were light as air. I dropped one without missing it until I got home and made a count.

Within the week I've seen thirty or so of these egg cases in a rose-grown field on Tinker Mountain, and another thirty in weeds along Carvin's Creek. One was on a twig of tiny dogwood on the mud lawn of a newly built house. I think the mail-order houses sell them to gardeners at a dollar apiece. It beats spraying, because each case contains between one hundred twenty-five to three hundred fifty eggs. If the eggs survive ants, woodpeckers, and mice— and most do—then you get the fun of seeing the new mantises hatch, and the smug feeling of knowing, all summer long, that they're out there in your garden devouring gruesome numbers of fellow insects all nice and organically. When a mantis has crunched up the last shred of its victim, it cleans its smooth green face like a cat.

In later summer I often see a winged adult stalking the insects that swarm about my porch light. Its body is a clear, warm green; its naked, triangular head can revolve uncannily, so that I often see one twist its head to gaze at me as it were over its shoulder. When it strikes, it jerks so suddenly and with such a fearful clatter of raised wings, that even a hardened entomologist like J. Henri Fabre confessed to being startled witless every time.

Adult mantises eat more or less everything that breathes and is small enough to capture. They eat honeybees and butterflies, including monarch butterflies. People have actually seen them seize and devour garter snakes, mice, and even *hummingbirds*. Newly hatched mantises, on the other hand, eat small creatures like aphids and each other. When I was in elementary school, one of the teachers brought in a mantis egg case in a Mason jar. I watched the new hatched mantises emerge and shed their skins; they were spidery and translucent, all over joints. They trailed from the egg case to the base of the Mason jar in a living bridge that looked like Arabic calligraphy, some baffling text from the Koran inscribed down the air by a fine hand. Over a period of several hours, during which time the teacher never summoned the nerve or the sense to release them, they ate each other until only two were left. Tiny legs were still kicking from the mouths of both. The two survivors grappled and sawed in the Mason jar; finaly both died of injuries. I felt as though I myself should swallow the corpses, shutting my eyes and washing them down like jagged pills, so all that life wouldn't be lost.

Koran the holy text of Islam

When mantises hatch in the wild, however, they straggle about prettily, dodging ants, till all are lost in the grass. So it was in hopes of seeing an eventual hatch that I pocketed my jackknife this afternoon before I set out to walk. Now that I can see the egg cases, I'm embarrassed to realize how many I must have missed all along. I walked east through the Adams' woods to the cornfield, cutting three undamaged egg cases I found at the edge of the field. It was a clear, picturesque day, a February day without clouds, without emotion or spirit, like a beautiful woman with an empty face. In my fingers I carried the thorny stems from which the egg cases hung like roses; I switched the bouquet from hand to hand, warming the free hand in a pocket. Passing the house again, deciding not to fetch gloves, I walked north to the hill by the place where the steers come to drink from Tinker Creek. There in the weeds on the hill I found another eight egg cases. I was stunned—I cross this hill several times a week, and I always look for egg cases here, because it was here that I had once seen a mantis laying her eggs.

It was several years ago that I witnessed this extraordinary procedure, but I remember, and confess, an inescapable feeling that I was watching something not real and present, but a horrible nature movie, a "secrets-of-nature" short, beautifully photographed in full color, that I had to sit through unable to look anywhere else but at the dimly lighted EXIT signs along the walls, and that behind the scenes some amateur moviemaker was congratulating himself on having stumbled across this little wonder, or even on having contrived so natural a setting, as though the whole scene had been shot very carefully in a terrarium in someone's greenhouse.

I was ambling across this hill that day when I noticed a speck of pure white. The hill is eroded; the slope is a rutted wreck of red clay broken by grassy hillocks and low wild roses whose roots clasp a pittance of topsoil. I leaned to examine the white thing and saw a mass of bubbles like spittle. Then I saw something dark like an engorged leech rummaging over the spittle, and then I saw the praying mantis.

She was upside-down, clinging to a horizontal stem of wild rose by her feet which pointed to heaven. Her head was deep in dried grass. Her abdomen was swollen like a smashed finger; it tapered to a fleshy tip out of which bubbled a wet, whipped froth. I couldn't believe my eyes. I lay on the hill this way and that, my knees in thorns and my cheeks in clay, trying to see as well as I could. I poked near the female's head with a grass; she was clearly undisturbed, so I settled my nose an inch from that pulsing abdomen. It puffed like a concertina, it throbbed like a bellows; it roved, pumping, over the glistening, clabbered surface of the egg case testing and patting, thrusting and smoothing. It seemed to act so independently that I forgot the panting brown stick at the other end. The bubble creature seemed to have two eyes, a frantic little brain, and two busy, soft hands. It looked like a hideous, harried mother slicking up a fat daughter for a beauty pageant, touching her up, slobbering over her, patting and hemming and brushing and stroking.

The male was nowhere in sight. The female had probably eaten him.

Fabre says that, at least in captivity, the female will mate with and devour up to seven males, whether she has laid her egg cases or not. The mating rites of mantises are well known: a chemical produced in the head of the male insect says, in effect, "No, don't go near her, you fool, she'll eat you alive." At the same time a chemical in his abdomen says, "Yes, by all means, now and forever yes."

While the male is making up what passes for his mind, the female tips the balance in her favor by eating his head. He mounts her. Fabre describes the mating, which sometimes lasts six hours, as follows: "The male, absorbed in the performance of his vital functions, holds the female in a tight embrace. But the wretch has no head; he has no neck; he has hardly a body. The other, with her muzzle turned over her shoulder, continues very placidly to gnaw what remains of the gentle swain. And, all the time, that masculine stump, holding on firmly, goes on with the business! . . . I have seen it done with my own eyes and have not yet recovered from my astonishment."

I watched the egg-laying for over an hour. When I returned the next day, the mantis was gone. The white foam had hardened and browned to a dirty suds; then, and on subsequent days, I had trouble pinpointing the case, which was only an inch or so off the ground. I checked on it every week all winter long. In the spring the ants discovered it; every week I saw dozens of ants scrambling over the sides, unable to chew a way in. Later in the spring I climbed the hill every day, hoping to catch the hatch. The leaves of the trees had long since unfolded, the butterflies were out, and the robins' first broods were fledged; still the egg case hung silent and full on the stem. I read that I should wait for June, but still I visited the case every day. One morning at the beginning of June everything was gone. I couldn't find the lower thorn in the clump of three to which the egg case was fixed. I couldn't find the clump of three. Tracks ridged the clay, and I saw the lopped stems: somehow my neighbor had contrived to run a tractor-mower over that steep clay hill on which there grew nothing to mow but a few stubby thorns.

So. Today from this same hill I cut another three undamaged cases and carried them home with the others by their twigs. I also collected a suspiciously light cynthia moth cocoon. My fingers were stiff and red with cold, and my nose ran. I had forgotten the Law of the Wild, which is "Carry Kleenex." At home I tied the twigs with their egg cases to various sunny bushes and trees in the yard. They're easy to find because I used white string; at any rate, I'm unlikely to mow my own trees. I hope the woodpeckers that come to the feeder don't find them, but I don't see how they'd get a purchase on them if they did.

Questions

1 The purpose of description is to communicate details about an object so that the reader can experience it concretely. How well has Dillard supplied

such details? Can you visualize a praying mantis egg case? Draw one; then compare your sketch to a photograph or to a scientific drawing (you might find an illustration in an encyclopedia or a book on insects).

2 Imagine this selection written as a narrative. To do so, remove all the purely descriptive material and read only the "story" of what Dillard did. Does it make as much sense without the description? Why, or why not?

3 Is Dillard's description objective or subjective? How do you know?

4 The introduction to this selection analyzes Dillard's use of description in paragraph 1. What uses of description do you find in the rest of the essay? Does the essay ever use a point-of-view organization? Are there examples of spatial organization and sensory organization? Where?

On Going Home

Joan Didion

Joan Didion was educated at the University of California at Berkeley and then worked in New York for a number of years on the staffs of Vogue, Esquire, Saturday Evening Post, *and* National Review. *She is the author of several novels and two collections of essays.*

In the following essay, Didion offers an extended description not only of home *and what it entails, but of the idea of* going *home. Explaining her own home, she describes a set of experiences that communicate the essence of these concepts. Sketched with brief strokes, these descriptions give only a glimpse of what Didion wishes us to see. They act as a kind of sensory shorthand. For example, the dust in her parents' home, the conversation on predictable subjects, the contents of the drawer she cleans out, the dry grass in the vandalized family graveyard, the visits to relatives—all give a glimpse of the* quality *of home. Taken together, they evoke the particular sights, sounds, and odors that mean* home *to each of us.*

The organization of the essay is partly sensory, partly spatial, and partly chronological. The main organizational pattern, though, is point of view. Didion's point of view is that of a returning member of a family. Still in *the family but no longer completely* of *the family, she has a new perspective from which to view the home.*

The essay expresses attitudes and emotions that many of us have felt or will feel. Native Californians may respond to it more intensely than, say, natives of Illinois, but the film of memory through which Didion relates her California homecoming has a counterpart in each of us that transforms our perceptions of the past. Didion's purpose is to make us understand that home is really an accretion of the past and that it cannot be fully recaptured or relived except in memory.

am home for my daughter's first birthday. By "home" I do not mean the house in Los Angeles where my husband and I and the baby live, but the place where my family is, in the Central Valley of California. It is a vital although troublesome distinction. My husband likes my family but is uneasy in their house, because once there I fall into their ways, which are difficult, oblique, deliberately inarticulate, not my husband's ways. We live in dusty houses ("D-U-S-T," he once wrote with his finger on surfaces all over the house, but no one noticed it) filled with mementos quite without value to him (what could the Canton dessert plates mean to him? how could he have known about the assay scales, why should he care if he did know?), and we appear to talk exclusively about people we know who have been committed to mental hospitals, about people we know who have been booked on drunk-driving charges, and about property, particularly about property, land, price per acre and C-2 zoning and assessments and freeway access. My brother does not understand my husband's inability to perceive the advantage in the rather common real-estate transaction known as "sale-leaseback," and my husband in turn does not understand why so many of the people he hears about in my father's house have recently been committed to mental hospitals or booked on drunk-driving charges. Nor does he understand that when we talk about sale-leasebacks and right-of-way condemnations we are talking in code about the things we like best, the yellow fields and the cottonwoods and the rivers rising and falling and the mountain roads closing when the heavy snow comes in. We miss each other's points, have another drink and regard the fire. My brother refers to my husband, in his presence, as "Joan's husband." Marriage is the classic betrayal.

Or perhaps it is not any more. Sometimes I think that those of us who are now in our thirties were born into the last generation to carry the burden of "home," to find in family life the source of all tension and drama. I had by all objective accounts a "normal" and a "happy" family situation, and yet I was almost thirty years old before I could talk to my family on the telephone without crying after I had hung up. We did not fight. Nothing was wrong. And yet some nameless anxiety colored the emotional charges between me and the place that I came from. The question of whether or not you could go home again was a very real part of the sentimental and largely literary baggage with which we left home in the fifties; I suspect that it is irrelevant to the children born of the fragmentation after World War II. A few weeks ago in a San Francisco bar I saw a pretty young girl on crystal take off her clothes and dance for the cash prize in an "amateur-topless" contest. There was no particular sense of moment about this, none of the effect of romantic degradation, of "dark journey," for which my generation strived so assiduously. What sense could that girl possibly make of, say, *Long Day's Journey into Night?* Who is beside the point?

That I am trapped in this particular irrelevancy is never more apparent to

Canton dessert plates antique dishes from China
assay scales scales for weighing gold and other precious metals

me than when I am home. Paralyzed by the neurotic lassitude engendered by meeting one's past at every turn, around every corner, inside every cupboard, I go aimlessly from room to room. I decide to meet it head-on and clean out a drawer, and I spread the contents on the bed. A bathing suit I wore the summer I was seventeen. A letter of rejection from *The Nation,* an aerial photograph of the site for a shopping center my father did not build in 1954. Three teacups hand-painted with cabbage roses and signed "E.M.," my grandmother's initials. There is no final solution for letters of rejection from *The Nation,* and teacups hand-painted in 1900. Nor is there any answer to snapshots of one's grandfather as a young man on skis, surveying around Donner Pass in the year 1910. I smooth out the snapshot and look into his face, and do and do not see my own. I close the drawer, and have another cup of coffee with my mother. We get along very well, veterans of a guerrilla war we never understood.

Days pass. I see no one. I come to dread my husband's evening call, not only because he is full of news of what by now seems to me our remote life in Los Angeles, people he has seen, letters which require attention, but because he asks what I have been doing, suggests uneasily that I get out, drive to San Francisco or Berkeley. Instead I drive across the river to a family graveyard. It has been vandalized since my last visit and the monuments are broken, overturned in the dry grass. Because I once saw a rattlesnake in the grass I stay in the car and listen to a country-and-Western station. Later I drive with my father to a ranch he has in the foothills. The man who runs his cattle on it asks us to the roundup, a week from Sunday, and although I know that I will be in Los Angeles I say, in the oblique way my family talks, that I will come. Once home I mention the broken monuments in the graveyard. My mother shrugs.

I go to visit my great-aunts. A few of them think now that I am my cousin, or their daughter who died young. We recall an anecdote about a relative last seen in 1948, and they ask if I still like living in New York City. I have lived in Los Angeles for three years, but I say that I do. The baby is offered a horehound drop, and I am slipped a dollar bill "to buy a treat." Questions trail off, answers are abandoned, the baby plays with the dust motes in a shaft of afternoon sun.

It is time for the baby's birthday party: a white cake, strawberry-marshmallow ice cream, a bottle champagne saved from another party. In the evening, after she has gone to sleep, I kneel beside the crib and touch her face, where it is pressed against the slats, with mine. She is an open and trusting child, unprepared for and unaccustomed to the ambushes of family life, and perhaps it is just as well that I can offer her little of that life. I would like to give her more. I would like to promise her that she will grow up with a sense of her cousins and of rivers and of her great-grandmother's teacups, would like to pledge her a picnic on a river with fried chicken and her hair uncombed, would like to give her *home* for her birthday, but we live differently now and I can promise her nothing like that. I give her a xylophone and a sundress from Madeira, and promise to tell her a funny story.

On Going Home   **119**

Questions

1 How does Didion describe the family graveyard? Can you visualize it? Is your mental image of the graveyard as sharp as your mental image of the drawer that Didion straightened?

2 Make a list of ten sensory details Didion supplies. Try to find at least one detail to represent each of the five senses.

3 How does Didion suggest to the reader that a large part of the meaning of home is the sense of the past?

4 What do you think Didion means when she says that she cannot give her daughter *home* for her birthday?

How to Get Your Money's Worth From Your Doctor

Mike Oppenheim

Mike Oppenheim is a physician in family practice in Los Angeles. The subject of his description here is an idea rather than an object; therefore, the rhetorical technique is somewhat more complex than it might be if he were describing, say, a new kind of stethoscope or a new treatment for a headache. Oppenheim in fact employs a wide variety of rhetorical methods, among them process, example, narrative, analysis, cause and effect, and definition. For example, the essay is organized around a few rules to observe in communicating with your doctor; thus it uses process. The steps in dealing with a doctor are explained through several other rhetorical methods. Stressing the need for clear talk between doctor and patient, Oppenheim describes and analyzes several situations in which poor communication existed. Some of his examples are narrative, others involve definition. And since the diagnosis of symptoms is central to medicine, cause and effect appears throughout the essay. Yet the whole development of the essay serves a descriptive function: to establish what is (and what is not) good communication between doctor and patient. In each instance Oppenheim is using detail to make us see, to make us experience, both poor communication and good communication. Indeed, his advice on describing medical problems can be applied to almost any exchange of information: be objective, be precise, be complete,

Oppenheim's article deals with a subject of importance to the general public, and it is written in a style that almost any adult can understand. Its language is simple and direct, and its gossipy tone adds to its appeal. Oppenheim also ensures his readers' interest by appealing to the common desire to get the most for one's money. He knows that providing the average patient with the best medical care possible requires the complete cooperation of the patient, and that a medical evaluation is only as good as the information upon which it is based. He is therefore trying to tell patients how to give their physician the most useful information they possibly can.

*S*ometimes doctors and patients have a hard time talking to each other. Here's a typical dialogue:

Doctor: "What brings you to the doctor, Mr. Jones?"

Patient: "I've been having trouble breathing."

Doctor: "Tell me about it."

Patient: "Sometimes I have trouble breathing. It's been worse since my vacation."

Doctor: "A couple of weeks ago?"

Patient: "No, eight months. I saw a doctor about it in San Diego. It got better when I moved to Los Angeles, but only for a month or so."

Doctor: "What happened when you saw the doctor?"

Patient: "He did tests."

Doctor: "What were the results?

Patient: "He gave me pills. They're the only thing that helps."

Doctor: "What sort of pills?"

Patient: "To help me breathe."

Doctor: "Do you know the name?"

Patient: "No, but they were little white ones."

I've had similar conversations again and again—conversations in which a patient does not describe his or her illness, cannot tell what previous doctors said or did, and does not know the name of medications. The patient may not be entirely to blame—his former doctor may have failed to supply important details—but the result is the same. Poor communication is all too common—and more harmful and costly to patients than many of them realize.

Many people believe that a doctor's examination and "tests" will get to the root of the problem. But 90 percent of a doctor's knowledge of a particular case comes from the patient. That's why it's important to give your doctor as much information as possible—and to give it accurately. Here are the main rules to keep in mind:

When you have a new illness, tell the doctor what's bothering you—not what you think it is.

Wrong: "I have a kidney infection."

Right: "I have a pain in this spot on my back."

Although patients who give their own diagnosis are often right, they're sometimes wrong. A conscientious doctor will investigate thoroughly and come to his own conclusion, but doctors are human. Under pressure they're sometimes tempted to take the patient's word for it—and that can be a big mistake.

Recently a patient told me, "My bladder infection just came back." I had seen her several times for the same problem and had no reason to doubt her. The office was crowded and I was falling behind on appointments, so I ex-

122 *Description*

pressed sympathy and wrote a prescription for an antibiotic. We were both pleased that it took so little time.

A week later she was back. The drug had not helped. I questioned her at length and discovered she did *not* have a bladder infection. A quick exam revealed that she had a minor vaginal infection that produces almost the same symptoms. The moral of this story is: Don't try to make your doctor's job easier by telling him or her your diagnosis. You may be sorry if he takes you up on it.

If you've had a significant medical problem in the past, give the doctor specific details about it.

I've often been frustrated by some patients' lack of knowledge about catastrophic events in their past. If I ask why they were hospitalized, for example, I might be told:

"For tests." (useless).

"For a heart condition." (not much better).

"For heart failure." (useful but too vague).

"Heart failure from a leaky valve." (pretty good).

"Heart failure from a leaky mitral valve; the doctor said I probably had rheumatic fever when I was young." (ideal).

Don't assume your doctor can "send for the records." That takes time and doesn't always succeed. Don't assume "it's in the chart" either. Your doctor's file may well contain a jumble of illegible handwriting and disorganized, incomplete data. Remember, it's *your* body. The best place for facts about it is your head.

"But my doctor didn't explain it," many patients complain. They're often right. Some doctors do a poor job of helping their patients understand what's going on. There's no excuse for that, but there's also no excuse for a patient's failure to ask for an explanation.

When I insist that patients know the names of their drugs or medical conditions, they often respond, "It's so long and complicated, I'll never remember it. . . ." But people remember what's important to them. How many inhabitants of Indianapolis or Guadalajara would say, "Sorry, I don't remember where I live. It's such a big word. . . ."

If you're changing doctors be sure to ask for a copy of your medical records to take with you. In many states they are legally your property, and the doctor must give them up if asked. And you can always get them if you're insistent.

Describe exactly how you feel, and tell the doctor everything you think he or she should know.

Never assume that your doctor will cleverly ferret out the necessary information by asking the right questions. And don't worry about giving too much data. You may not think your headache is related to your stomach problem, but tell your doctor about it anyway. Remember that your family's problems are pertinent to your own. If you're concerned about a lump in your breast, the doctor should know whether your mother had breast cancer.

Do your homework.

The doctor's office is not a witness stand, but the experience is more pleasant if you can answer pertinent questions. For example, if a patient has pain I always ask for a description (sharp? dull? throbbing? squeezing? knife-like? . . .). He or she may insist it can't be described, but it always can—provided there's enough time and encouragement.

Other questions that should be answered (even if the doctor doesn't ask them) are: How long have you had the problem? How has it changed? What have you done about it? What makes it better? What makes it worse? Does anyone around you have it?

Preparation is enormously helpful. When a patient comes to me with a problem, I sit back and listen to it without interruption. Some patients are so well organized that I never have to ask any questions. But occasionally a story goes on and on with hardly a scrap of useful information.

Here is an example: "I woke up last night and felt terrible. Then I threw up. I couldn't get back to sleep, so I watched TV for a while and made myself some cocoa. I couldn't keep it down. I took my temperature and had a little fever. I went back to bed, but my stomach kept me awake. I took some bicarbonate of soda and a tranquilizer and that seemed to help. I slept a couple of hours. I still feel awful, but the diarrhea isn't quite so bad. It's probably something I ate."

Such a patient could have food poisoning, a stomach virus, appendicitis, typhoid fever, a drug reaction, a hangover or a dozen other problems. The story is not much help in narrowing them down.

Always tell the doctor why you did whatever you did.

Patients often describe their self-treatment in great detail—without explaining their reasons. In the previous example the patient says, "I couldn't get back to sleep . . ." (Why?) ". . . my stomach kept me up." (How?) "I took some bicarbonate of soda. . . ." (For what symptom?) "I slept a couple of hours." (Why only a couple?)

This patient also said she "had a little fever." Statements like that are confusing to doctors, because people have different ideas about fever. Most of us know that 98.6 is a normal temperature, but 99 can also be normal. Does the patient realize that, or does she think 98.8 is "a little fever"?

Here's how a doctor would love to hear the same situation described: "I woke up at 3 A.M. feeling nauseated. I vomited three times in the next hour. I took my temperature; it was 99. At four I went back to bed, but I couldn't sleep. I had cramps in my lower abdomen. I vomited again around five and started to have diarrhea. I took some bicarbonate of soda and a tranquilizer, and the cramps seemed to get better. I slept for two hours but then the diarrhea kept me running. I still feel queasy and tired, but the cramps are gone. I haven't vomited since five A.M., but the diarrhea still hits me every hour or so."

From this story it's clear the patient has a mild case of food poisoning and should continue to improve. Notice that the description did not require a large vocabulary or any knowledge of medicine—which leads to the next rule.

Keep it simple.

Your doctor may be a brilliant person with a wealth of scientific knowledge, but it's better to talk about your problems as if he or she is a little dim. Avoid using medical terminology to describe an illness because doctors can never be certain what laymen mean. Some patients think, for example, that a medical term is another way of saying "serious." (A severe headache is a "migraine"; a bad sore throat is a "strep throat.") This is wrong.

Try not to use words that mean different things to different people. When I hear "indigestion," a dozen symptoms come to mind. I have no clear idea of what a "nervous breakdown" is. And I'm not entirely sure what a patient has in mind when I hear he or she as a "cold."

Here are some examples:

Wrong: "My indigestion is acting up."

Right: "I have a burning pain here in my stomach and I've been doing a lot of belching."

Wrong: "My husband had a nervous breakdown."

Right: "My husband became very depressed and had to be hospitalized."

Make sure your doctor communicates with you.

Although it's the doctor's responsibility to communicate with you, no one is perfect. If you're the sixth patient with low back pain he's seen that day, his discussion may well be shorter than it was for the first patient. If it leaves you uncertain about what to do, the doctor has not done his job properly—but you will be the one to suffer.

In sheer self-defense, you must make sure you're satisfied with the doctor's explanation and instructions. You should know the answers to the following questions:

What is my problem? It should have a name—and the name should tell you something about it. If the doctor tells you you have a sprained back, what have you learned? Is it an injured muscle, a pinched nerve or a slipped disc? Don't accept meaningless descriptions like "weak bladder," "nervous stomach" or "poor circulation."

If the doctor's answer is "I don't know," that may be proper—provided you're told what he or she intends to do next. For example, "I don't know, but call me if it doesn't go away in a few days." Or "I don't know, but we'll do some tests."

What caused it? If you've just fallen down the stairs, it's clear why your ankle hurts. But often it's not so obvious. Never be satisfied with vague scientific terms such as "anemia" or "arthritis." And don't assume you know the cause of the problem. Many people think anemia is caused by a poor diet, but that's wrong. Almost all anemia in young women is from excessive bleeding. Diet is hardly ever responsible except in pregnancy. If you're told you have anemia, it's critically important to find out why. Where are you bleeding? What should you do about it? Getting the proper medication is far less crucial. Many patients tell me they have "anemia" and take vitamins or iron for it. Fortunately most of them are *not* anemic, but that's another subject.

What should I do about it? Most doctors will tell you what to do, but make sure you remember. Researchers have asked patients leaving doctor's offices to repeat what the doctor told them. Invariably, they recalled only a fraction of what they were told. Don't be afraid to take notes or to ask the doctor to write down the instructions. I recently had a wisdom tooth extracted. Several times the following day I had to refer to the instruction sheet the dentist gave me. He had told me what to do, but in the anxiety of the moment I forgot.

When should I get better and what should I do if I don't? If more patients asked these questions, it would eliminate much worry and many phone calls. At the end of a visit I routinely say, "If you're not better in three (or whatever) days, let me know."

Do you want to see me again for this problem? If the doctor has not already told you when to return, ask. There is always an answer, even if it is "no."

Do I really need this? The majority of all doctor visits are for minor problems that medical science cannot cure. Colds, the flu, viral infections and upset stomachs run their course no matter what medicine is given. Bumps, bruises and minor sprains heal in their own time. Medication for these ills may make the discomfort more tolerable, but it's not essential.

Doctors often overtreat these conditions because they've learned that most patients feel better if they receive something: a shot, a prescription, "a treatment," anything. When I prescribe cough medicine, I tell my patients that it will not cure their colds. Only rarely does someone say, "If it's not necessary, I'll do without it." If relief of your symptoms is not important, ask whether the medication is necessary. But don't decide on your own whether or not you need it.

Knowing your answers to these questions may not cure you more quickly, but it will take the mystery out of your illness and help you deal more confidently with it and with your doctor. It can also save you the cost of unnecessary visits and medications.

We are all conscious of our health these days. The average person recognizes the importance of a nourishing diet, regular exercise and avoidance of smoking and excessive drinking. Most would add a good relationship with a doctor—and that involves communication. A doctor can learn some things by examining you and other facts through lab tests. But the greatest source of information is what you tell him. The most useful thing you can do at the doctor's office is to talk to him—and make sure he talks to you.

Description

Questions

1 Oppenheim's article appeared in *Woman's Day,* a magazine sold in grocery stores and containing recipes, craft ideas, and beauty and fashion information. Considering its subject matter and tone, do you think the article appeared in the right publication? Why, or why not?

2 What is the purpose of beginning the article with a dialogue between a hypothetical doctor and patient? Are there other dialogues in the article? Is their use effective?

3 What do you find amusing in the opening dialogue? Are there other humorous passages in the article? Does the humor add or detract from the author's serious purpose? Why?

4 Are the rhetorical techniques used here too fragmented and inconsistent? Would the article be improved if it relied more consistently upon a single method of development? Why, or why not?

Fluid Inclusion Research:
An Informal Proposal

Roger Kolvoord

Roger Kolvoord is a geologist and president of his own consulting firm, Diversified Exploration Services, Inc., located in Denver, Colorado. The proposal he offers in this selection uses several rhetorical techniques in discussing the equipment and steps necessary for a particular type of research. Description is the primary technique used to explain the problems and the expense connected with the optical and heating systems involved. Kolvoord is very selective, though; he describes only the parts of the microscope or heating stage necessary for the work he is proposing. To describe such equipment in further detail would not suit the purpose of the proposal. If we make an effort to understand the terminology, the descriptions become very clear. They are analytical descriptions—that is, they are presented for the purpose of evaluating.

Kolvoord begins with a statement of the problems one encounters in doing this sort of research: the object to be researched is very small and thus requires high magnification, and it must be examined at very high temperatures which could damage the optical system used. He then describes the petrographic microscopes ordinarily used, stressing the problems that they might cause. His description is objective, and moves spatially within what he calls the "working distance," the space between the viewing stage and the objective of the lens. The description of heating stages is also objective and is perhaps even more selective than the description of microscopes. Kolvoord explains the problems presented by commercially available heating stages, and then describes the differences between the heating stages. Thus Kolvoord's proposal could also serve as an example of process analysis.

The proposal was sent by Kolvoord to a fellow geologist, an engineer at the Last Ditch Mining Company (ficticious names are used to protect the confidentiality of a business arrangement, but the proposal is an actual one). The presentation of informal proposals in letter form is increasingly common in industry, as is informal language. It may seem a bit jarring to read technical language side by side with highly colloquial expressions; indeed, were Kolvoord writing a paper to be delivered at a professional meeting, he would undoubtedly use a more formal style. In this letter, however, he is interested not only in providing a suggestion and an analysis of procedure and cost, both of which must be phrased technically, but in maintaining a cordial relationship with a prospective client. To use a formal style might imply pomposity or arrogance.

129

Dr. Joe Blow   March 27, 19--
Last Ditch Mining Company
P. O. Box 733
Leadville, CO 80462

Dear Joe:

I have given some thought to our March 15 telephone discussion on the possibility of doing some fluid inclusion research for Last Ditch. In this letter, I have explained some of the considerations that go into setting up for fluid inclusion work and some "ballpark" figures on the cost of setting up a fluid inclusion capability. A serious commitment on our part would be required to significantly reduce these costs.

As we discussed, I have looked at a system that was designed to do relatively low-temperature (less than 300°C) homogenization temperature determinations and freezing point measurements for determination of salinities. There are basically four instrumentation aspects that need to be considered in designing a system. These are:

1. Sample preparation;
2. Optical system;
3. Heating stage; and
4. Cooling stage.

I propose to consider these separately below.

1. *Sample Preparation.*

Unless one wants to be limited to working solely with single crystals of very high quality, it is necessary to be able to cut and polish specimens for examination. This needs to be done in a manner which does not mechanically overstress the sample (since this will tend to open inclusions) or does not excessively heat the sample. Excessive heating can induce sufficient pressure in the inclusions to open them. The most satisfactory system involves use of a diamond dicing saw, such as is sometimes used for study of semiconductors, to slice thin slabs from the sample material. With most heating stages, this material must then be polished to obtain suitable optics for examination of the inclusions. Therefore, polishing equipment is also required. In operation, the time

---

fluid inclusion small amounts of fluids present in minerals which may be trapped within the mineral grains when minerals crystallize. Most are microscopic and may also contain a small bubble of gas.
homogenization temperature determinations determinations of the temperature at which all the physical parts of the rock under study take on the same structure
salinities measures of the quantity of total dissolved solids in water

required to prepare a sample for examination is comparable to the time required to prepare a sample for polished section analysis in ore microscopy. I estimate that suitable equipment would cost about $2,000.

2. Optical System.

Most fluid inclusions are very, very small, and it is desirable to be able to examine the sample under as high a magnification as is possible. This is complicated by the fact that the optical system of the microscope must be protected from the heat of the sample. In practice, what one desires is a microscope with very high magnification but a very long working distance. This is, of course, a very difficult optical combination at which to arrive. This problem can be simplified somewhat through the design of the heating stage, but it is still difficult. Petrographic microscopes are usually used for heating/cooling stage work, but have several disadvantages. The working distance between the objective and the sample is very short for most petrographic 'scopes. For example, for a Leitz NPl P 20x objective, the working distance is only 0.90 mm, and the next higher powered objective, 50x, has a working distance of only 0.38 mm (0.015 inches). It is barely possible to get some working space between sample and cover glass, plus a thin cover glass, plus a small gap between the cover glass and the object, and do it in 0.90 mm (the cover glass is needed to prevent bad thermal gradients across the sample). When that is all done, however, there is almost no room for working distance down into the sample. Thus, conventional objectives are out of the question in a practical sense. My experience has been that Universal Stage objectives are more useful, but even the most powerful, e.g., a Leitz UTK 50, has only 32x magnification in the absence of a Universal Stage Hemisphere segment. Thus, the maximum practical magnification is on the order of 500x, using a petrographic 'scope. One disadvantage of using a petrographic 'scope is that it is a very expensive piece of gear to tie up on inclusion work.

Another possibility that might well be evaluated is the use of some of the more modern binocular microscopes, such as some of the Wild or Bausch and Lomb microscopes, which provide reasonable magnification (250 to 280x) and long working distances. For larger inclusions (to about 10 microns) such a microscope would probably be adequate. Much (most?) vein material carries a reasonable number of inclusions in this size range. A mechanical stage is sometimes a very

---

heating stage a mechanical device to bring rocks to a desired temperature
petrographic having to do with the classification of rocks
objective the lens end of a microscope closest to the object to be viewed
gradients slopes or curves that show how a quantity changes in value from point to point
vein material ores deposited by underground water in cracks or fissures

desirable adjunct in relocating individual inclusions during the course of the experiment. A fiber illuminator is almost essential to get good lighting into an inclusion. Depending upon the brand of microscope to be eventually selected, a petrographic 'scope equipped for fluid inclusion work would probably cost about $8,000, while a binocular might be had for about $2,500–$3,000.

3. Heating Stage.

Several sorts of stages are commercially available. Most of these heat the surface upon which the sample is placed. Sometimes a passive heat shield is placed around the sample to try to maintain an even temperature (see the last issue of *Economic Geology*, p. 335). These stages are generally very unsatisfactory since, for obvious reasons, movement of air across the stage can cause the sample to be at significantly different temperatures than the surface of the stage. Furthermore, extreme temperature gradients are frequently encountered across the stage and it is difficult to establish a simple correlation between the apparent stage temperatures and the sample temperature.

A few heating stages are commercially available in which the sample is enclosed within a small oven, and the microscope optics are protected by circulating air around this oven. Mettler makes a stage, the FP 52, of this type. Its advantages are reasonable temperature range (−20 to 300C); low thermal mass (so that the temperature can be changed very rapidly); availability as a single unit with stage, temperature controller, and temperature measuring equipment; and good claimed accuracy (± 0.3C in the 200–300C range). Disadvantages are that only one sample can be heated at a time, the maximum sample thickness is limited, and high quality sample preparation is needed.

A third type of heating stage uses a hot liquid that is circulated into a cell on the microscope stage. One cell of this type was described by Roedder (*Economic Geology*, vol. 57, p. 1045), and I designed and constructed a modified version for study of samples from Pachuca when I was at the University of Texas. The advantage of these cells is that they provide very accurate temperature measurements and a number of samples can be studied on a single run to elevated temperatures. Disadvantages are that they have extremely high thermal interia, the maximum temperature is limited to about 275C (the heating liquid decomposes at higher temperatures), and they are not commercially available.

I have been involved in numerous "do-it-yourself" projects that involve design and construction of apparatus. If one enjoys building,

---

fiber illuminator a device with which light can be directed at a variety of angles to illuminate an object for microscopic viewing

Description

rebuilding, redesigning, and improving things, such projects can be a lot of fun. However, if the objective is to get results, it is much more satisfactory to buy off-the-shelf items, even if they aren't perfect, and put them to use. For this reason, I would investigate the Mettler stage as my first choice. It is fairly expensive, about $6,750, and I would want some more technical data before I made a final decision, but it would probably be the most satisfactory piece of equipment for the job.

4. Cooling Stage.

One of the major problems in estimating fluid salinities by measurement of freezing point depression is that metastable supercooling of the fluid inclusion usually occurs. To beat this, the sample is first frozen in a dry ice–acetone bath, and then gradually warmed. The heating stage can be used to control the temperature by circulating cold gas or liquid past the sample and back-heating the cooling medium using the hot stage heating elements. The major elements of such a system consist of a small refrigeration unit (several are commercially available), and a suitable heat exchanger to transfer the "cool" to the circulating medium. As far as I know, it is not possible to buy a complete, ready-to-go cooling stage. I would estimate that about $1,500 would be required to set up for freezing point work, including equipment for freezing the samples.

SUGGESTED APPROACH

If we were to agree to do fluid inclusion work, I would want to begin the project gradually. I think that a high-powered binocular microscope would probably work, and would be much cheaper than using a petrographic 'scope. It is much more convenient to do sample preparation in-house because not all slices from a sample have good fluid inclusions, and a technician can't always be relied on to get a good specimen the first time, but a qualified person could probably be located to do this work for us and major expense would be the heating stage and freezing equipment. I would estimate equipment costs to be:

Microscope and accessories	$ 2,000
Heating stage	6,750
Cooling equipment	1,500
Misc. equipment and supplies	250
TOTAL:	$10,500

freezing point depression a lowering of the freezing point
metastable existing temporarily under conditions of change; for example, a piece of ice in hot water

Fluid Inclusion Research

133

The time to get a system purchased, set up, calibrated and operational should take 10 to 15 man-days of professional effort. If we multiply that by 2.6 (Roedder's factor) to get an estimate of the time it would really take, we're looking at about a month's work to get going. Presumably, a small research project could be done in the course of getting operational.

A further consideration is that much of this discussion evaporates if we will be looking at certain types of samples. For instance, Carlin-type ores typically contain very small inclusions. If a great deal of work on such rocks is contemplated, the equipment would have to be designed to allow maximum magnification, and, therefore, a petrographic 'scope would be essential.

Finally, as we have discussed, if Last Ditch were to support our entry into this area, we could work out an arrangement so that you would recoup your original investment through discounts on services rendered.

If Last Ditch is hesitant to make the kind of investment outlined above, I would like to suggest an alternate arrangement that might be worth investigating. There is a rather large, but very diffuse, literature on fluid inclusions in precious metal deposits. Evaluation of this information would provide some useful background information on the "state-of-the-art" and some insight into what might be expected to come out of a more intensive research program. In addition, as I told you over the phone yesterday, I think I could borrow the use of a heating stage at the University of Texas in Austin for a short project. If we ran homogenization temperatures on the small batch of samples that you have on hand, we could combine a short research project with the literature search. With this in hand, it might be easier to assess what place fluid inclusion work might have in your research program and determine the requirements for equipment that would best fill your anticipated needs. I would estimate that 15–20 days would be required to do these tasks.

Cordially,

DIVERSIFIED EXPLORATION SERVICES, INC.

Roger W. Kolvoord, Ph.D.
President

RWK:kk

calibrate to adjust the graduations of a measuring device systematically
Roedder's factor the factor of 2.63 by which any estimate of the time needed to do a particular task should be multiplied to determine the actual time that task will take
Carlin-type ores a type of gold deposit

Questions

1 Why isn't it appropriate to describe the petrographic microscope and the heating stages in greater detail for "Dr. Blow"?

2 What examples of description are used in the proposal in addition to those discussed on page 129? What kinds of descriptive technique do they represent?

3 Discuss the use of the letter format to present the proposal. What are its advantages? What are its disadvantages?

4 Do you think the use of such colloquialisms as *"ballpark" figure, 'scope* for *microscope, a very expensive piece of gear, (most?), "do-it-yourself," off-the-shelf items,* and so on is justified by the desire to remain friendly and informal? What other expressions and other ways of maintaining a warm, cordial presentation could have been used? Rewrite the proposal employing your suggestions.

DEFINITION

Definition is one of the fundamental processes of logical thinking. Written discourse tends to make use of three main types of definition: *lexical, stipulative,* and *formal.*

A lexical definition, the sort found in the dictionary, is usually brief and arrived at in any of four ways. We can create a lexical definition by citing the capacities that determine the use of the thing being defined—that is, by pointing out its most important connotations. We can also create one by examining physical qualities; this approach is, of course, limited to concrete objects. The lexical definition can also consist of an example or enumeration of subclasses; this is its least reliable form. For example, we can define *citrus fruit* by enumerating oranges, lemons, limes, grapefruit, and tangerines. Finally, we can create a lexical definition by making clear the meanings of important terms in the concept.

A stipulative definition is a proposal to use a word in a specific way. It most often deals with a new word or one whose meaning is ambiguous or vague. For example, when Alexander Fleming chose to name his discovery "penicillin," he presented the word as a stipulative definition for "mold broth filtrate," which is what penicillin is. The stipulative definition that deals with a common word makes it more precise by putting it into a context.

A formal definition attempts to classify and uniquely identify something. For example, we can classify a *square* as a "four-sided figure." There are other four-sided figures, however, and to say that a square has four sides simply sets it into a group of things with that characteristic—rectangles, parallelograms, and so forth. To uniquely identify a square, we need to say that a square has four sides and that they are all equal and joined so as to form right angles. Similarly, classifying a *submarine* as a naval vessel does not provide a formal definition; destroyers and aircraft carriers are also naval vessels. To distinguish it from all others in this class, we need to say that a submarine is a naval vessel that can operate not only on the surface of the water but also below the surface.

Several ways of using formal definition are common. Sometimes the differentiation is accomplished by describing the way a thing works; the definition of *submarine* given above is such a *functional definition*. We can also differentiate an object from others in its class by relating how it is made or its place of origin. For example, an *earthquake* can be explained as "a cataclysmic geologic occurrence resulting from the collision of tectonic plates." This kind of definition is called a *theoretical definition*. (Scientists are not certain what causes earthquakes, but accepted theory suggests that the cause is such a collision.) To define *broth* as the liquid in which meat, fish, or a vegetable has been boiled is to state a *generic definition*. A *persuasive definition* is one whose purpose is not to inform but to influence attitudes, beliefs, or actions. Often it is not really logical, although it appears to be. "Religion is the opiate of the people" is such a definition.

All definitions should be undertaken very carefully. A powerful tool, definition can easily be abused and overused. In this regard, there are five major cautions. First, the phrase that describes the meaning should be a synonym for and interchangeable with the word being defined. Second, that synonym should be neither broader nor narrower than the word being defined. Consider definitions of the word *house:* "something used for shelter" is too broad because many things other than houses are used for shelter; but "a wooden structure used for shelter" is too narrow because brick, stucco, or stone houses are excluded. Third, a definition should not be circular; it should not hinge on any form of the term it attempts to clarify. Defining *washing machine* as "a machine that washes clothes" is not very helpful. Fourth, a definition should not be expressed in obscure or figurative language. It needs to be understood and understandable. Samuel Johnson's definition of *network,* while humorous, does not clarify what a network is: "anything reticulated or decussated, at equal distances, with interstices between the intersections." If we define politics as "the art of the possible," we have said something interesting, but only to those who already know what politics is. Finally, a definition should not be expressed in negative terms unless the term being defined is in the negative. It may be all right to define *unmarried* as "not having a spouse," but it is not very useful to define a building as "an object that is not an automobile."

Definition

Work, Labor, and Play

W. H. Auden

W. H. Auden (1907–1973), renowned poet, essayist, and playwright, was an Oxford-educated Englishman who in 1946 became a citizen of the United States, where he spent most of his remaining years. Honored on both sides of the Atlantic, he was the recipient of many of America's literary awards, among them the 1948 Pulitzer Prize for poetry and the National Book Award in 1956.

The following brief essay by Auden begins with functional definitions of labor *and* play: *labor is activity society values but that the individual does only to earn a living; play is activity the individual enjoys but society does not value. Auden then moves to a* precising *definition, one that sets the limits of the term being defined. He sets* work *between* labor *and* play, *defining it as activity society values but that the individual enjoys doing. Next, he compares work with labor in order to clarify the differences.*

Work, labor, and play are here grouped by Auden into one class, differentiated according to a single set of factors. Because they are all activities, they differ not so much in kind as in degree, each representing a different section along a graph that indicates social value and enjoyment. The more social value and the less enjoyment, the more nearly the activity approaches labor; the more enjoyment and the less social value, the more nearly the activity approaches play.

The last part of the essay relies upon stipulative *definitions, those in which the meaning shifts according to circumstance. Auden observes that the meaning of work changes according to the needs of society because the value society places upon an activity shifts.*

Auden is writing for well-educated readers, and perhaps chiefly for himself. The value of such a personal exercise is established partly by Auden's description of a worker: "what from the point of view of society is necessary labor is from his own point of view voluntary play."

So far as I know, Miss Hannah Arendt was the first person to define the essential difference between work and labor. To be happy, a man must feel, firstly, free and, secondly, important. He cannot be really happy if he is compelled by society to do what he does not enjoy doing, or if what he enjoys doing is ignored by society as of no value or importance. In a society where slavery in the strict sense has been abolished, the sign that what a man does is of social value is that he is paid money to do it, but a laborer today can rightly be called a wage slave. A man is a laborer if the job society offers him is of no interest to himself but he is compelled to take it by the necessity of earning a living and supporting his family.

The antithesis to labor is play. When we play a game, we enjoy what we are doing, otherwise we should not play it, but it is a purely private activity; society could not care less whether we play it or not.

Between labor and play stands work. A man is a worker if he is personally interested in the job which society pays him to do; what from the point of view of society is necessary labor is from his own point of view voluntary play. Whether a job is to be classified as labor or work depends, not on the job itself, but on the tastes of the individual who undertakes it. The difference does not, for example, coincide with the difference between a manual and a mental job; a gardener or a cobbler may be a worker, a bank clerk a laborer. Which a man is can be seen from his attitude towards leisure. To a worker, leisure means simply the hours he needs to relax and rest in order to work efficiently. He is therefore more likely to take too little leisure than too much; workers die of coronaries and forget their wives' birthdays. To the laborer, on the other hand, leisure means freedom from compulsion, so that it is natural for him to imagine that the fewer hours he has to spend laboring, and the more hours he is free to play, the better.

What percentage of the population in a modern technological society are, like myself, in the fortunate position of being workers? At a guess I would say sixteen per cent, and I do not think that figure is likely to get bigger in the future.

Technology and the division of labor have done two things: by eliminating in many fields the need for special strength or skill, they have made a very large number of paid occupations which formerly were enjoyable work into boring labor, and by increasing productivity they have reduced the number of necessary laboring hours. It is already possible to imagine a society in which the majority of the population, that is to say, its laborers, will have almost as much leisure as in earlier times was enjoyed by the aristocracy. When one recalls how aristocracies in the past actually behaved, the prospect is not cheerful. Indeed, the problem of dealing with boredom may be even more difficult for such a future mass society than it was for aristocracies. The latter, for example, ritualized their time; there was a season to shoot grouse,

Hannah Arendt a political scientist and philosopher particularly known for her ideas on Jewish matters and totalitarianism
antithesis exact opposite
grouse a plump, brownish game bird often hunted in Scotland

Definition

a season to spend in town, etc. The masses are more likely to replace an unchanging ritual by fashion which it will be in the economic interest of certain people to change as often as possible. Again, the masses cannot go in for hunting, for very soon there would be no animals left to hunt. For other aristocratic amusements like gambling, dueling, and warfare, it may be only too easy to find equivalents in dangerous driving, drug-taking, and senseless acts of violence. Workers seldom commit acts of violence, because they can put their aggression into their work, be it physical like the work of a smith, or mental like the work of a scientist or an artist. The role of aggression in mental work is aptly expressed by the phrase "getting one's teeth into a problem."

Questions

1 What feature do work, labor, and play have in common? When you have determined that feature, you will have classified them. The next step is to differentiate them. What details of differentiation does Auden use?
2 What details does Auden offer for his functional definition of *labor?* of *play?* of *work?*
3 How does Auden convey exactly what he means by *work?*
4 What purpose does the discussion of technology and the division of labor serve in the last part of the essay?

Why I Want a Wife

Judy Syfers

Judy Syfers spent a number of years as a wife. She is now divorced, a feminist, and working as a secretary in the financial district of San Francisco. The definition of a wife in her essay is an operational one; she defines what a wife is by what a wife does. In her view, there are several categories of wifely work: governess, housemaid and nurse, helpmate, social director, and mistress.

The tone of this essay is as important as its organization. Syfers' definition of wife is presented so ironically that the reader is encouraged to assume a particular kind of husband—selfish, lazy, insensitive, and amoral, the typical "male chauvinist pig." One soon realizes that Syfers is offering a highly subjective view of marriage, and that her definition has an argumentative point. The definition proceeds logically, but the things left out of it make the cumulative effect pseudological.

Published in the first issue of Ms. *magazine, the essay projects the new liberationist attitudes of many women during the late 1960s and early 1970s. Syfers was writing for all the women who had done what was expected of them (that is, marry and raise children). Her purpose was to question, and to get other women to question, the goals that had been set for them, goals that they had accepted and were struggling to fulfill. The audience for whom Syfers originally wrote, however, may have changed somewhat in the last decade or so. To be sure, there are many women to whom the definition still applies; but they are fewer than they were, more and more women having modified their roles, often with the help of cooperative and caring men.*

belong to that classification of people known as wives. I am A Wife. And, not altogether incidentally, I am a mother.

Not too long ago a male friend of mine appeared on the scene fresh from a recent divorce. He had one child, who is, of course, with his ex-wife. He is obviously looking for another wife. As I thought about him while I was ironing one evening, it suddenly occurred to me that I, too, would like to have a wife. Why do I want a wife?

I would like to go back to school so that I can become economically independent, support myself, and, if need be, support those dependent upon me. I want a wife who will work and send me to school. And while I am going to school I want a wife to take care of my children. I want a wife to keep track of the children's doctor and dentist appointments. And to keep track of mine, too. I want a wife to make sure my children eat properly and are kept clean. I want a wife who will wash the children's clothes and keep them mended. I want a wife who is a good nurturant attendant to my children, who arranges for their schooling, makes sure that they have an adequate social life with their peers, takes them to the park, the zoo, etc. I want a wife who takes care of the children when they are sick, a wife who arranges to be around when the children need special care, because, of course, I cannot miss classes at school. My wife must arrange to lose time at work and not lose the job. It may mean a small cut in my wife's income from time to time, but I guess I can tolerate that. Needless to say, my wife will arrange and pay for the care of the children while my wife is working.

I want a wife who will take care of *my* physical needs. I want a wife who will keep my house clean. A wife who will pick up after me. I want a wife who will keep my clothes clean, ironed, mended, replaced when need be, and who will see to it that my personal things are kept in their proper place so that I can find what I need the minute I need it. I want a wife who cooks the meals, a wife who is a *good* cook. I want a wife who will plan the menus, do the necessary grocery shopping, prepare the meals, serve them pleasantly, and then do the cleaning up while I do my studying. I want a wife who will care for me when I am sick and sympathize with my pain and loss of time from school. I want a wife to go along when our family takes a vacation so that someone can continue to care for me and my children when I need a rest and change of scene.

I want a wife who will not bother me with rambling complaints about a wife's duties. But I want a wife who will listen to me when I feel the need to explain a rather difficult point I have come across in my course of studies. And I want a wife who will type my papers for me when I have written them.

I want a wife who will take care of the details of my social life. When my wife and I are invited out by my friends, I want a wife who will take care of the babysitting arrangements. When I meet people at school that I like and want to entertain, I want a wife who will have the house clean, will prepare a special meal, serve it to me and my friends, and not interrupt when I talk about the things that interest me and my friends. I want a wife who will have arranged that the children are fed and ready for bed before my guests arrive

Definition

so that the children do not bother us. I want a wife who takes care of the needs of my guests so that they feel comfortable, who makes sure that they have an ashtray, that they are passed the hors d'oeuvres, that they are offered a second helping of the food, that their wine glasses are replenished when necessary, that their coffee is served to them as they like it. And I want a wife who knows that sometimes I need a night out by myself.

I want a wife who is sensitive to my sexual needs, a wife who makes love passionately and eagerly when I feel like it, a wife who makes sure that I am satisfied. And, of course, I want a wife who will not demand sexual attention when I am not in the mood for it. I want a wife who assumes the complete responsibility for birth control, because I do not want more children. I want a wife who will remain sexually faithful to me so that I do not have to clutter up my intellectual life with jealousies. And I want a wife who understands that *my* sexual needs may entail more than strict adherence to monogamy. I must, after all, be able to relate to people as fully as possible.

If, by chance, I find another person more suitable as a wife than the wife I already have, I want the liberty to replace my present wife with another one. Naturally, I will expect a fresh, new life; my wife will take the children and be solely responsible for them so that I am left free.

When I am through with school and have a job, I want my wife to quit working and remain at home so that my wife can more fully and completely take care of a wife's duties.

My God, who *wouldn't* want a wife?

Questions

1 You may have noticed that loving one's husband is not mentioned as an essential activity of a wife. Why do you think it was omitted?

2 According to Syfers, what is the sex of a *wife*? How does she indicate her notion to the reader? What purpose does this handling of a wife's gender serve?

3 What kind of audience would be most likely to appreciate Syfers' article today? Is it the same audience that probably appreciated the article a decade ago? Name two groups that might be hostile to Syfer's definition.

4 Is the article an accurate appraisal of an American wife's duties. Is Syfers being fair? Is her definition exaggerated? Why, or why not?

The Third Most Powerful Man in the World

Norman Cousins

Norman Cousins, formerly editor of Current History *and* Saturday Review, *is now chairman of the board of editors of* Saturday Review *and chairman of the National Programming Council of Public Television. He is also the author of many books and articles and the recipient of several literary awards.*

The essay by Cousins reprinted here defines the third most powerful man in the world; it is essentially a persuasive definition. In calling attention to this position, Cousins relies upon our natural inclination to think of powerful statesmen and international leaders as the probable candidates. However, here this somewhat dubious honor is bestowed upon the commander of a Trident submarine.

The definition is developed by means of carefully chosen psychological and emotional appeals. First, the submarine itself is described as possessing truly awesome power. Cousins follows this emotional appeal by presenting two advantages of the Trident and then what he apparently considers an overriding disadvantage, the possibility of a psychological defect in an individual allowed so much seemingly unrestricted power.

The next appeal appears to be a logical one, but is in fact as emotional as the first. Cousins raises the question of America's need to defend against almost equally destructive weapons in the hands of a Soviet psychopath. Of course, the implication of these comments is that no one person ought to have total access to such power. Men who believed themselves to be patriotic have at times acted contrary to the orders of their governments. What if such a person happened to have sole control over the launching of a thermonuclear bomb?

The essay's final appeal is to tradition and authority. When Cousins recounts the efforts of John Adams and Alexander Hamilton to circumscribe the amount of power any one person might command, we are reminded of Lord Acton's famous aphorism, "Power corrupts, and absolute power tends to corrupt absolutely."

The culminating effect of all these appeals is to define a commander of a Trident submarine as some sort of political psychopath roaming the oceans of the world with a finger poised above a very dangerous button. In reading and analyzing this defini-

tion, we must understand that Cousins is presenting an extreme case and that he is carefully slanting the information he gives. In the first place, a single officer cannot launch a missile. Such a launching requires the cooperation of the weapons officer and the executive officer, to say nothing of the ship's navigator and the engineer. Second, that several of a submarine's senior officers would experience the kind of severe mental breakdown Cousins postulates is highly unlikely.

Cousins' audience is the well-educated, moderately liberal public, generally people well disposed toward decreases in defense budgets and limitations on nuclear armament. The essay is an editorial, and as such relies heavily on personal opinion. Cousins hopes to persuade the American people to reconsider and reject the Trident program; in his opinion, it poses an intolerable threat to human life and to civilization itself.

Next to Gerald Ford and Leonid Brezhnev, the most powerful man in the world is not Mao Tse-tung or the head of any other government. The third most powerful man in the world is a commander of a Trident submarine.

A single Trident submarine today carries more destructive force than all the military establishments of Great Britain, Italy, Spain, Brazil, Argentina, West Germany, Japan, the Philippines, India, and Pakistan put together.

A Trident has built into it an undersea launching platform for thermonuclear bombs, some of which contain more explosive force than a thousand atomic bombs of the kind that destroyed Hiroshima in 1945.

Theoretically, the American people ought to feel completely secure in the fact of such power being deployed in their behalf. The Trident has almost unlimited mobility; it can launch an attack on any country of its choosing, yet it is practically immune to counter-attack by being able to hide in the seas.

But there are problems. A Trident has both the advantages and the disadvantages of being an autonomous war machine. The men who operate it are in a position, theoretically at least, to make their own decisions about the use of the total power at their command. Suppose one of them decides, out of what he believes to be a higher patriotism, to activate a thermonuclear bomb. Trident commanders are human beings subject to all the stresses and quirks of human personality that make other mortals fallible and unpredictable. We can be certain that every test for stability and reliability has been applied in the selection of Trident officers. But psychologists cannot guarantee that any individual will not be seized at some point by a totally irrational idea or by an aberration. All we know for sure is that the Trident officers have in their hands more power than had been accumulated by human beings in recorded history up through 1945.

autonomous independent
fallible capable of error
aberration a deviation from a proper course of action

Definition

Meanwhile, the Soviet Union may not have submarines with Trident capability, but what they have is ominous enough—snorkel-type subs with launching platforms for intermediate-range missiles. This relative lack of range does not prevent the Soviet submarines from getting close enough to our shores to make every major American city a potential target. And the same questions must be raised about the danger that a Soviet submarine commander might take it into his head to trigger a holocaust.

Military and political annals are replete with examples of men—from the lowliest orderlies to generals and rulers—who took it upon themselves to use available force for an insane purpose. As recently as the Vietnam War, there was the example of the bombing of Hanoi without the express order of the President. Some years ago a French colonel flying over Algeria dropped bombs without authorization on a populous target.

The main threat to human life in this world has invariably been represented by the irresponsible use of force. Even well-intentioned men have lost their sensibilities when they have had unchecked power at their disposal. Nothing was of greater concern to the American Founding Fathers than the ease with which men in authority collect power and then abuse it. If John Adams and Alexander Hamilton were alive today, what would they say about the fact that submarines of the United States and Soviet Union are roaming the oceans and that their commanders have the ready means to annihilate an entire population and start civilization on a downward spiral?

The Trident submarine is a logical development in an illogical situation. Given the existence of an explosive that can incinerate a million human beings, it is logical in military terms to try to devise highly mobile delivery systems that enjoy a wide margin for error and that cannot be easily hunted down and destroyed.

But there is a higher logic that needs to be asserted today. That logic must begin with a full understanding of what nuclear war is all about. Historically, the main purpose of a nation's foreign policy is to protect the lives, values, and property of its citizens. If this purpose becomes impossible because of the nature of nuclear explosives, then much of the official policy on national security is not security at all but an illogical venture in mass suicide. The hard truth is that the only security for the American people today, or for any people, is to be found through the control of force rather than the pursuit of force. In turn, such control of force must be connected to the existence of a world order capable of administering justice and dealing with basic causes of war.

This is a good time for anyone who is running for the Presidency to talk sense about the connection between world peace and a workable world order. And unless a Presidential candidate understands the global nature of most of our other problems, he disqualifies himself to deal with the major issues of our time.

Is it too much to hope that the Presidential candidates will address them-

replete with full of

Third Most Powerful Man in the World   149 selves to the question of a world made safe and fit for human habitation? This is the main test. Everything else is peripheral.

Questions

1 What important logical facts does Cousins ignore in his definition?
2 Notice that often the essay concentrates on describing not the position being defined but an object closely associated with it. This literary technique is known as *metonymy*. Is its use in this kind of writing justified? Why, or why not?
3 Consider Cousins' purpose. How well does this editorial fulfill that purpose?
4 How is Cousins' definition a *persuasive* definition?

Shipboard Electrical Safety Program

Don C. LaForce

Don C. LaForce, a lieutenant commander currently stationed at Bremerton, Washington, has served on several of the U.S. Navy's submarines. When he wrote the following electrical safety program, he was weapons officer on the precommissioning crew of a Trident submarine.

LaForce's Shipboard Electrical Safety Program makes use of several definitions. The program itself is actually a manual on how to maintain electrical safety, but within that rhetorical focus some rather technical and complex objects and occurrences are defined.

Section 3a, for instance, provides a simple and concise operational definition of electrical shock by describing how it works. In the course of the definition LaForce explains that electrical shock can occur even when one does not touch both leads; the circuit can still be completed, at least aboard ship. Section 3b then defines the limits of safety by describing what happens when electrical current reaches a certain level. This, too, is an operational definition. Section 3c focuses on the process of ensuring safety; and in Section 3d, a discussion of how to extinguish electrical fires, LaForce again makes use of operational definitions to explain two agents often used to put out electrical fires.

In Section 4, "Installation and Testing Program," definition is also evident; here LaForce defines by enumerating subclasses. He defines portable electrical equipment and personal equipment in this way. In Section 5, "Miscellaneous Precautions," he defines what a safe electrical environment is by explaining how to maintain it. This use of definition is less direct than any other in the manual, but it increases the reader's understanding nonetheless.

The manual's purpose is stated in Sections 1 and 2, and quite directly. The audience that LaForce expects is clearly indicated in a note near the beginning of the manual: "THIS SECTION IS INTENDED PRIMARILY FOR THOSE WHO HAVE LITTLE OR NO ELECTRICAL OR ELECTRONIC TRAINING." The format used is perhaps less than graceful, but LaForce is following Navy regulations regarding communications of this kind. (This obligatory format has the virtue of being completely without ambiguity, and other writers would do well to have their audience and purpose so clearly formulated before beginning to write.) Expecting his readers to be sailors who know little or nothing about the subject, LaForce presents his information as simply and nontechnically as possible and even tries to anticipate likely questions.

---

1. *Purpose.* To emphasize the dangers of electrical shock and to establish education, installation and testing programs to minimize shipboard electrical safety hazards.

2. *Discussion.* Deaths by electrocution have been largely due to the disregard for or the unfamiliarity with electrical safety requirements. . . . A number of shipboard fatalities have been reported due to contact with 115-volt portable tools and equipment. Despite a fairly widespread but totally unfounded belief to the contrary, low voltage circuits are very dangerous and can cause death where resistance of the body is lowered by moisture and especially when a current passes through the chest. Shipboard conditions are particularly conducive to severity of shock because the body is likely to be in contact with the ship's metal structure and the body resistance may be low because of perspiration or damp clothing.

3. *Background.*

NOTE

THIS SECTION IS INTENDED PRIMARILY FOR THOSE WHO HAVE HAD LITTLE OR NO ELECTRICAL OR ELECTRONIC TRAINING.

a. Electrical shock occurs when the body forms part of a complete electrical circuit and electrical current flows through the body. In addition to flash burns and general tissue damage, electrical current can induce cardiac arrest—the major cause of death in electrocution cases.

It is NOT necessary to touch both leads of a system to complete the circuit. Specifically, if a system is "grounded" (i.e., one or more points present a low resistance to the ship's structure, or "ground"), current will flow from one lead, through the body to the ground (hull), then via the low resistance path back to the other lead. Although ships' electrical systems are theoretically ungrounded, and are constantly monitored for ground faults, there is still a current path which will not show up on typical D.C. ground detectors or Meggers. This is the unavoidable "capacitance" of A.C. systems, which permits A.C. current to "leak" from the distribution system to ground. Thus, the effect of touching a supposedly ungrounded 115 volt or 440 volt lead can produce a current through the body of 5 to 10 times the value generally considered lethal.

resistance opposition to the flow of electrical current
ground faults a flaw in the grounding of a circuit

Definition

b. The effect of varying levels of current are as follows:

1 milliamp—may be able to feel current flow

10 milliamps—may lose voluntary muscular control and, therefore, may be unable to let go of the current source

100 milliamps—generally considered lethal, especially if current passes through the chest

A common household lamp can carry ten times the current considered lethal.

If the body is wet or damp (due to perspiration, moisture, etc.), body resistance can be as low as 300 ohms. Therefore ANY VOLTAGE IN EXCESS OF 30 VOLTS SHOULD BE CONSIDERED POTENTIALLY LETHAL.

c. Since the majority of the current in a circuit will take the path of least resistance, there are two methods of protecting personnel from shock.

(1) Insulate personnel from the system and/or the ground by use of rubber gloves, mats, insulated tools, etc.

(2) For all electrical equipment, provide a short circuit from the metal casing to the ground via a third prong in the plug, or a permanent grounding strap. Thus, if a faulty lead contacts the case, the current will preferentially travel through the grounding wire (vice through the users body).

d. Electrical Fires: It is generally useless to attempt to extinguish an electrical fire until the circuit is de-energized, since the source of the heat has not been removed. However, if there is an unavoidable delay in de-energizing the affected gear, application of CO_2 can minimize the spread of flames and help limit damage. It is best to use fire-fighting agents as follows:

(1) CO_2 is by far the most desirable agent, since it is non-conductive, leaves no residue, is almost always totally effective in extinguishing the fire, and can be applied through vents or louvers. Exercise caution not to touch the metal part of the extinguisher to the affected panel, since shock may result.

(2) Dry Chemical (PKP) is a non-conductive, extremely effective extinguishing agent. However, it is a fine powder which quickly coats surfaces, enters cracks and crevices, and leaves behind a residue which could necessitate complete equipment replacement. Furthermore it easily becomes airborne, where it can become a lung and eye irritant and enter other, nearby equipment. Even a short burst can quickly make the atmosphere of a confined space unbreathable. Therefore, PKP should be used ONLY AS A LAST resort, if CO_2 fails to control the casualty.

c. Water, foam or other liquid extinguishing agents are NOT recommended for electrical fires. The shock hazards, and additional damage incurred, can easily worsen, vice alleviate the casualty.

amp ampere, a unit of electrical current
ohm a unit of electrical resistance
vice military jargon for *instead, instead of,* or *rather than*
CO_2 carbon dioxide

Shipboard Electrical Safety Program   **153**

4. *Installation and Testing Program.*

a. *Portable Equipment.* Any portable or semi-permanent electrical equipment (tools, extension cords, coffee pots, toasters, adding machines, hotplates, sterilizers, hair clippers, flatirons, etc.) which does not have a cord with a grounding conductor and grounded plug, except that equipment which is double-insulated and certified by Underwriters Laboratories (UL), shall be provided with the appropriate multiconductor flexible cable and grounded plug as specified in paragraph 300-2.10 of reference (a). Cords need not be replaced on apparatus that are positively and adequately grounded through their mounting, nor on portable lights and other equipment having no exposed metal parts that may become energized.

b. *Personal Equipment.* Personal radios, television sets, record players, and tape recorders may be used aboard ship if the equipment is equipped with a power transformer as described in paragraph 300-2.12 of reference (a) and is provided with a grounded plug and suitable cord. Personally owned or non-navy standard electric lights, fans and tools shall not be used aboard ship inasmuch as adequate numbers and types of navy equipment are available to meet all needs. Hobby equipment may be used aboard ship as an exception to the foregoing, subject to the precautions of paragraph 300-2.12 of reference (a). Grounded plugs are not required for electric shavers having completely insulated housings and isolated cutting blades or other equipment having no exposed metal parts which could become energized.

c. All applicable ship's portable equipment and all personal electrical equipment shall be safety-checked prior to first use aboard ship, and semi-annually. Therefore, in accordance with the procedures of the Preventive Maintenance System to ensure proper grounding and insulation integrity, all Division Officers or owners are asked to inform the Electrical Division of any new equipment brought aboard or put into service.

d. A ground continuity test of each installed grounded receptacle for proper connections shall be performed in accordance with procedures and periodicity of the Preventive Maintenance System and:

(1) After installation or repairs involving lifted leads.

(2) Whenever physical damage or wetting is suspected.

(3) After each shipyard overhaul.

5. *Miscellaneous Precautions:*

a. If slight shocks are felt on any portable or permanent electrical equipment, inform the watch officer and have the equipment TAGGED OUT.

b. Cords on portable electrical equipment should be no longer than twenty-five feet.

c. Extension cords should be no longer than twenty-five feet and should consist of three-conductor flexible cable with grounded type connectors. When used, it should have been properly tested.

Definition

d. Wear high voltage rubber gloves and rubber lineman's sleeves when replacing high voltage electron tubes, resistors, fuses, etc., and if manipulating the interlocks of the removed panel covers to de-energize and energize the equipment. If intricacy of the work makes wearing of gloves unfeasible, make doubly sure equipment is de-energized and stays de-energized. An alternative is to remove the affected/damaged smallest subassembly and perform work in an area which affords proper electrical insulation.

e. Keep protective covers on electric and electronic equipment tightly closed at all times except during actual inspection and servicing of equipment.

f. Only personnel duly qualified by the department head having cognizance over the applicable equipment shall be assigned to operate, repair or adjust electrical or electronic equipment.

6. *Action.* All personnel shall:

a. Adhere to the requirments of enclosure (1) whenever performing maintenance on electrical or electronic equipment.

b. Prior to using portable electrical equipment, ensure it has been safety-checked, and tagged, within the required period.

c. Inspect equipment and receptacles for damage to the casing, leads, plug, and insulation prior to each use. Turn in all dropped, damaged or "jury-rigged" equipment to the Electrical Division for repair and/or testing.

d. Notify the Electrical Officer or Electrical Division Leading Petty Officer whenever an electrical safety hazard is noticed.

e. Never drill or otherwise penetrate any bulkhead, deck or panel until it has been verified there are no cable runs on the other side.

Questions

1 What two important rhetorical considerations does LaForce observe in his safety manual?
2 Is it significant that LaForce's manual shows a mixture of definition and process? What importance might that fact have rhetorically?
3 Is the format discouraging to the reader? Why, or why not?
4 In general, do you find the manual understandable? What points need clarification, if any?

CLASSIFICATION

Classification is similar to analysis in that it concerns itself with categories; however, in movement and impetus this pattern of development is almost the opposite of analysis. In classification, the task is to group objects or ideas that are seemingly diverse into categories which allow us to see their similarities. This grouping begins with the specific object or idea and moves to a general observation about it. It attempts, in some ways, to discover universal properties, and as such it is a way of organizing not only our writing but also our world. In classification, the recognition of common features leads to a systematic and logical arrangement of objects into groups.

Classification is an extremely useful pattern of development, and the writers represented in this section use it for a wide variety of purposes. For example, James Austin uses classification to identify the four kinds of chance involved in scientific discovery; Eric Berne classifies people according to body type in order to explore how we respond to physical appearance; George Ladd, an agricultural economist, classifies research tools for other scientists; and Marvin Segal, a businessman who writes on the wholesale apparel business, classifies fibers for the benefit of clothing manufacturers.

When classification is used in writing, certain guidelines should be observed. First, we must be sure that our system of classification is consistent. The things we are classifying must relate to each other in some way; at least one feature must be common to all members of the class. We cannot apply one basis of classification to some potential members of a class and a different basis of classification to others. For example, in classifying *apples* we cannot create a coherent group called Number One Fancy if we say that Number One Fancy apples can be either three inches in diameter or red. We would have to say that red apples three inches in diameter are Number One Fancy, while red apples two inches in diameter and green apples of any size are not. Second, we must be careful to make our class cover the whole field, to make it complete. If color is not important to our apple-sorting and size is the only necessary criterion, then we can consider three-inch green apples Number One Fancy as well. Third, we must be sure that classes are mutually exclusive. Let us suppose we decide that Number Two Fancy apples are apples that are sour. How do we classify an apple that is red, three inches in diameter, and sour? Is it Number One Fancy or Number Two Fancy? Our dilemma suggests that the categories are not mutually exclusive: three-inch apples can be sour or sweet. Finally, we must be sure that all of the criteria on which we base our categories are significant. In the marketing of apples, the only significant factors are those that influence taste and price. That an apple was grown in the state of Washington is relevant on both grounds, but the type of truck on which it was shipped is usually irrelevant.

Thus, in any classification, we need to keep purpose in mind. The introductory paragraph of a written classification should provide several kinds of information: the basis for classification, a list of classes to be considered, and the reason for choosing them. Subsequent paragraphs should consider each class separately, defining it and providing an explanation of it. The conclusion should explain how the classification satisfies the purpose stated in the introduction.

Can People Be Judged
By Their Appearance?

Eric Berne

Eric Berne, who died in 1970, was a psychiatrist on the staff at Mt. Sinai Hospital in New York City. The author of a number of popular books and articles, he is probably best known for the book, Games People Play.

In the following excerpt from another of his books, A Layman's Guide to Psychiatry and Psychoanalysis, *Berne sets forth a classification of people according to body type. In his view, human beings can be described in terms of three physical types—ectomorph, mesomorph, and endomorph. However, some individuals may not fit neatly into one group. Indeed, as Berne acknowledges, it is easier to find a person who is a mixture of body types than it is to find one who exhibits only a single type. Nevertheless, Berne restricts his classification to the three basic body types. His categories are well-defined, but they are not thorough; the world's many ectomorph-mesomorphs and mesomorph-endomorphs are not described. Thus, his classification is useful in a somewhat limited way; it does not explain the mixed body types. But, Berne asserts, whenever we encounter a person who demonstrates only one of the three basic body types, we can rather easily predict that person's general pattern of behavior. Even this limited application is enough to make the classification a significant one.*

Berne's intended reader is the average American curious about and at least partly in sympathy with psychoanalytical techniques. Conscious of writing for the general reader, Berne makes certain that his presentation of concepts is simple and clear. Except for the terms that label his categories—endomorph, mesomorph, *and ecto-morph—and their accompanying stomach-, muscle-, or brain-mindedness, medical or psychological jargon is avoided. The purpose of the essay is to explain something important about human behavior in terms of human appearance, and thereby to de-mythologize the methods of the psychiatrist. Berne wants his message to reach as large a portion of the general public as possible. He works toward this end by always offering a clear rhetorical focus and a very careful selection of details.*

veryone knows that a human being, like a chicken, comes from an egg. At a very early stage, the human embryo forms a three-layered tube, the inside layer of which grows into the stomach and lungs, the middle layer into bones, muscles, joints, and blood vessels, and the outside layer into the skin and nervous system.

Usually these three grow about equally, so that the average human being is a fair mixture of brains, muscles, and inward organs. In some eggs, however, one layer grows more than the others, and when the angels have finished putting the child together, he may have more gut than brain, or more brain than muscle. When this happens, the individual's activities will often be mostly concerned with the overgrown layer.

We can thus say that while the average human being is a mixture, some people are mainly "digestion-minded," some "muscle-minded," and some "brain-minded," and correspondingly digestion-bodied, muscle-bodied, or brain-bodied. The digestion-bodied people look thick; the muscle-bodied people look wide; and the brain-bodied people look long. This does not mean that the taller a man is the brainier he will be. It means that if a man, even a short man, looks long rather than wide or thick, he will often be more concerned about what goes on in his mind than about what he does or what he eats; but the key factor is slenderness and not height. On the other hand, a man who gives the impression of being thick rather than long or wide will often be more interested in a good steak than in a good idea or a good long walk.

Scientists use Greek words to describe these types of body-build. For the man whose body shape mostly depends on the inside layer of the egg, they use the word *endomorph*. If it depends mostly upon the middle layer, they call him a *mesomorph*. If it depends upon the outside layer, they call him an *ectomorph*. We can see the same roots in our English words "enter," "medium," and "exit," which might just as easily have been spelled "ender," "mesium," and "ectit."

Since the inside skin of the human egg, or endoderm, forms the inner organs of the belly, the viscera, the endomorph is usually belly-minded; since the middle skin forms the body tissues, or soma, the mesomorph is usually muscle-minded; and since the outside skin forms the brain, or cerebrum, the ectomorph is usually brain-minded. Translating this into Latin and Greek, we have the *viscerotonic endomorph*, the *somatotonic mesomorph*, and the *cerebrotonic ectomorph*.

Words are beautiful things to a cerebrotonic, but a viscerotonic knows you cannot eat a menu no matter what language it is printed in, and a somatotonic knows you cannot increase your chest expansion by reading a dictionary. So it is advisable to leave these words and see what kinds of people they actually apply to, remembering again that most individuals are fairly equal mixtures and that what we have to say concerns only the extremes. It is easier to study these types in men than in women.

Viscerotonic endormorph. If a man is definitely a thick type rather than a broad or long type, he is likely to be round and soft, with a big chest but

Classification

a bigger belly. He would rather eat than breathe comfortably. He is likely to have a wide face, short, thick neck, big thighs and upper arms, and small hands and feet. He has overdeveloped breasts and looks as though he were blown up a little like a balloon. His skin is soft and smooth, and when he gets bald, as he does usually quite early, he loses the hair in the middle of his head first.

The short, jolly, thickset, red-faced delegate with a cigar in his mouth, who always looks as though he were about to have a stroke, is the best example of this type. The reason he makes a good delegate is that he likes people, banquets, baths, and conventions; he is easygoing, soothing, and his feelings are easy to understand.

His abdomen is big because he has lots of intestines. He likes to take in things. He likes to take in food, and affection and approval as well. Going to a banquet with people who like him is his idea of a fine time. It is important to understand the natures of such men. One mistake to avoid is taking them at face value. They often make jokes about themselves when they are feeling good. In such cases, it is a good idea to smile politely, but refrain from laughing, because later, when they are feeling bad, they may feel angry at someone who laughed, even though they themselves invited it by making a joke.

Somatotonic mesomorph. If a man is definitely a broad type rather than a thick or long type, he is likely to be rugged and have lots of muscle. He is apt to have big forearms and legs, and his chest and belly are well formed and firm, with the chest bigger than the belly. He would rather breathe than eat. He has a bony head, big shoulders, and a square jaw. His skin is thick, coarse, and elastic, and tans easily. If he gets bald, it usually starts on the front of the head.

Li'l Abner, and other men of action belong to this type. Such people make good lifeguards and construction workers. They like to put out energy. They have lots of muscles and they like to use them. They go in for adventure, exercise, fighting, and getting the upper hand. They are bold and unrestrained, and love to master the people and things around them. Knowing the things which give such people satisfaction, one can understand why they may be unhappy in certain situations.

Cerebrotonic ectomorph. The man who is definitely a long type is likely to have thin bones and muscles. His shoulders are apt to sag and he has a flat belly with a dropped stomach, and long legs. His neck and fingers are long, and his face is shaped like a long egg. His skin is thin, dry, and pale, and he rarely gets bald. He looks like an absent-minded professor and often is one.

Though such people are jumpy, they like to keep their energy and don't fancy moving around much. They would rather sit quietly by themselves and keep out of difficulties. Trouble upsets them, and they run away from it. Their friends don't understand them very well. They move jerkily and feel jerkily. The person who understands how easily they become anxious is often able to help them get along better in the sociable and aggressive world of endomorphs and mesomorphs.

Can People Be Judged By Their Appearance?   **161**

In the special cases where people definitely belong to one type or another, then, one can tell something about their personalities from their appearance. When the human mind is engaged in one of its struggles with itself or with the world outside, the individual's way of handling the struggle will be determined partly by his type. If he is a viscerotonic he will often want to go to a party where he can eat and drink and be in good company at a time when he might be better off attending to business; the somatotonic may want to go out and do something about it, master the situation, even if what he does is foolish and not properly figured out; while the cerebrotonic may go off by himself and think it over, when perhaps he would be better off doing something about it or seeking good company to try to forget it.

Since these personality characteristics depend on the growth of the layers of the little egg from which the person developed, they are difficult to change. Nevertheless, it is worthwhile for a person to know about these types, so that he can have at least an inkling of what to expect from those around him, and can make allowances for the different kinds of human nature, and so that he can become aware of and learn to control his own natural tendencies, which may sometimes guide him into making the same mistakes over and over again in handling his difficulties. The "egg layer" system is the best one known at present for judging people by general appearance.

Questions

1 Does the failure to establish comprehensive categories invalidate Berne's essay? Why, or why not?
2 Berne uses at least six rhetorical techniques in addition to classification. What are they, and where are they used?
3 Evaluate the quality of detail in the essay. How well does it support the author's purpose? What details are the most effective?
4 What techniques does Berne use to maintain interest throughout the essay?

The Roots of Serendipity

James Austin

James Austin, head of the neurology department at the University of Colorado Medical School, is the author of the book Chase, Chance, and Creativity: The Lucky Art of Novelty. *In the following essay on how creative people manipulate chance, Austin uses classification as his primary rhetorical technique. The essay also defines* chance *and demonstrates both the process of manipulating it and the cause-and-effect relationships inherent in its operation. Austin considers motor activity and sensory receptivity the significant factors in all kinds of chance and thus offers these two qualities as the basis for his classification. Chance I is passive and requires no sensory receptivity; Chance II is active and requires no sensory receptivity; Chance III, like Chance I, is passive, but it requires the sensory receptivity of "the prepared mind," as does Chance IV, which is active.*

Along with explaining the four kinds of chance clearly and in great detail, Austin encourages anyone possessed of an inquiring, active mind to manipulate chance rather than be manipulated by it. He hopes his audience will be, primarily, those with enough intellectual energy to convert his classification system into a plan of action. He is trying to persuade us that we can indeed make our own luck.

It is never entirely in fashion to mention luck in the same breath as science. Science is considered a rational endeavor, and the investigator is supposed to make discoveries for logical reasons by virtue of his own intellectual hard work. As everyone no doubt knows, however, discoveries *do* come about through chance, but this fact becomes more impressive only when it happens to you personally.

Take, for example, something that happened to me a few years ago. A physician-investigator, I was directing a laboratory team studying a rare form of hereditary epilepsy. The disorder is called Lafora's disease, after its discoverer, and in it the nerve cells contain distinctive round, red-staining particles, called Lafora bodies. We knew if we could discover the chemical composition of these tiny spherules, it would help us eventually understand the metabolic cause of the disease. However, when we first analyzed the Lafora bodies isolated by my colleague, Dr. Yokoi, we drew a blank. We were up a blind alley, asking the wrong questions, using the wrong analytical method.

At this point, my dog, Tom, led us to the answer—but only by a curious combination of circumstances. Tom was a high-spirited Brittany spaniel which frequently coursed far afield. One day we were out hunting—his hobby and mine—in thick cover, and to know where he was, I took the precaution of tying a bell to the front of his collar. The bell is worth noting.

A few days later I noted a rapidly growing mass on the front of Tom's neck. The mass was hard enough to be a malignant growth, and my surgical colleague, who was doing research on malignant tumors in dogs, suggested that it be removed at once.

Tom turned only a few dog hairs during the operation and quickly returned to his usual frisky self. The mass, to everyone's surprise, was not a malignant tumor after all. Instead, the microscopic slides showed a subacute inflammatory response involving some lymph glands in Tom's neck. We were baffled as to what might be the cause of this inflammation. Tuberculosis? Yeast? Fungi? Searching for these organisms, I asked the technicians to treat further sections of the tissue with special staining methods. These new sections showed an "unusual round fungus." Under the microscope round structures were indeed there. Curiously, they lay around the outside of the mass. None lay inside. No one had ever seen a fungus quite like this before. Finally, someone on the surgical service brightened with a happy thought. Perhaps these were not fungi but round spherules of starch! Starch? Starch, we all now recalled, is used to dust surgical gloves. Some of it could have remained on the gloves used during Tom's operation and could have been transferred to the outside of the mass when it was resected.

When I checked out this possibility and looked at starch dust under the microscope, I finally realized that it is made up of round spherules. Moreover, because starch is composed of many sugar molecules, the starch in Tom's biopsy also turned red when stained with a special histochemical stain for sugars. In fact, the starch spherules looked very much like the human Lafora bodies we were trying to identify! When these elementary facts entered my awareness, they completely transformed our approach to Lafora's disease.

Lafora bodies in humans not only looked like starch but also could be a kind of starch! Starting afresh from this new working hypothesis, we could next apply the appropriate chemical tests for sugar to the small amounts of Lafora bodies Dr. Yokoi had isolated. The tests permitted us to confirm our hypothesis. Some weeks later we finally knew that Lafora bodies, like starch, were essentially made up of many sugar units linked together in a long chain to form a polymer.

Now, nothing in this story is intended to convey the view that raising dogs and running them afield is better than being hard-working, persistent, curious, imaginative, or enthusiastic. Nor would we downgrade the sudden flash of insight that illuminates the scene or the whiff of intuition that inclines us in the right—or wrong—direction.

But when this is said and done, much that is really novel in our creative efforts will still be decided at the pivotal moment when we confront chance. Like the lowly turtle, man, too, lurches forward only if he first sticks his neck out and chances the consequences.

What is chance? Dictionaries define it as something fortuitous that happens unpredictably without discernible human intention. Chance is unintentional and capricious, but we needn't conclude that chance is immune from human intervention. Indeed, chance plays several distinct roles when humans react creatively with one another and with their environment.

We can readily distinguish four varieties of chance if we consider that they each involve a different kind of motor activity and a special kind of sensory receptivity. The varieties of chance also involve distinctive personality traits and differ in the way one particular individual influences them.

Chance I is the pure blind luck that comes with no effort on our part. If, for example, you are sitting at a bridge table of four, it's "in the cards" for you to receive a hand of all 13 spades, but it will come up only once in every 6.3 trillion deals. You will ultimately draw this lucky hand—with no intervention on your part—but it does involve a longer wait than most of us have time for.

Chance II evokes the kind of luck Charles Kettering had in mind when he said: "Keep on going and the chances are you will stumble on something, perhaps when you are least expecting it. I have never heard of anyone stumbling on something sitting down."

In the sense referred to here, Chance II is not passive, but springs from an energetic, generalized motor activity. A certain basal level of action "stirs up the pot," brings in random ideas that will collide and stick together in fresh combinations, lets chance operate. When someone, *anyone,* does swing into motion and keeps on going, he will increase the number of collisions between events. When a few events are linked together, they can then be

polymer a molecular compound composed of millions of simple molecules
fortuitous happening by chance, lucky
capricious fickle, unpredictable
Charles Kettering American electrical engineer and inventor (1876–1958)

exploited to have a fortuitous outcome, but many others, of course, cannot. Kettering was right. Press on. Something will turn up. We may term this the Kettering Principle.

In the two previous examples, a unique role of the individual person was either lacking or minimal. Accordingly, as we move on to Chance III, we see blind luck, but in camouflage. Chance presents the clue, the opportunity exists, but it would be missed except by that one person uniquely equipped to observe it, visualize it conceptually, and fully grasp its significance. Chance III involves a special receptivity and discernment unique to the recipient. Louis Pasteur characterized it for all time when he said: "Chance favors only the prepared mind."

Pasteur himself had it in full measure. But the classic example of his principle occurred in 1928, when Alexander Fleming's mind instantly fused at least five elements into a conceptually unified nexus. His mental sequences went something like this: (1) I see that a mold has fallen by accident into my culture dish; (2) the staphylococcal colonies residing near it failed to grow; (3) the mold must have secreted something that killed the bacteria; (4) I recall a similar experience once before; (5) if I could separate this new "something" from the mold, it could be used to kill staphylococci that cause human infections.

Actually, Fleming's mind was exceptionally well prepared for the penicillin mold. Six years earlier, while he was suffering from a cold, his own nasal drippings had found their way onto a culture dish, for reasons not made entirely clear. He noted that nearby bacteria were killed, and astutely followed up the lead. His observations led him to discover a bactericidal enzyme present in nasal mucus and tears, called lysozyme. Lysozyme proved too weak to be of medical use, but imagine how receptive Fleming's mind was to the penicillin mold when it later happened on the scene!

One word evokes the quality of the operations involved in the first three kinds of chance. It is *serendipity*. The term describes the facility for encountering unexpected good luck, as the result of: accident (Chance I), general exploratory behavior (Chance II), or sagacity (Chance III). The word itself was coined by the Englishman-of-letters Horace Walpole, in 1954. He used it with reference to the legendary tales of the Three Princes of Serendip (Ceylon), who quite unexpectedly encountered many instances of good fortune on their travels. In today's parlance, we have usually watered down *serendipity* to mean the good luck that comes solely by accident. We think of it as a result, not an ability. We have tended to lose sight of the element of sagacity, by which term Walpole wished to emphasize that some distinctive personal receptivity is involved.

There remains a fourth element in good luck, an unintentional but subtle personal prompting of it. The English Prime Minister Benjamin Disraeli summed up the principle underlying Chance IV when he noted that "we make

sagacity shrewdness

Classification

our fortunes and we call them fate." Disraeli, a politician of considerable practical experience, appreciated that we each shape our own destiny, at least to some degree. One might restate the principle as follows: *Chance favors the individualized action.*

In Chance IV the kind of luck is peculiar to one person, and like a personal hobby, it takes on a distinctive individual flavor. This form of chance is one-man-made, and it is as personal as a signature. Indeed, it is to motor behavior what Chance III is to sensory receptivity. But Chance IV connotes no generalized activity, as bees might have in the anonymity of a hive. Instead, it comprehends a discrete behavioral performance focused in a unique manner. Chance IV has an elusive, almost mirage-like quality. Like a mirage, it is difficult to get a firm grip on, for it tends to recede as we pursue it and advance as we step back. But we still accept a mirage when we see it, because we vaguely understand the basis for the phenomenon. A strongly heated layer of air, less dense than usual, lies next to the earth, and it bends the light rays as they pass through. The resulting image may be magnified as if by a telescopic lens in the atmosphere, and real objects, ordinarily hidden far out of sight over the horizon, are brought forward and revealed to the eye. What happens in a mirage then, and in this form of chance, not only appears farfetched but indeed is farfetched.

About a century ago, a striking example of Chance IV took place in the Spanish cave of Altamira.* There, one day in 1879, Don Marcelino de Sautuola was engaged in his hobby of archaeology, searching Altamira for bones and stones. With him was his daughter, Maria, who had asked him if she could come along to the cave that day. The indulgent father had said she could. Naturally enough, he first looked where he had always found heavy objects before, on the *floor* of the cave. But Maria, unhampered by any such preconceptions, looked not only at the floor but also all around the cave with the open-eyed wonder of a child. She looked up, exclaimed, and then he looked up, to see incredible works of art on the cave ceiling! The magnificent colored bison and other animals they saw at Altamira, painted more than 15,000 years ago, might lead one to call it "the Sistine Chapel of Prehistory." Passionately pursuing his interest in archaeology, de Sautuola, to his surprise, discovered man's first paintings. In quest of Science, he happened upon Art.

Yes, a dog did "discover" the cave, and the initial receptivity was his daughter's, but the pivotal reason for the cave paintings' discovery hinged on a long sequence of prior events originating in de Sautuola himself. For when we dig into the background of this amateur excavator, we find he was an exceptional person. Few Spaniards were out probing into caves 100 years ago. The fact that he—not someone else—decided to dig that day in the cave

---

* The cave had first been discovered some years before by an enterprising hunting dog in search of game. Curiously, in 1932 the French cave of Lascaux was discovered by still another dog.

mirage an illusion resulting from distortion of light

of Altamira was the culmination of his passionate interest in his hobby. Here was a rare man whose avocation had been to educate himself from scratch, as it were, in the science of archaeology and cave exploration. This was no simple passive recognizer of blind luck when it came his way, but a man whose unique interests served as an active creative thrust—someone whose own actions and personality would focus the events that led circuitously but inexorably to the discovery of man's first paintings.

Then, too, there is a more subtle matter. How do you give full weight to the personal interests that imbue your child with your own curiosity, that inspire her to ask to join you in your own musty hobby, and that then lead you to agree to her request at the critical moment? For many reasons, at Altamira, more than the special receptivity of Chance III was required—this was a different domain, that of the personality and its actions.

A century ago no one had the remotest idea our caveman ancestors were highly creative artists. Weren't their talents rather minor and limited to crude flint chippings? But the paintings at Altamira, like a mirage, would quickly magnify this diminutive view, bring up into full focus a distant, hidden era of man's prehistory, reveal sentient minds and well-developed aesthetic sensibilities to which men of any age might aspire. And like a mirage, the events at Altamira grew out of de Sautuola's heated personal quest and out of the invisible forces of chance we know exist yet cannot touch. Accordingly, one may introduce the term *altamirage* to identify the quality underlying Chance IV. Let us define it as the facility for encountering unexpected good luck as the result of highly individualized action. Altamirage goes well beyond the boundaries of serendipity in its emphasis on the role of personal action in chance.

Chance IV is favored by distinctive, if not eccentric, hobbies, personal life-styles, and modes of behavior peculiar to one individual, usually invested with some passion. The farther apart these personal activities are from the area under investigation, the more novel and unexpected will be the creative product of the encounter.

For some classic examples of the four Chances in biology and medicine, let us again turn to Fleming.

Good examples of Chance I (pure blind luck) do not leap out from the medical literature, because researchers always feel a little guilty when they mention that luck has replaced more rational approaches. However, we can rely on Fleming for his candor as he described how it was to be visited by Chance I. He said: "There are thousands of different molds, and there are thousands of different bacteria, and that chance put that mold in the right spot at the right time was like winning the Irish Sweepstakes."

Many investigators are as energetic as bees, so their fast mental and physical pace stirs up a certain amount of Chance II for this reason alone. Examples of Chance II are surely all around us, but it is difficult to prove with

candor frankness, honesty

scientific certainty that they exist, because studies of twins would be required. No researcher seems to have a twin who is indolent, but equal in all other abilities, to serve as a basis for comparison.

We have already considered Fleming under Chance III, and for an example of the subtle workings of the personality in Chance IV, we can return to him. In Fleming's background was a boyhood shaped by the frugal economy of a Scottish hill farm in Ayrshire. Later, we find that much of his decision to train and work at old St. Mary's Hospital in London was not based on the excellence of its scientific facilities. Instead, his decision hinged on the fact that he liked to play water polo and St. Mary's had a good swimming pool. Without the hobby that drew him to St. Mary's, Fleming would never have discovered penicillin! Still later, when he is 47, let us observe this same thrifty Scot at his laboratory at St. Mary's. His research facilities are primitive by today's standards. His bench stands beneath a window, covered by a clutter of old culture dishes, for Fleming is still reluctant to throw any dish out until he is certain that everything possible has been learned from it. He then picks up one culture dish of staphylococci that, with ingrained thrift, he has hoarded for many days. The delay has been crucial. Had he thrown the dish out earlier, on schedule like the rest of us, the penicillin mold might not have had the opportunity to grow. But there the mold is now, growing in the over-age culture dish, and he alone also has the prepared mind to realize its implications.

We have now seen Sir Alexander Fleming's modest comment about his Irish Sweepstakes luck under Chance I, and can infer that Chance II entered his life from his many industrious years in the laboratory. We later observed how receptive he was (Chance III) and finally how his hobby and his thrifty habits coalesced in Chance IV. Fleming's discovery earned him the Nobel Prize in Physiology and Medicine in 1945. (He shared it with Florey and Chain, who achieved the large-scale production of penicillin.) In Fleming's life, then, we see a fusion of all four forms of chance, and from this there follows a simple conclusion: The most novel, if not the greatest, discoveries occur when several varieties of chance coincide. Let us call this unifying observation the Fleming Effect. His life exemplifies it, and it merits special emphasis.

Why do we still remember men like Fleming? We venerate them not as scientists alone. As men, their total contribution transcends their scientific discoveries. In their lives we see demonstrated how malleable our own futures are. In their work we perceive how many loopholes fate has left us—how much of destiny is still in our hands. In them we find that nothing is predetermined. Chance can be on our side, if we but stir it up with our energies, stay receptive to its very random opportunity, and continually provoke it by individuality in our hobbies and our approach to life.

venerate to admire, regard with respect
malleable able to be shaped or influenced

The Roots of Serendipity

Questions

1 What rhetorical techniques does Austin use besides classification? Explain your answer.

2 What is the rehetorical purpose of the account of the dog's operation?

3 Why does Austin discuss Alexander Fleming at such great length?

4 Do the bases for classification used in this essay lead to significant, mutually exclusive, complete categorizations? Explain.

Artistic Research Tools for Scientific Minds

George W. Ladd

George W. Ladd is a professor of economics at Iowa State University. The research tools discussed in his essay are placed in three categories: subconscious mental processes, chance, and writing. These categories suggest a classification system even though the relationships among the three are not entirely consistent.

Ladd divides each of the research tools into its components: Subconscious mental processes are divided into imagination and intuition; these in turn are categorized, according to their use and their occurrence, as "four stages of invention" and "conditions stimulating to subconscious mental processes." He discusses four kinds of chance—the same as those in Austin's classification—and then explains the use of problemsolving to handle different types of tasks. Finally, Ladd discusses the third research tool, writing. He points out writing activities that can stimulate research and then briefly discusses how writing techniques can make research more efficient.

Ladd's essay is much more rambling than the tight and controlled classifications presented in the Berne essay and the even more formal Austin essay. One reason for its diffuse quality may be that Ladd wrote the essay first as a paper to be delivered at a seminar, and thus deliberately adopted an informal approach to the subject. As Ladd announces in the paper, he is addressing himself mainly to students—graduate students. His purpose is to help such students become more efficient and creative researchers.

Two criteria that we teachers apply in selecting topics that we want students to learn are (*a*) frequency of application and (*b*) versatility. But, in violation of our own criteria, we pay little attention in our courses to the research tools that are the most versatile and frequently used of all.

The topics of this paper are some frequently used, versatile tools: subconscious mental processes (imagination, intuition, hunch), chance (including serendipity), and writing. These topics receive little attention in our courses.

On the criteria of frequency of use, consider. In the twenty-three years that I have been doing economic research, I have made six different applications of linear programming. Some applications took a few weeks. Others lasted about a year. If we allow one year per application—a generous figure—we find that in sixteen of the twenty-three years, I have not been using linear programming. But I use subconscious mental processes daily, and write at least weekly, and take advantage of chance whenever I can, which has been more than six times. A similar condition prevails for others with whom I have talked. They use subconscious mental processes and writing more frequently than they use quantitative tools that they were taught as students, and their careers are affected by luck.

On the criteria of versatility, consider. Linear programming is one of the most versatile tools available to economists. But there are a number of problems for which it is inappropriate. Linear programming has not proved useful for estimating consumer demand functions or for solving truck routing problems. Neither is it useful for obtaining the data needed for a linear program. Each research tool we teach students is, like linear programming, inappropriate for many problems. But subconscious mental processes, writing, and chance are useful for any problem, at every stage of every research project.

Application of the criteria of frequency of use and versatility leads me to conclude that students need to be exposed to the topics of this paper. This paper is addressed mainly to students. But even an experienced investigator who knows the importance of the tools discussed here may find a systematic discussion to be helpful.

Evidence on the usefulness of these tools can be found in books of Austin (a neurologist), Beveridge (an animal pathologist), Hadamard and Polya (mathematicians), Young (a biologist), and Porterfield (a sociologist), and in writings cited in these books. Wiener's (p. 72) first stage in the inductive research process is "the imagination of a theory to fit the facts." Even philosophers of science acknowledge the importance of subconscious mental processes in research. See for example Braithwaite (p. 27) and Popper (pp. 31, 32). Hicks' reaction to Keynes' *General Theory* is appropriate here. Hicks wrote:

> I must confess that, as I have worked with Mr. Keynes's book, I have been amazed at the way he manages, without the use of any special apparatus, to

linear programming laying out a flow of information as a manual or computer model cut through the tangle of difficulties that beset him, and to go straight for the really important things. He succeeds in doing so just because he makes free use of his superb intuition and acute observation of the real world, in order to be able to discard the inessentials and go straight for the essentials. (p. 4)

Intuition is subconscious. Observation involves the conscious and the subconscious.

The purpose of this paper is to present ways of making subconscious mental processes, chance, and writing more productive.

SUBCONSCIOUS MENTAL PROCESSES

Have you ever had an experience like this? You are talking and making a point that requires you to talk for two minutes. Halfway through the two minutes you become conscious of a useful idea, but by the time you complete the two minutes of talk you have lost the idea. And you are unable to remember or recreate the idea. Your subconscious mental processes created a suggestion and put it forward for your conscious mind to catch, and your conscious failed to catch and hold the idea.

In the "Born Loser" comic strip of 6 October 1977, Mr. Born Loser is walking along mumbling to himself, "Backward, turn backward, Oh time in thy flight, I just thought of a comeback I needed last night." Perhaps this has happened to you. An hour after an argument, a good idea occurs to you that would have won your case.

These experiences are typical of subconscious processes. The term "subconscious" describes mental processes such as thoughts, ideas, and feelings that occur in our mind without our being conscious of them. Freud's comparison of the human mind to an iceberg illustrates the view held by many psychologists of the subconscious (or unconscious as they call it). Only one-eighth of the mass of an iceberg is above the water; the remaining seven-eights is below the surface of the water. Only a small fraction of our mental processes are conscious—above the surface of consciousness. A large fraction of our mental processes are below the surface: subconscious (or unconscious) processes.

Normally, we are not aware that our subconscious is operating because the thoughts it throws up to our conscious combine with our conscious thoughts to provide an orderly, reasonable, ordinary stream of consciousness. It is only when the subconscious puts up a new, exciting, extraordinary thought that we are made aware of its operation, or when it puts up a thought on a topic other than the one we are consciously pondering.

Many of our concepts and thoughts originate in the subconscious. Conscious reason is used to examine and accept or reject the proposal from the subconscious.

Given Freud's comparison of the mind to an iceberg and given that ideas originate in the subconscious, it is desirable to increase the productivity of the subconscious. This can be done because the subconscious does respond to stimuli. And a person can exercise some control over the amount, variety, and strength of the stimuli his subconscious receives. By controlling these stimuli, he exercises some control over his subconscious.

It is not enough, however, to stimulate one's subconscious. One must also sensitize one's conscious mind to the operations of the subconscious in order to minimize the number of ideas from the subconscious that are lost before they penetrate the conscious. Some of the things a person does to stimulate his subconscious to create ideas also stimulate his conscious to grasp the ideas.

Most of the ideas generated by our subconscious processes turn out, upon evaluation by our conscious mental processes, to be useless, or at least useless in the context in which they came to mind. This means that, because the subconscious is often wrong, the person who desires to increase its usefulness must have more ideas, knowing that a large proportion of them will be bad ideas. And he must use his conscious mind to discriminate.

Imagination and Intuition

Psychologists speak of several kinds of imagination. Daydreams and nightdreams are instances of passive imagination. Reproductive imagination is the capacity to form mental pictures of past experiences. The kind of imagination of most concern in science is productive or creative imagination. Senator Robert F. Kennedy is reported to have said, "Some people see things as they are and wonder why. I see things that never were and ask why not?" To "see things that never were" is an act of creative imagination. The product of creative imagination is a new invention. The new invention may be something physical like the wheel. It may be an artistic piece. It may be a new concept or new idea or new model, (e.g., autoregressive least squares). Frequently the product of the imagination is a link between things that were not formerly seen to be connected in any way. "A thing learned in certain connections is torn out of the context in which it was learned, for use in some new context" (Guilford, p. 100). Ideas, facts, relationships, or concepts become dissociated from their previous contacts and become associated together in new ways.

Porterfield discusses synopsis and synthesis as processes of imagination. Synopsis or "whole-sight" provides a view of the whole of a problem or situation. Synthesis provides understanding of relations among the parts of the whole. Hadamard (p. 23) argues: "The unconscious has the important property of being manifold; several and probably many things can and do occur in it simultaneously. This contrasts with the conscious ego which is unique." Because of the uniqueness of the conscious and the manifold character of the subconscious, the act of synthesis is performed in the subconscious rather than in the conscious. In discussing creative imagination, Weld writes:

autoregressive least squares an exotic statistical concept

Without warning but usually after long incubation and as the result of some chance situation, or some grouping of associative tendencies, a new meaning, a happy thought, is born. . . . In view of the suddenness of its initiation, its unaccountableness, its feeling of strangeness and the joy which it sometimes brings, the new idea often seems to come as an inspiration from on high. Sometimes the new conception comes in its complete form. . . . But at other times and more frequently, the new idea is vague, incomplete or only in outline. . . . (p. 707)

The terms suddenness, unaccountableness, strangeness, joy, inspiration are terms sometimes used to describe intuition. In philosophy, intuition is defined as immediate knowledge attained without conscious deliberation or reasoning. In the theory of knowledge, intuition is the immediate apprehension of truth. It is "knowing without knowing why I know." Beveridge (p. 91) defines it as "a sudden enlightenment or comprehension of a situation, a clarifying idea which springs into the consciousness, often, though not necessarily, when one is not consciously thinking of the subject. . . . Ideas coming dramatically when one is not consciously thinking of the subject are the most striking examples of intuition, but those arriving suddenly when the problem is being consciously pondered are also intuitions."

We all have these intuitions. Subconscious mental processes are research tools, just as is linear programming, and the subconscious mental processes that create intuitions can be stimulated to be more productive.

FOUR STAGES OF INVENTION

Wallas has described the inventive process as consisting of four stages: preparation, incubation, illumination, and verification.

Preparation is a conscious, voluntary, willful effort that is required to stimulate the subconscious. The rules for the preparation stage include "the whole traditional art of logic, the mathematical forms of which are the logic of the modern experimental sciences, and the methods of systematic and continuous examination of present or recorded phenomena . . . and the voluntary choice of a 'problem-attitude.' Our mind is not likely to give us a clear answer to any particular problem unless we set it a clear question . . ." (Wallas, p. 84).

The incubation stage is a stage of subconscious mental activity. "During incubation we do not voluntarily or consciously think on a particular problem and . . . a series of unconscious and involuntary . . . mental activities take place" (Wallas, p. 86). Illumination is the same as Beveridge's "sudden enlightenment or comprehension."

Wallas discusses verification as a conscious, voluntary, willful effort. It is guided by the same rules as preparation. One purpose of verification is to test the illumination against logic or mathematical rules, experience, and other knowledge. Another purpose is to express the results in language. A third purpose is to "precise" the results, that is, to state the results completely and precisely. A fourth purpose is to prepare for using the illumination. What Wallas calls verification, some people would call verification and validation.

Typically a person is simultaneously engaged in two or more of these stages on two or more problems. Conscious verification of an answer to one problem is preparing him for subconscious effort on a second problem while his subconscious is incubating on a third problem. Work on any single problem does not follow these steps in strict sequence. Rather, investigators jump back and forth from one step to another.

CONDITIONS STIMULATING TO SUBCONSCIOUS MENTAL PROCESSES

Reading, discussions, and introspection lead to the belief that many people's subconscious minds respond to the stimuli discussed here.

Doubt

In those instances when you are most doubtful of accepted modes of thought or of conventional questions or approaches, your subconscious is more apt to generate novel ideas than when you are satisfied with the conventional wisdom.

Venturesome Attitude

You are not going to break ground by developing something new if you are paralyzed by the fear of making a mistake. Don't be afraid to make mistakes. There are plenty of people around who will delight in pointing out your errors. Think how much pleasure you will afford those people if you do make a mistake! I think it was John Maynard Keynes who astutely observed, "It is not so terrible to make a mistake. What is terrible is not to be found out." By the time each of us finishes formal schooling, he has been caught in enough mistakes that he knows that being found out does not destroy one's ego or self-esteem. Being caught in a mistake after leaving school is not more destructive of one's self-esteem than being caught in a mistake while in school.

Probably fear of failure also inhibits us. But if a failure now and then is going to ruin your career or your self-esteem, your successes must not be worth much. Perhaps this suggests a career that is a mixture of some "safe" projects and some "risky" projects so that successes on the "safe" projects can compensate for possible failures on the "risky" projects. But failure is unpredictable. On some projects you will fail to achieve what you initially thought were modest objectives. In some cases you will achieve objectives that you initially had no idea how to achieve.

One reason for this may be some sort of compensatory principle. A greater curiosity about or interest or challenge in the risky project elicits more preparation and effort. Too, a magnificent failure can be more exciting than a modest success.

Few things in life are more gratifying than accomplishing a task that you once believed to be impossible. It is appropriate to recall that Pogo (in Walt Kelly's comic strip of the same name) once observed, "We are confronted with insurmountable opportunities."

Diverse Experiences, Memories, and Interests

One condition favorable to a fruitful subconscious is diversity of memories, experiences, and interests. A fruitful intuition is often the perception of a connection between things that were previously unconnected. A varied store of memories and experiences makes it possible for your subconscious to perceive connections between things that you would not even be aware of if your experiences were less varied. One of the advantages an experienced investigator has over a young researcher is that the former has a more varied store of memories and experiences to draw on.

From his studies of problem solving, the psychologist Raaheim has concluded, "The more experienced you are, the more problems you are likely to be faced with. And . . . the more problems you are likely to solve" (p. 87).

The diversity need not all be in professional interests and experiences. Austin emphasizes that research results are the accomplishments of the whole person, not just of a compartmentalized "professional" portion of a person, and presents examples to show that his hobbies of music, watercolor painting, and hunting have contributed to his research in neurology. A person can acquire diverse experiences vicariously by reading on a variety of topics. Mighell argued that economists should read widely.

Variety in experience does not come simply from living. You must make an effort to obtain it. A young assistant professor had failed to make this conscious effort. He had been at one school for three years when he learned that a desirable position was open at another university. He quickly applied for the position. In his application, he emphasized the benefit of his three years of experience. His department head, however, saw it differently. In his letter of reference he wrote. "This young man claims to have had three years of experience. This is not so. He has had one year of experience three times."

Thorough Preparation

Preparation precedes subconscious mental activity. The more thoroughly your conscious mind has grasped the problem—in general outline and in detail—the better is the chance that your subconscious will produce fruitful ideas. Subconscious processes are stimulated by vigorous conscious processes.

How does one go about preparing thoroughly? Some relevant considerations were presented under the section "Four Stages of Invention." Careful formulation of the problem is an important part of preparation.

vicariously through imaginative participation

Artistic Research Tools for Scientific Minds 177

Tension

Conscious absorption of a problem, teamed with an intense desire to know, provides a strong stimulus to your subconscious. In discussing the creative person, Maslow (p. 47) has written of "this total fascination with the matter-in-hand, this getting lost in the present, this detachment from time and place." Such total immersion in a problem bespeaks of intense concentration and overpowering desire for a solution. The stereotype of the absentminded professor has a factual basis in the actual behavior of professors experiencing "this detachment from time and place" while in the throes of "tense thought," to use Hadamard's term.

What are sources of a strong desire for a solution? One is certainly curiosity. It seems to me that curiosity has an aesthetic component: an intellectual aesthetic sense, or a yearning for intellectual tidiness. Beveridge (p. 77) wrote of the "love of order and logical connection between facts." Polya (p. 45) expressed it, "The feeling that harmonious simple order cannot be deceitful guides the discoverer both in the mathematical and in the other sciences." An aesthetic tension is created by an incomplete or broken pattern of facts and ideas or a pattern with discordant pieces. This tension is discomforting. When you finally see the pattern complete and unbroken, you experience a delightful release of the tension. You perceive something soothing or delightful to your sense of intellectual aesthetics. Curiosity may also have a component of the naive, open-eyed wonder of a child at the marvels of the world. Another source of strong desire for a solution may be your ego. Obtaining a solution gives you a sense of mastery. Your desire for a solution may rise from a feeling of frustration: frustration with the inadequacies of present answers to a question, or irritation over the lack of an answer.

Temporary Abandonment

A practice that most people find favorable to subconscious activity is temporary conscious abandonment of the problem. Upon returning to the problem later, one frequently finds that he has acquired new ideas or insights in the interim. One undesirable result of over-long conscious pondering of a problem is conditioned thinking. Conditioned thinking is like cycling in solving a degenerate linear program: the mind continually retraces the same established (and fruitless) patterns of thought. Temporary abandonment helps to break these fruitless patterns. The value of temporary abandonment is reflected in the old proverb "Sleep on it."

The essence of Wallas' second stage in inventive thought—incubation—is temporary conscious abandonment. You may also temporarily abandon a problem during the preparation stage. You may alternate between conscious thought and temporary abandonment several times before finally coming up with a solution.

One student working on his dissertation told me that when he was having difficulty, he would concentrate on the problem for the last fifteen to thirty minutes of his evening's work before going home, and then not think about the problem any more that evening. The problem frequently would be clarified, and sometimes solved, by the time he returned to his office the next morning.

A colleague has told me that he works most effectively when engaged in intense concentration if he takes a five-minute break every half-hour. During that five minutes he may take a coffee-break or walk to the water fountain for a drink. After the five-minute break, he returns to work refreshed.

You may temporarily abandon conscious efforts on one problem in order to turn your conscious mind to other problems. But you may also temporarily abandon conscious efforts on all research.

Relaxation

Some people find a period of relaxation or light effort—driving, shaving, walking—immediately following a period of serious effort to be a favorable time for intuitions. The subconscious processes of some people are active at night, and these people will be awakened during the night by bright ideas, or ideas will spring to mind just after waking in the morning. Some people find lying in bed in the morning while half-awake to be favorable to the appearance of intuitions. Some people find a combination of mental relaxation and physical exercise to be conducive to the appearance of intuitions.

Writing

Young expressed the attitude of many people toward writing when he wrote, "The scientist does not usually think of the writing of books or preparing of lectures as research. Writing seems to him to be a rather tiresome labour that he must do after the fun of laboratory research is over" (p. 1). But, later in the same paragraph that contained this statement, Young wrote, "I came to realize the extent to which having to describe the results of one's thoughts to others is a part of the process of discovery itself."

Many of my intuitions come to me when I am writing. It frequently happens that "I don't know what I think until I write it." It sometimes happens, for example, that I start to write a paragraph knowing only the first sentence and having only a vague idea of the central theme. But by the time I reach the end of the paragraph I will have expressed some ideas that I did not have when I started the paragraph, or at least did not know I had.

Clardy beautifully expresses my attitude toward writing. She says, "I have acquired many things by writing them. There are allegedly those who know what they have to say before saying it, but I have never counted myself in their number. Argument seems to me a means of developing rather than merely demonstrating theories, and articulation a means of amassing rather than just disseminating insight. Writing is as much the cause as the result of having something to say."

The process of learning from your own writing does not end at the first draft. In discussing rewriting and restating the evidence, Penfield (p. 106) states, "Often, once I get my thoughts truly expressed, I see things I never suspected before."

Precising the results and preparation for using the illumination are two purposes of the verification stage of invention. Precising the results involves stating them completely and precisely writing them. The writing helps you to prepare to use the results.

We usually think of writing as something that one does to report to others. What is being advocated here is writing to yourself to generate or discover knowledge. This position is similar to the one you have probably heard (and may have expressed yourself): "The best way to learn something is to have to teach it." For some statistical support for this view, see Siegfried. He concluded that proctoring an introductory economics course significantly improves the student-proctor's understanding of economics principles.

Exchange with Colleagues

Discussion with others can be helpful in various ways. Your colleagues' or students' comments can bring out points you had missed. They may bring a new perspective that provides you with new insight. They may point out an incorrect assumption you were making, and show you a correct alternative. They may complete a partial idea of yours.

Discussion has other values. Keynes wrote (p. vii): "It is astonishing what foolish things one can temporarily believe if one thinks too long alone. . . ." Discussion with colleagues provides a useful defense against believing foolish things. Take care, however, lest your colleagues teach you foolish things that you did not know before.

Some people find the most stimulating exchange with colleagues to be the exchange that occurs in a "pressurized environment," as when presenting and defending a paper before a friendly but critical audience. These people commonly say, "I think better on my feet."

The difference between "writing" and "exchange with colleagues" is that writing represents an exchange with one's self.

Freedom from Distraction

Another condition favorable to the subconscious is freedom from distraction: interruption by others, intrusive noises, pressures to be working on several other jobs in addition to the one currently occupying you. Intrusive influences that distract your conscious mind inhibit the operation of your subconscious mind. These influences also make it more likely that ideas generated by your subconscious will be overlooked by your conscious.

It is a common experience that putting in eight hours on research in two four-hour stretches is more productive than eight one-hour stretches. The reason may be that changing tasks requires redirecting your subconscious. Changing from one task to another shortly after the first task is initiated requires your subconscious to be redirected before it has time to accomplish anything on the original task.

In addition, frequent changing of tasks makes it difficult for your subconscious mind to absorb thoroughly any single problem. You might say that prolonged concentration on one problem permits the conscious to transmit information to the subconscious. When you change tasks frequently, the messages transmitted from your conscious are received by your subconscious as random noise.

Both temporary abandonment and distraction mean changing the course of your conscious thoughts. One is voluntary and the other is involuntary. If you do it to yourself, it is temporary abandonment. If I do it to you, it is distraction.

Deadlines

Some scientists do their best work when facing deadlines imposed from outside. For deadlines to have this effect, you must be able to work without distraction. It is questionable whether self-imposed deadlines do stimulate the subconscious. Such deadlines so easily can be set back by a few days or a few weeks.

The conditions most stimulating of all to your subconscious are those that combine a number of the individual conditions presented here, e.g., interdisciplinary brainstorming sessions in preparation for writing a report due the fifteenth of next month. This involves diversity, exchange with colleagues, and pressure of meeting a deadline.

Capturing Intuitions

It does you no good to have a fertile subconscious if your conscious fails to grasp the results of your subconscious processes. Intuitions frequently appear on the edge of your conscious and willful effort is required to grasp them before they are lost. You need to be alert to grasp these intuitions as soon as they appear. Commonly an intuition lost once is lost permanently. Some people wisely make a habit of jotting down notes as soon as an intuition appears.

CHANCE

Beveridge has written, "New knowledge very often has its origin in some quite unexpected observation or chance occurrence arising during an investigation. The importance of this factor [chance] in discovery should be fully appreciated and research workers ought deliberately to exploit it" (p. 55). And the mathematician Polya writes: "The first rule of discovery is to have brains and good luck" p. 172).

Nelson (p. 256) reports:

After he discovered the tuberculosis bacillus [Pasteur] was very often given evidence of the acute jealousy of people in his or in related fields. At a big reception at which Pasteur was the guest of honor one of his colleagues came up and said, "Isn't it extraordinary these days how many scientific achievements of our century are arrived at by accident?" Pasteur said, "Yes, it really is remarkable when you think about it, and furthermore, did you ever observe to whom the accidents happen?"

Pasteur's response becomes more meaningful if you know that Pasteur believed that "Chance favors only the prepared mind."

Four Forms of Chance

Austin finds four kinds of chance that play roles in creative research. Chance I represents blind luck, completely accidental. In Chance II, good luck is the result of general exploratory behavior. Its major premise is that "*un*luck runs out if you persist" (p.73). Its main feature is general exploratory actions in promising directions. In Chance III, good luck is the result of personal sagacity. It occurs to the "prepared mind" when "some special receptivity born from past experience permits you to discern a new fact or to perceive ideas in a new relationship" (p. 78). Austin classifies Chance I, II, and III as serendipity, "the facility for encountering unexpected good luck as the result of accident, sagacity or general exploratory behavior" (p. 71). Chance IV "is the kind of luck that develops during a probing action that has a distinctive personal flavor" (p. 75). Chance II involves generalized motor activity. Chance III involves one's personal sensory receptivity. Chance IV involves personalized motor behavior (action) that is focused in a specific manner that results from the investigator's own unique combination of skills, interests, background, aptitudes, personality, values, beliefs: from the person the investigator is. Austin's classification can make you aware of the different ways that chance can benefit your research and can thereby increase the likelihood that you will recognize those situations when you can be the beneficiary of chance.

The results of chance are not all beneficial in research; results of chance can also be harmful. The existence of "Murphy's Laws," their correlatives and variations are evidence of the awareness of the negative effects of chance. Austin (pp. 95–96) presents twenty such laws. The simplest version of Murphy's Law is, "If anything *can* go wrong, it will."

You do have some control over your luck. You cannot determine, but you can influence, your luck. Possession of a lively curiosity, active imagination, acute perception, diverse experiences, a retentive memory, and persistence will do a great deal to improve your luck.

One Solution Solves Several Problems

In one sort of serendipity, a method used to solve one problem turns out to be appropriate for solving a second problem that was not previously perceived as having any relation to the first; or a solution to one problem turns out to be a solution to an apparently unrelated problem. This justifies Polya's advice (p. 65): "Having made some discovery, however modest, . . . we should not miss the possibilities opened up by the new result, we should try to use again the procedure used. Exploit your success! *Can you use the result, or the method, for some other problem?*"

Polya's suggestion would worry some economists. These people are concerned that "too many agricultural economists are tool-oriented rather than problem-oriented. They learn a method or tool and then search around for problems to try it on." I think Polya's proposal is justified, and their concern is justified. These economists are concerned, I believe, about people practicing cookbookery or mathematistry, in Box's terms. The symptoms of cookbookery are "a tendency to force all problems into the molds of one or two routine techniques, insufficient thought being given to the real objectives of the investigation or to the relevance of the assumptions of the imposed methods" (p. 797). "Mathematistry is characterized by development of theory for theory's sake, which since it seldom touches down with practice, has a tendency to redefine the problem rather than solve it" (p. 797). It is possible to follow Polya's advice without engaging in cookbookery or mathematistry.

Hadamard (p. 50) lamented his missed opportunities when he "happened to overlook results which ought to have struck me blind." Following Polya's advice will reduce the frequency with which you miss opportunities to use your discoveries.

Problem Solving

It will give us greater insight into the various forms of chance if we consider some findings of psychologists on problem-solving behavior. Raaheim differentiates among three kinds of tasks. He first conceives of a series of earlier situations of the same sort. A problem situation is "the deviant member of a series of earlier situations of the same sort" (p. 22). The definition focuses at once on the elements that are common to the problem situation and the earlier situations, and the difference between the problem situation and the earlier situations. This definition treats as problems those "tasks which may eventually be solved by *intelligently* utilizing one's past experience" (p. 50), because intelligent behavior depends on an ability to reformulate one's past experience to meet the requirements of the present.

A second kind of task is a routine task. A routine task has no detectable difference from previous situations of the same sort. Solution of such tasks does not require application of intelligence, but use of memory.

The third kind of task is a novel task in which "the deviation from what are the familiar features is too great . . . when a familiar pattern is no longer recognizable" (Raaheim, p. 83). Intelligence is not a factor in solving such totally unfamiliar tasks. Application of intelligence to solution of such tasks can delay or even prevent finding a solution. "For the effective handling of very unfamiliar tasks, an exploratory activity is more rewarding than intelligent reflection" (Raaheim, p. 84). In experimental studies of people faced with novel tasks, the successful experimental subjects were more active, more persistent, and tried out more methods of attacking the task than the subjects who failed to solve the novel task. This categorization of tasks helps us to see one of the benefits of experience. What is a novel task to a novice may only be a routine task to an experienced person.

This categorization also implicitly focuses on the characteristics and experiences of the decision maker involved. For example, academic economists and businessmen face different sets of tasks. The same decision-situation that presents a businessman with a problem because it deviates somewhat from a series of earlier, similar situations would present an academic economist with a novel task because he has experienced no earlier, similar situations.

Chance in Solving Problems

Chance II and IV involve movement, action, trying, persistence: things that are important in solving novel tasks. In facing a task, one thing you do is search for a series of similar situations that have been encountered earlier. This may involve attempts to form different series and attempts to reformulate some past experiences. In carrying out these activities, you are liable to do a good deal of searching (of memory, notes, books, journal articles, of colleague's ideas, and experience) and some trial and error. This involves the motion of Chance II and Chance IV. And the prepared mind and ability to form significant associations of Chance III can have a deciding effect on the success or failure of the quest.

WRITING

Many people look upon writing as purely a research-reporting tool; they neglect its role as a research tool. Everything presented earlier on writing as a stimulus to the subconscious argues that writing is a valuable research tool. Certainly if you share with me the trait of not knowing what you think until you write it down, you should view writing as a research tool. Writing serves other functions in addition to stimulating the subconscious. Writing out in detail the statement of the problem, how you plan to solve the problem and why you plan to solve it in the way you do, can save work, time, money, and embarrassment.

Preparing a report covering statement of the problem, review of literature (if appropriate), theoretical analysis (economic, statistical, econometric, or operation research), data used, method of data collection, method of empirical analysis of the data—everything but results, summary, and conclusions—before beginning to collect and analyze data has several beneficial results. It causes you to solve many problems before they ever arise, and to solve them in a consistent, coherent way. It reduces the collection of unnecessary data, likelihood of failure to collect needed data, number of false starts, and performance of unneeded computations.

An alternative to writing before doing research is to do and decide simultaneously: while doing research you are also deciding how to do research. A common result is that doing gets ahead of thinking and when you finally begin to think about what you did last week, you discover that you did it wrong and last week's work has to be redone. Access to electronic computers handicaps the student, or any other researcher, who tries to plan research and perform research simultaneously. If you try to keep the computer busy, and many seem to feel the need to do so, your own busyness keeps you from doing adequate planning.

A common objective of research is the testing of hypotheses. Before you ever start testing, you ought to know which hypotheses you will test, how you will test them, why you will test them, and how you will interpret results of the tests. Writing a report before doing the research increases your chances of knowing these things and, consequently, of correctly performing and interpreting the tests of hypotheses that are most relevant for your problem. Every research project involves use of maintained hypotheses, i.e., of things that are assumed to be true for the purposes of, and during the duration of, the study. Sometimes the question of whether a specific hypothesis should be tested or maintained is critical. You are more apt to make a proper choice if you write before you act.

A reason for having my students write their theses before doing their research is this. When public funds have been assigned to me and I am responsible for them, and a student is spending those funds to gather data or perform computations, I am not comfortable unless I know what he is doing and am confident that he knows what he is doing.

Austin (p. 171) presents another reason for doing the writing before the research is completed. He writes, "The investigator must finally put all the information into a manuscript for publication complete with tables, figures, and bibliography, and must try to anticipate which editors of which journals will be the most receptive. By now, . . . *months* have gone by. The original ideas have lost their luster. Completing the manuscript is like giving birth to a cactus that has bloomed long before." Writing is much less painful if done as an early step in research than if left to the end.

REASONS MOST COURSES IGNORE THESE TOOLS

Why do the research tools covered here receive so little attention in our graduate programs? This section represents my (speculative) explanations.

First, special purpose research tools (multiple regression, linear programming, etc.) are "public property." They are in the public domain. The tools discussed in this chapter are "private property." They are in the private domain. Thus, you can discuss my linear program or regression analysis as well as I can. And I can discuss yours as well as you can. But you cannot study and discuss my subconscious mental activities or writing habits. Nor can I study yours.

Logical analysis is public property (we all know and use the rules); intuitive analysis is private. One consequence is that "scientific types tend to downgrade subconscious mental activities because they try to keep things 'rational, within reason' (that is, consciously workable)" Austin (p. 162).

Perhaps a more fundamental reason relates to differences between the left and right halves of the mind. Austin (pp. 138–39) reports:

> Our left cerebral hemisphere "thinks" in verbal, auditory terms, is good at translating symbols, including those of mathematics as well as language, and works best when analyzing a sequence of details. . . . In contrast, our right hemisphere "thinks" in visual, *non*verbal terms, particularly in terms involving complex spatial relationships, and specializes in three dimensional depth perception. It also recognizes structural similarities, and works best in Gestalt: that is, drawing conclusions based on a grasp of the total (visual) picture. . . . While its left partner proceeds, piecemeal, to examine the irregular bark on each tree, our right hemisphere grasps in one sweep the shape of the whole forest, relates it adroitly to the contours of the near landscape, then to the line of the horizon. . . . Hidden away, almost out of reach of language [in the right hemisphere], can be the source of intuitive insights that are of fundamental importance in solving a problem. And this hemisphere . . . is mute.

We see that education addresses itself almost entirely to the left half of the brain. Scientists tend to be "outward-oriented" rather than "inward-oriented." They ask, "How does the world out there work?" and not, "How does the world inside me work?" As individuals, they may be curious about the latter question; but they view this as an individual concern, not a scientific concern. Related to this is the scientific constraint that research reports are to focus on the investigation, not on the investigator.

Questions

1 Why do you think Ladd gives so many examples, illustrations, and explanations?

2 How does Ladd use "subconscious mental processes," "chance," and "writing" as categories? Can you find any classifications within these categories?

3 What rhetorical techniques other than classification can you find in Ladd's paper? Why are they used?

4 Do the many references to sources detract from the clarity of the presentation? Why, or why not? Why did Ladd include them?

Fiber Facts

Marvin Segal

Marvin Segal is president of the Southwest Apparel Manufacturers' Association and editor of the association's newsletter. He is also the author of a text on fashion entrepreneurship, From Rags to Riches *(1982). His "Fiber Facts" is a brief column in the newsletter that publicizes the properties of various kinds of fibers to those interested in using them in the making of garments and in marketing those garments. In the segment reprinted here, Segel classifies Celanese fibers according to the amount of stretch that each will produce. His use of classification is entirely utilitarian. If the stretchability of a fabric is as important to the consumer as the column implies, manufacturers and buyers need to know which fibers and fabrics will give their garments the kind and degree of stretch that fashion demands.*

Segal's expected audience is a very limited one: the manufacturers of clothing in the Southwest and clothing buyers. The purpose of the column is simply to inform, and its classification is presented factually and succinctly.

187

COTTON, INC.

The Spring/Summer 1981 Pret A Porter is always an excellent source for styling ideas, fabric news and color innovation. Cotton, Incorporated was there and can now offer you the benefits at the **Cottonworks.**Come and see the slides from the latest European shows, both the Pret A Porter and the SEHM menswear show.

Cotton sweaters will be strong items for spring '81 because of their versatility and wide color spectrum, according to specialty and department store retailers. Stores point out that because these sweaters take color so well and clearly, they have good point-of-purchase appeal. The fact that the sweaters can stand alone or be used to accessorize a suit or sport coat is another factor which contributes to their popularity.

DUPONT

A new **"Quina"** product has been introduced by **DuPont.**

Designed primarily for weaving applications, the new product will permit the silk-like esthetics of **"Quina"** to be available in a broader range of fashion fabrics and garments than ever before.

The new product is a combination of nylon and polyester spun into a single, unique splittable bicomponent fiber. The initial offering will be 70 denier, 26 filament.

"Quina" is a registered DuPont trademark used with nylon fiber. The new product, T-483, which combines nylon and polyester polymers, will require a revision of the company's trademark approach.

The product will be targeted toward retail business in Holiday 1981 and Spring 1982 markets.

CELANESE

Stretch fabrics made of Celanese Fortrel/polyester predominates many Womenswear lines for Spring/Summer '81 and will increase in importance in Fall '81. Stretch fabrics may be classified as follows:

Non-stretch—0–10%

All spun woven fabrics, and rigid textured polyesters fall into this category. Spun fabrics stretch approximately 5%, textured woven 8–12%.

Pret A Porter European women's fashion showings; literally, "ready to wear"
SEHM European menswear fashion showings
denier unit of fineness for synthetic yarn
filament thinly spun thread

Mechanical Stretch—10–15%

All textured and all spun fabrics can be finished to fit this category; fabrics with less than 15% stretch are not considered merchandisable stretch fabrics.

Comfort Stretch—15–25%

All textured and spun fabrics can be treated in weaving and finishing to produce fabrics in this category. The most innovative in comfort stretch fabric is Fortrel/cotton and filament Fortrel fabrication.

Active Stretch—Above 25%

This category requires the use of astomeric yarn. These fabrics are excellent for active sportswear, are the most expensive stretch fabrics and exhibit much greater "growth" than other types of stretch fabrics.

Questions

1 Is the information in "Fiber Facts" likely to be helpful to most of its audience? Why, or why not?
2 What rhetorical technique is Segal using in the section headed "Cotton, Inc."? In the section headed "DuPont"?
3 If you were assigned to write a column containing the information in "Fiber Facts," how would you do it? Write one.

"growth" stretchability

COMPARISON

As a pattern of development in writing, *comparison* relies upon one of the most basic aspects of thought, the ability to see relationships and differences. Several types of comparison occur frequently in writing: *logical comparison*, the process of seeing similarities between objects or ideas of the same class: *analogy*, the process of seeing similarities between objects or ideas of different classes; *difference in degree*, which explores the relative extent to which two or more ideas or objects possess a trait; and *difference in kind*, which involves seeing what traits or aspects are not shared by two or more objects or ideas.

Comparison is one of the primary means by which we make decisions—that is, in any decision-making we compare one alternative with another. It can also be used to explain or to persuade; however, these uses are less common than its use in evaluation. A constant feature of our personal lives—we compare when we select steaks, or cars, or clothes—comparison is also used in our work lives.

The selections in this section offer several types of comparisons. Professional writer Larry McMurtry uses comparison to give the reader a fuller understanding of a particular American city; essayist E. B. White compares country schools with private city schools; Atuhiro Sibatani, a scientist, uses comparison to make a point about the way the brain processes knowledge: Joseph Wilson, a policeman, compares television cops to real ones; and scientist Lewis Thomas compares human beings to computers.

Comparison used to develop ideas in writing usually takes one of two traditional approaches: part-by-part or whole-by-whole. Let us suppose that you have reason to demonstrate the equivalence of two college courses—you want your school's permission to substitute a junior-level course in Shakespeare for a required sophomore-level course in types of drama. You have personal reasons for preferring the Shakespeare course: you love Elizabethan drama, you have played several of Shakespeare's major characters in high school and college productions, and you have heard how wonderful the professor who teaches the Shakespeare course is. None of those reasons, however, will be acceptable to those who determine the school's general graduation requirements. So you will have to show that the Shakespeare course is academically equivalent to the types-of-drama course. You can choose to construct your justification by the part-by-part method or the whole-by-whole method. If your approach is part-by-part, you might acknowledge that the types-of-drama course teaches students about comedy, tragedy, and tragicomedy, but then point out that Shakespeare wrote plays in all three subgenres. You might also suggest that, while the mixed-dramas course also teaches the classical approach to tragedy as explained by Aristotle, the Shakespeare course includes some of the very plays that the other course uses to explain such Aristotelian concepts as *hamartia, peripeteia,* and *anagnorisis.* Since so many of the concepts taught in the types-of-drama course are also taught in the Shakespeare course, you could maintain that your education would hardly be shortchanged if you took only the Shakespeare course. If you were to choose to make your plea by comparing the courses whole-by-whole, then you would simply describe the types-of-drama course completely and then describe the Shakespeare course completely, taking up comparable details for each in the same order. Your choice of the part-by-part technique will emphasize the specific points of similarity. Your choice of the whole-by-whole technique will emphasize the overall picture of the two courses.

Showing the similarity between two very different things constitutes analogy. You may want to imply that, if two things are alike in some ways, they are likely to be similar in others as well. Generally the reason for using analogy is to explain an unfamiliar idea by comparing it with a familiar one. Sometimes the purpose of an analogy is to explain a concept in a humorous way. For example, it has been said that owning and racing a sailboat is like standing fully dressed in the shower tearing up thousand dollar bills. Owning and racing a sailboat is an experience that relatively few people have had. But almost everyone has taken a shower, and almost everyone realizes the value of thousand dollar bills and the folly of destroying them. Thus the analogy emphasizes two rather negative aspects of sailing—the tendency to get wet and the expense.

We would be using difference in degree if we were to write a comparison of the compact automobile with what the industry calls the midsize automobile. We might choose as our bases of comparison price, economy of operation, comfort, and safety. Then we might show the differences in the two sizes of automobiles according to the degree of difference in price, in estimated

192   *Comparison*

fuel efficiency, in smoothness of ride and interior commodiousness, and in relative protection afforded by larger and heavier construction versus smaller and lighter.

Difference in kind, the companion to difference in degree, also requires that we define clearly the basis of comparison; but with difference in kind we are comparing the differences between common traits or aspects of a thing. For example, we might compare T-bone steaks with New York strip sirloins. T-bones have bones, New York strips do not; T-bones also have more fat on them than New York strips. Or you might compare the differences between your parents and the stereotypical mother and father. Perhaps your mother is ambitious, aggressive, a wretched housekeeper, a whiz at finance, and your father is easy-going, patient, very tidy, and hopeless with money. The two are different in kind from each other, and they are different in kind from the stereotypes.

Whenever you write a comparison, keep in mind the purpose for which you are writing. Your purpose should be closely allied with the kind of comparison you are using, and it will dictate the technique of presentation you should use. Further, be careful to avoid two mistakes that can destroy the effectiveness of a comparison. First, do not dwell upon the obvious. If the basis for comparison is something that everyone recognizes, think some more about your subject. Second, choose bases of comparison that are relevant. A comparison of athletes based upon length of hair and mode of dress serves very little purpose. The significant differences are left unexplored.

Dallas

Larry McMurtry

Larry McMurtry, who was born into a cattle ranching family in Wichita Falls, Texas, is a graduate of North Texas State and Rice universities. A writer of novels, short stories, and film scripts, he is perhaps best known as the author of The Last Picture Show, *which was made into a widely acclaimed motion picture, and of* A Horseman Passed By, *the story on which the movie* Hud *was based.*

In the following selection from In a Narrow Grave, *McMurtry compares the cities of Dallas and Houston. His contrast is organized in a loose part-by-part scheme, and Dallas does not compare favorably according to the criteria that McMurtry applies. Contending that Houston is more secure about itself than Dallas is, he supports his claim by describing the behavior of the well-to-do citizens of each city.*

Even similar features have different overtones, McMurtry asserts. Both Dallas and Houston are business towns that strive for cultural sophistication; but Houston does it crudely and honestly, in his view, whereas Dallas deludes itself into thinking that it values culture over money. McMurtry emphasizes how conformist Dallas disapproves of anything eccentric or different by telling the tale of writer Ken Kesey's visit to Dallas, and moves from that into a discussion of the sources of conservatism in the two cities. McMurtry closes by comparing the quality of violence in Dallas with that in Houston or the rest of the state. The metaphor he uses to describe the nature of Dallas' violence is both apt and unusual. He compares it to a particular kind of oil well, the gusher, which explodes with great force when the oil reservoir is tapped.

McMurtry assumes a reader who has some acquaintance with Dallas and Houston—an acquaintance made directly by having actually lived or visited there, or indirectly by exposure to films or written works about these two cities. He assumes that the reader will have sensed intangible differences between the two, and his comparison attempts to clarify the attitudes and situations that produced such differences. Maintaining a highly sophisticated antiestablishment tone, he brings to the task a great deal of his own bias regarding Dallas and Houston and clearly hopes to entertain as well as to inform.

D allas is more like Houston than either city would readily admit, but there are a few crucial differences. Houston doesn't mind being thought a boom town; it feels damn good about itself and tends to be completely convinced by its own publicity. Houstonians are secure to the point of smugness about their city: they expect people to like it (and them) and are amazed and perplexed when someone doesn't.

Not so Dallas. It is one of the uneasiest cities in the country, and was that way long before the assassination. Well-to-do Houstonians are not only convinced that they are valuable, they are convinced they are wonderful. Well-to-do Dallasans regard themselves with considerable less certainty. They are tentative, not quite sure who they are supposed to be, not really confident that who they are supposed to be is worth being. It is, consequently, the city of the instant put-down, and the higher one goes in the Dallas establishment the more true this is likely to be. Nowhere else in the state does one find so many bitter, defensive, basically insecure people in positions of power.

What well-to-do Dallasans *are* very often convinced of is that they are right. The Kennedy assassination and the Johnson presidency made self-questioners of many Texans; but the citizens of Dallas, now that the city's economy has survived the assassination, seem almost as self-righteous as ever. Indeed, part of the civic unease may be a result of the city's own very effective publicity. Dallas was the first Texas city to publicize itself heavily as a center of culture and sophistication, a campaign which seems to have contributed to the confusion of the populace. Such sophistication and culture as Dallas has is mostly hybrid, not indigenous. Like Houston, it is a business town, and always has been. For a generation or so its more affluent children have been provided with Eastern educations, and those of them who return to Dallas have to work at culture like mad to keep from feeling they are wasting themselves. The citizens of Dallas have the strain of maintaining the delusion that in their city culture, not money, counts most. As in Houston, wealth and ostentation are respected, even adored, while art is dutifully (and on the whole, crudely) patronized. Art is not really as important as money, but it is nonetheless something to be taken Very Seriously. The eccentric is not welcomed; the patrons are not confident enough to be comfortable in the presence of someone radically unlike themselves.

A year or so ago, for example, the energetic young novelist and psyche-delist Ken Kesey flew into Dallas for a Book-and-Author affair. Mr. Kesey responds very acutely to his surroundings, and after a day or two of Dallas parties, where tensions and hostilities flicker like prairie lightning, he decided that the way to survive Dallas would be to get above it. Accordingly, he got high and stayed high, and, just before his speech, took the further precaution of supplying himself with a bag full of red rubber balls. His speeches tend to be loosely extemporized, and this one, I judge, was no exception. He was only getting plane fare for his trouble, and had felt under no obligation to write anything. Now and then, as he spoke, he threw the red rubber balls at what he judged to be hostile faces in the crowd, a tactic which disconcerted his audience and left his sponsors highly dismayed. It was clearly no way to approach High Culture. Upon consultation, the sponsors decided that such irregularity ought to be punished, so they withheld the plane fare and told Mr. Kesey he could get back to California as best he could. He responded by threatening to invade a Murchison party, where he proposed to scrounge ticket-money from the guests. The thought of such indecorous proceedings had the desired effect, and the sponsors grudgingly forked over.

Otherwise, most of what I have said about Houston and Houston's pretensions could simply be repeated for Dallas. Houston is open, an opportunist's delight. Dallas is cleaner than Houston; cleaner because more tightly controlled. In Dallas the ruling oligarchy is old, cagey, and so well entrenched as to be practically invulnerable to rude invasion. The newspapers in both cities are languid and establishmentarian, but politically Dallas is the more extreme. The savagery of its perfervid conservatives is so well known that most politicians now give the town a wide berth.

This conservatism is compounded of fear and boredom and in tone closely resembles religious hysteria. In Dallas a flavorless Protestantism seems to have yielded super-patriotism as by-product. The Dallas true-believers have made conservatism a religion-surrogate: they hate liberals the way passionate religious dogmatists once hated heretics. Orthodoxy is the American way of life as lived in Highland Park, and Earl Warren, among others, should be sent to the stake. Indeed, J. Evetts Haley drew wild applause in Dallas for suggesting that Warren should be hanged.

The city contains one of the more picturesque skid rows in the state, a section known as Deep Ellum. There is a glossy picture of Jack Ruby in the window of a pawnshop there—a picture taken in his glossy days, such as they were. His head is enfolded between the breasts of one of his strippers. Nearby, apropos of nothing, is a yellowing newspaper picture of the Kennedy brothers, and nearby that a photograph of the bullet-riddled body of some gangster, Dillinger or Pretty Boy Floyd or perhaps Clyde Barrow, whose grave is across the Trinity in Oak Cliff. A few windows away there is, or used to be, a shiny, nickel-plated submachine gun, of the type Bonnie and Clyde were said to use. And if one walks west along Pawn Shop Row, past windows full of pistols and ankle-knives with twelve-inch blades, one comes in a few blocks to the junction of Elm and Ervay and can turn north and see the famous gold-bannistered staircase in the lobby of the Republic National Bank.

Wealth, violence, and poverty are common throughout Texas, and why the combination should be scarier in Dallas than elsewhere I don't know. But it is: no place in Texas is quite so tense and so tight. Violence in Houston is extremely common, but there it lies close to the surface and is easily predicted and fairly easily avoided. Dallas is a city of underground men: the violence there lies deeper, and is under greater pressure. It may not surface for a long time, but when it does, as we all know, it surfaces like Spindletop.

languid lacking energy or vitality
perfervid impassioned, zealous
surrogate substitute

Questions

1 Does McMurtry provide comparable information on Houston with every point he makes about Dallas? Why, or why not?

2 What bases of comparison does McMurtry use in contrasting Dallas and Houston?

3 Is the prominence given to the Ken Kesey incident rhetorically effective? Why, or why not?

4 What methods of development does the essay use in addition to comparison? Cite three.

Computers

Lewis Thomas

Lewis Thomas, a distinguished physician and successful author, has been president of the Sloan Kettering Cancer Center in New York and dean of the Yale Medical School. His collections of essays include The Lives of a Cell, *which received the National Book Award in 1975, and* The Medusa and the Snail *(1979).*

In the following adroit and humane comparison of human beings with computers, Thomas does not expose his rhetorical technique to open view. He begins with an understated comparison of humans and computers; he lists a variety of tasks a computer can perform even better than humans can, but then sets out to remind us of all the things we can do better than computers. We need not fear that computers will replace us, he maintains: there are more of us than there are of them, and we humans are wired together in a way that computers are not. Thomas also points out that humans can deal with much greater levels of probability than computers can. He lists the disadvantages of long-range planning that humans cannot at present manage and, by implication, praises human unpredictability and improbability partly because they lead to creativity.

After listing several tasks it would be pleasant to have computers around to help with, Thomas notes that, while humans can take in a great deal of information, they have trouble getting it out. We rarely know what other people are thinking. Thomas suggests that communication is the area in which to begin improving human beings.

In this essay the comparison technique operates by indirection. When Thomas discusses the advantages of the human, he implies the disadvantages of the computer, and vice versa. He does not often state his comparison openly.

Thomas counts on an audience familiar with the growth of computers but not intimately acquainted with them. Such people are likely to be nervous about the possibility of computers making humans obsolete—and they constitute a large segment of the general population. While entertaining his readers, Thomas hopes to allay their fears by helping them recognize how truly complex and powerful a thinking "machine" the human is.

You can make computers that are almost human. In some respects they are superhuman; they can beat most of us at chess, memorize whole telephone books at a glance, compose music of a certain kind and write obscure poetry, diagnose heart ailments, send personal invitations to vast parties, even go transiently crazy. No one has yet programmed a computer to be of two minds about a hard problem, or to burst out laughing, but that may come. Sooner or later, there will be real human hardware, great whirring, clicking cabinets intelligent enough to read magazines and vote, able to think rings around the rest of us.

Well, maybe, but not for a while anyway. Before we begin organizing sanctuaries and reservations for our software selves, lest we vanish like the whales, here is a thought to relax with.

Even when technology succeeds in manufacturing a machine as big as Texas to do everything we recognize as human, it will still be, at best, a single individual. This amounts to nothing, practically speaking. To match what we can do, there would have to be 3 billion of them with more coming down the assembly line, and I doubt that anyone will put up the money, much less make room. And even so, they would all have to be wired together, intricately and delicately, as we are, communicating with each other, talking incessantly, listening. If they weren't *at* each other this way, all their waking hours, they wouldn't be anything like human, after all. I think we're safe, for a long time ahead.

It is in our collective behavior that we are most mysterious. We won't be able to construct machines like ourselves until we've understood this, and we're not even close. All we know is the phenomenon: we spend our time sending messages to each other, talking and trying to listen at the same time, exchanging information. This seems to be our most urgent biological function; it is what we do with our lives. By the time we reach the end, each of us has taken in a staggering store, enough to exhaust any computer, much of it incomprehensible, and we generally manage to put out even more than we take in. Information is our source of energy; we are driven by it. It has become a tremendous enterprise, a kind of energy system on its own. All 3 billion of us are being connected by telephones, radios, television sets, airplanes, satellites, harangues on public-address systems, newspapers, magazines, leaflets dropped from great heights, words got in edgewise. We are becoming a grid, a circuitry around the earth. If we keep at it, we will become a computer to end all computers, capable of fusing all the thoughts of the world into a syncytium.

Already, there are no closed, two-way conversations. Any word you speak this afternoon will radiate out in all directions, around town before tomorrow, out and around the world before Tuesday, accelerating to the speed of light, modulating as it goes, shaping new and unexpected messages, emerging at the end as an enormously funny Hungarian joke, a fluctuation in the money market, a poem, or simply a long pause in someone's conversation in Brazil.

syncytium a protoplasmic mass having many nuclei but no cell boundaries

Comparison

We do a lot of collective thinking, probably more than any other social species, although it goes on in something like secrecy. We don't acknowledge the gift publicly, and we are not as celebrated as the insects, but we do it. Effortlessly, without giving it a moment's thought, we are capable of changing our language, music, manners, morals, entertainment, even the way we dress, all around the earth in a year's turning. We seem to do this by general agreement, without voting or even polling. We simply think our way along, pass information around, exchange codes disguised as art, change our minds, transform ourselves.

Computers cannot deal with such levels of improbability, and it is just as well. Otherwise, we might be tempted to take over the control of ourselves in order to make long-range plans, and that would surely be the end of us. It would mean that some group or other, marvelously intelligent and superbly informed, undoubtedly guided by a computer, would begin deciding what human society ought to be like, say, over the next five hundred years or so, and the rest of us would be persuaded, one way or another, to go along. The process of social evolution would then grind to a standstill, and we'd be stuck in today's rut for a millennium.

Much better we work our way out of it on our own, without governance. The future is too interesting and dangerous to be entrusted to any predictable, reliable agency. We need all the fallibility we can get. Most of all, we need to preserve the absolute unpredictability and total improbability of our connected minds. That way we can keep open all the options, as we have in the past.

It would be nice to have better ways of monitoring what we're up to so that we could recognize change while it is occuring, instead of waking up as we do now to the astonished realization that the whole century just past wasn't what we thought it was, at all. Maybe computers can be used to help in this, although I rather doubt it. You can make simulation models of cities, but what you learn is that they seem to be beyond the reach of intelligent analysis; if you try to use common sense to make predictions, things get more botched up than ever. This is interesting, since a city is the most concentrated aggregation of humans, all exerting whatever influence they can bring to bear. The city seems to have a life of its own. If we cannot understand how this works, we are not likely to get very far with human society at large.

Still, you'd think there would be some way in. Joined together, the great mass of human minds around the earth seems to behave like a coherent, living system. The trouble is that the flow of information is mostly one-way. We are all obsessed by the need to feed information in, as fast as we can, but we lack sensing mechanisms for getting anything much back. I will confess that I have no more sense of what goes on in the mind of mankind than I have for the mind of an ant. Come to think of it, this might be a good place to start.

Questions

1 Does Thomas' avoidance of the usual structure of comparison make the essay difficult to follow? Why, or why not?

2 What makes the essay interesting? Is it Thomas' use of detail? Is it his main idea? Explain.

3 Does Thomas tell us directly what his purpose is in this essay? If not, how do we know? If so, where?

4 What is the main basis of comparison applied to humans and computers?

Education—March 1939

E. B. White

E. B. White, an essayist, short-story writer, and novelist, has been for over fifty years a contributor to the New Yorker *and other prestigious magazines; his works include* One Man's Meat, Charlotte's Web, *and* Here is New York.

The following comparison by White of two schools his son attended—a country school and a private school in New York City—follows a careful and well-structured pattern. The qualities of the country school are discussed in the first, fourth, and fifth paragraphs; the qualities of the city school in the second and third paragraphs. Essentially, White presents the two schools in a whole-by-whole structure, except that he divides the description of the country school into two parts.

In the second paragraph, before the description of the private school begins, White discusses his own reaction to public schools and his wife's to private schools. A number of aspects of the private school are then explored: the modern plumbing, the decor, the extracurricular activities, the clothing, transportation, nutrition, academics, and its way of coping with childhood diseases. All these points are taken up in the description of the country school, but not necessarily in the same order.

What White manages to convey in this comparison is that the boy likes the country school better, and so do the parents once they are assured that the child is being taught all a third-grader ought to know. The lack of facilities and specialized activities is more than compensated for by the human caring and love the children receive in the country school.

White is writing for an audience that may, perhaps, be aware of the advantages of a private school, or at least of a suburban public school, but will probably know little, if anything, about a country school. His purpose is to make clear an important fact about education: the kind of facilities a school has is not nearly as important as the kind of teachers it hires and their attitude toward their students.

have an increasing admiration for the teacher in the country school where we have a third-grade scholar in attendance. She not only undertakes to instruct her charges in all the subjects of the first three grades, but she manages to function quietly and effectively as a guardian of their health, their clothes, their habits, their mothers, and their snowball engagements. She has been doing this sort of Augean task for twenty years, and is both kind and wise. She cooks for the children on the stove that heats the room, and she can cool their passions or warm their soup with equal competence. She conceives their costumes, cleans up their messes, and shares their confidences. My boy already regards his teacher as his great friend, and I think tells her a great deal more than he tells us.

The shift from city school to country school was something we worried about quietly all last summer. I have always rather favored public school over private school, if only because in public school you meet a greater variety of children. This bias of mine, I suspect, is partly an attempt to justify my own past (I never knew anything but public schools) and partly an involuntary defense against getting kicked in the shins by a young ceramist on his way to the kiln. My wife was unacquainted with public schools, never having been exposed (in her early life) to anything more public than the washroom of Miss Winsor's. Regardless of our backgrounds, we both knew that the change in schools was something that concerned not us but the scholar himself. We hoped it would work out all right. In New York our son went to a medium-priced private institution with semi-progressive ideas of education, and modern plumbing. He learned fast, kept well, and we were satisfied. It was an electric, colorful, regimented existence with moments of pleasurable pause and giddy incident. The day the Christmas angel fainted and had to be carried out by one of the Wise Men was educational in the highest sense of the term. Our scholar gave imitations of it around the house for weeks afterward, and I doubt if it ever goes completely out of his mind.

His days were rich in formal experience. Wearing overalls and an old sweater (the accepted uniform of the private seminary), he sallied forth at morn accompanied by a nurse or a parent and walked (or was pulled), two blocks to a corner where the school bus made a flag stop. This flashy vehicle was as punctual as death: seeing us waiting at the cold curb, it would sweep to a halt, open its mouth, suck the boy in, and spring away with an angry growl. It was a good deal like a train picking up a bag of mail. At school the scholar was worked on for six or seven hours by a half a dozen teachers and a nurse, and was revived on orange juice in midmorning. In a cinder court he played games supervised by an athletic instructor, and in a cafeteria he ate lunch worked out by a dietitian. He soon learned to read with gratifying facility and discernment and to make Indian weapons of a semi-deadly nature. Whenever one of his classmates fell low of a fever the news was put on

Augean filthy (from the legend in which the stables of Augeas, neglected for thirty years, were laboriously cleaned by Hercules)
sallied went out on a trip or excursion

Comparison

the wires and there were breathless phone calls to physicians, discussing periods of incubation and allied magic.

In the country all one can is that the situation is different, and somehow more casual. Dressed in corduroys, sweatshirt, and short rubber boots, and carrying a tin dinner-pail, our scholar departs at crack of dawn for the village school, two and a half miles down the road, next to the cemetery. When the road is open and the car will start, he makes the journey by motor, courtesy of his old man. When the snow is deep or the motor is dead or both, he makes it on the hoof. In the afternoons he walks or hitches all or part of the way home in fair weather, gets transported in foul. The schoolhouse is a two-room frame building, bungalow type, shingles stained a burnt brown with weather-resistant stain. It has a chemical toilet in the basement and two teachers above stairs. One takes the first three grades, the other the fourth, fifth, and sixth. They have little or no time for individual instruction, and no time at all for the esoteric. They teach what they know themselves, just as fast and as hard as they can manage. The pupils sit still at their desks in class, and do their milling around outdoors during recess.

There is no supervised play. They play cops and robbers (only they call it "Jail") and throw things at one another—snowballs in winter, rose hips in fall. It seems to satisfy them. They also construct darts, pinwheels, and "pick-up sticks" (jackstraws), and the school itself does a brisk trade in penny candy, which is for sale right in the classroom and which contains "surprises." The most highly prized surprise is a fake cigarette, made of cardboard, fiendishly lifelike.

The memory of how apprehensive we were at the beginning is still strong. The boy was nervous about the change too. The tension, on that first fair morning in September when we drove him to school, almost blew the windows out of the sedan. And when later we picked him up on the road, wandering along with his little blue lunch-pail, and got his laconic report "All right" in answer to our inquiry about how the day had gone, our relief was vast. Now, after almost a year of it, the only difference we can discover in the two school experiences is that in the country he sleeps better at night— and *that* probably is more the air than the education. When grilled on the subject of school-in-country *vs.* school-in-city, he replied that the chief difference is that the day seemed to go so much quicker in the country. "Just like lightning," he reported.

Questions

1 What purpose is served by breaking the description of the country school and inserting the information about the city school? Does it impair the rhetorical technique?

esoteric meant to be understood only by a select few; mysterious

2 Find an example of each of the following in the essay: narration, description, cause and effect, process, example.

3 Why do you think White chose to use comparison instead of argument or cause and effect to make his point?

4 What is the purpose of the information in the concluding paragraph about how the boy felt going to school and returning?

The Japanese Brain

Atuhiro Sibatani

Atuhiro Sibatani is a developmental biologist in the Molecular and Cellular Biology Unit of the Commonwealth Scientific and Industrial Research Organization in Sydney, Australia. Sibantani's discussion here of the differences in the way the Japanese process sensory information in the brain and the way Westerners process such information is essentially a part-by-part comparison. The article begins with the revolutionary theory suggested by a Japanese hearing specialist, Tadanobu Tsunoda; Tsunoda proposed that the language one learns in childhood determines to a large extent the way the brain stores and uses information. Applying this theory, Sibatani compares the way Westerners, Koreans, Chinese, and Bengalis process vowels with the way Japanese and Polynesians process them. Next, he examines their handling of mechanical sounds and music and then contrasts the way in which speakers of European languages process nonverbal human sounds with the way Japanese-speaking people process them. Sibatani further compares Americans brought up in Japan and Japanese brought up in America to determine if the processing pattern is hereditary or acquired. The final part of the essay continues the examination of how well Tsunoda's theory accounts for many cultural differences, including how different language groups handle the relationship between logic and emotion.

Along with its fascinating subject matter, the essay offers a remarkable display of rhetorical technique. Sibatani carefully limits himself as much as is practical to the comparative technique, an unusual restriction in an essay of this length. Although some elements are presented narratively and descriptively, and while process and cause and effect are implicit in the essay, the primary rhetorical device remains comparison.

Sibatani expects an audience at least slightly familiar with the idea that different hemispheres of the brain control different actions. The idea, as he points out, is not a new one. He also expects his audience to be aware that the hemispheric activity of the brain controls language functioning. The purpose of his article is to explain a new theory about the interaction between language and brain function. The implications of Tsunoda's findings, Sibantani suggests, may have great significance in the debate over genetic determinism.

The idea that the Japanese live in harmony with their surroundings, turning everyday rituals into art forms, has been ascribed sometimes to genetic inheritance, sometimes to cultural conditioning. But in recent years a clever new technique designed to study speech and hearing defects has yielded one of the most tantalizing—and controversial—theories to date: that Japanese brains function differently from other people's not because of inheritance or conditioning but because of the peculiarities of the Japanese language. If this provocative hypothesis proves to be correct, we may have to revise some of our venerable convictions, for it may turn out that the language we learn alters the physical operation of our brains.

The startling assertion that language shapes the neurophysiological pathways of the brain is the thesis of a dry academic tome that, amazingly, became a best seller in Japan when it appeared in 1978. Written by Tadanobu Tsunoda, *The Japanese Brain: Brain Function and East-West Culture* has yet to be translated into English, but information about its contents has crossed the oceans and is provoking a good deal of discussion in Western circles. What Tsunoda has found, he claims, is that the language one learns as a child influences the way in which the brain's right and left hemispheres develop their special talents.

That the brain's hemispheres specialize in different tasks has been recognized since the 19th century. Neurologists studying men injured by strokes or battle wounds found that damage to the brain's left side often interfered with speech. Since then, scientists have demonstrated hemispheric specialization with techniques such as dichotic listening tests, which present different words simultaneously to both right and left ears to determine which ear "excels" at which tasks.

For most right-handed people, the left hemisphere appears to be the main seat of language, as well as of precise manual manipulations, mathematics, and other analytic functions. The right hemisphere is superior in dealing with spatial concepts, recognition of faces, musical patterns, environmental sounds, and perhaps intuitive and artistic processes. For left-handed people, it is harder to generalize about the brain's organization. . . .

These are observations made by Western scientists working with Caucasian subjects. Tsunoda's research with Japanese patients, on the other hand, seems to have revealed fundamental differences in the way that Caucasian and Japanese brains divide up the labor of processing sensory data.

One of Tsunoda's findings is that in the brains of right-handed Westerners, Koreans, Chinese, and Bengalis, vowel sounds usually get processed in one side of the brain if they occur in isolation, but in the other half if the vowels occur in a spoken context, that is, if they are surrounded by consonants. But right-handed Japanese and Polynesians, Tsunoda discovered, usually process all vowels in the left or dominant half, whether they occur in a spoken context or not.

Mechanical sounds—bells, whistles, and helicopter noises—are among the

dichotic divided into two parts

Comparison

few sounds that Japanese and Polynesians handle in the right hemisphere, as do other ethnic groups. Western instrumental music is also processed in the right hemisphere. By contrast, Japanese subjects handle Japanese music in the left hemisphere, possibly because Japanese music attempts to mimic the human voice.

The Japanese and Polynesians also tend to depend on their left brains for processing nonverbal human utterances that express emotions—sounds such as laughter, crying, or sighing—along with natural sounds such as cricket chirps, cow calls, bird songs, and ocean waves. By contrast, those who speak European languages handle all these sounds in their right hemispheres.

Tsunoda suggests that the Japanese may utilize the left hemisphere more heavily because the Japanese and Polynesian languages are particularly rich in vowels. One can make up complex sentences in Japanese using vowels only: *"Ue o ui, oi o ooi, ai o ou, aiueo"* means "A love-hungry man who worries about hunger hides his old age and chases love." Polynesians also use lots of vowels, as in the cry of distress, *"Oiaue!"* leading some experts to suggest that the Japanese race has Polynesian roots.

A fundamental discovery of Tsunoda is that the Japanese, in contrast to Westerners, process far more sounds in only one hemisphere. Furthermore, if a sound normally processed in the left hemisphere, whether voices or insect chirps, is buried amidst other background noises, the entire load of processing all the sounds is switched to the left. This switching process, characteristic of all human brains, is not surprising, since a first priority of the brain is language.

Curiously enough, certain odors, including perfumes, alcohol, and tobacco smoke, also seem to trigger this switching ability. Because Tsunoda associates the effects of these chemicals with emotional reactions, he infers that the Japanese process emotion in the dominant hemisphere, apparently opposite to Westerners.

A specialist in hearing difficulties at Tokyo Medical and Dental University, Tsunoda was studying patients whose speech was damaged, testing the possibility that he might somehow transfer language processing to the undamaged part of the brain. In the course of his research, Tsunoda devised a unique dichotic listening test designed to be independent of the subject's conscious awareness. The test required subjects to tap simple, regular patterns on a Morse code key. Tones keyed by the tapping process were then fed back to each ear through earphones. One ear received the sound directly; the other ear received the signal delayed by two-tenths of a second. Tsunoda gradually increased the loudness of the delayed signal until it interfered with the subject's key-tapping performance. The purpose was to ascertain whether one ear—and its associated brain hemisphere—predominated in registering this interference.

In addition to the time delay, Tsunoda also supplied each ear with different kinds of sounds—not only pure tones but also such sounds as spoken words, animal noises, Japanese and Western musical instruments, and ocean waves.

Tsunoda is convinced that the switching stimulus is not inherited, but is acquired by every child through the use of the language that he or she speaks. Japanese people brought up in the United States, for example, have the characteristic Caucasian brain lateralization. That is, they process consonants on the left and vowels on the right. Conversely, Americans brought up in Japan and fluent in the language acquire typically Japanese brains. Tsunoda shows that the response of the natively blind, and hence illiterate, Japanese is exactly the same as that of the literate members of the population. From this he concludes that the emergence of the Japanese brain is not triggered simply by learning to read and write Japanese but rather by listening to the language and speaking it.

Tsunoda's results have been heralded by some as beautiful and clear-cut; others have adopted a wait-and-see attitude, since his results have so far not been replicated. Still, brain researchers are intrigued with Tsunoda's hypothesis that language affects the way the brain's two halves process language.

However, Western scientists are frankly skeptical about some of Tsunoda's sweeping speculations. He conjectures, for example, that in the Japanese brain, logical thinking and emotional responses are not partitioned into separate hemispheres as they seem to be in the West, but are tucked into one and the same verbal hemisphere. This may cause the Japanese to depend more on inutitive and emotional reactions than on logical trains of thought.

Nor do the Japanese distinguish analytic problems and natural sensations in the clear-cut way that Westerners do, according to Tsunoda. The Japanese seem to have a psychological need to live immersed in natural sounds such as bird and insect songs, animal cries, snow thudding off tree branches, ocean waves beating against the shore, and winds whistling through forest pines. That harmony of nature and environment is evident in all aspects of Japanese life, from their calligraphy to the tea ceremony to Noh drama and Ikebana flower arranging. In Japanese landscape and architecture, physical objects melt into the character of space rather than oppose it. For example, the Japanese use few partitions, rooms combine into sweeping space, and the garden may recess into the house so that dwellers can be outdoors while sitting indoors. Tsunoda believes that this blurring of physical barriers and natural elements may help explain the deep sense of harmony within the group that results in the social cohesion of the Japanese nation.

The negative aspect, however, is that the Japanese may be overtaxing the left hemisphere, particularly when forced to learn a variety of foreign languages. After speaking other languages for a few days or months at a time, the Japanese brain seems to switch sounds normally processed on the right to the opposite hemisphere. This undoubtedly places a tremendous burden on the over-utilized verbal hemisphere.

One of the most intriguing spin-offs of Tsunoda's work may be its impli-

lateralization division into two parts, one on each side of a midline
replicated duplicated, repeated
calligraphy decorative handwriting

cations for sociobiology, the science that studies the genetic predisposition of social behavior. Tsunoda argues that some differences in brain function are conditioned by the mother tongue, rather than by genetic factors of ethnic origin. If Tsunoda is right, the patterns of each individual's perceptions, cognitions, mental acts, and social behavior can be dramatically affected during early childhood by one of the most human of activities—language. The debate over strict genetic determinism, so heated on this side of the ocean, has not thus far troubled the Japanese. Whether or not this indifference results from the "inscrutable" nature of the Japanese brain may constitute another absorbing chapter for those interested in Japan's role in modern society.

Questions

1 What rhetorical consideration might have caused Sibatani to rely as fully as he does upon comparison?

2 How are you led to understand that the article is intended for people who have at least a minimal understanding of the concepts of language acquisition and hemispheric functioning of the brain?

3 Can you find a reason for writing this article other than the one suggested on page 207?

4 Evaluate Sibatani's two introductory paragraphs and concluding paragraph according to the rules for writing good beginnings and endings. Are Sibatani's well done? Why, or why not?

Real Cops, Not "Reel" Cops

Joseph Wilson

Joseph Wilson is a sergeant in the New York City Police Department's Office of Public Information. The main rhetorical technique used by Wilson in the following brief tribute is comparison, although the article also relies heavily on narration and definition. To establish the context, he presents three incidents in which police officers behaved with courage and propriety; then he compares these officers, described as real *cops, with their television counterparts, the* reel *cops. Wilson assumes a knowledge among his readers of the way police officers are portrayed by the media. Relying on such knowledge, he can establish his comparison with a brief reference to the television cops and devote most of his article to a detailed account of* real *cops.*

The purpose of the article is primarily to inform. Wilson has two messages to convey: first, most real police officers behave responsibly and with restraint in critical situations; second, the officers of the New York City Police Department appreciate realistic portrayals of police by the media. The essay was written to appear in a police department newsletter, but it could just as well have been addressed to the general public. The information is interesting enough and the rhetorical focus and the language are clear enough to appeal to any reader.

August 28, 1973—0045 hours—46 Pct.   P.O. Frank Buono, off duty and in civilian clothes, observed a dispute between two men. He overheard one of them, hurrying away, say that he was "going to get a gun too." P.O. Buono, identifying himself, approached the other man, who turned and fired one shot from a 9 mm automatic hitting P.O. Buono in the left forearm. As P.O. Buono attempted to take shelter behind a parked car, he was shot again, in the left thigh. P.O. Buono did not return fire because of the risk of hitting innocent bystanders. Officer Buono, who was removed to Jacobi Hospital, is recovering, His assailant is being sought.

September 1, 1973—1830 hours—48 Pct.   Police officers responded to the scene of a shooting. The victim had been shot in the leg by a bullet that came through an apartment window. While a search was being conducted for the perpetrator, P.O. Walter O'Reilly was fired upon four times from a nearby building. The perpetrator was apprehended and a 25 cal. automatic was recovered. The arrest was made without any shots being fired by police officers.

September 2, 1973—2000 hours—25 Pct.   A woman was chasing another woman down the street and firing a revolver at her. P.O.'s Rudolph Scalla and Lawrence Wagers, responding to the scene, ordered her to drop the gun. She turned and fired two shots at them. They succeeded in arresting her without firing their guns.

These are REAL cops. In each case they could have been killed. In each case they could have justifiably returned fire, but they didn't. They put the life and safety of innocent bystanders ahead of their own. They used admirable restraint and excellent judgement. This is a far cry from the latest fashion in REEL cops, the ones the entertainment media portray as incompetent, violent, sadistic, and corrupt. These portrayals do the thousands of everyday hardworking officers of our department a great injustice. Any resemblance between REAL cops and REEL cops is purely imaginary. As with all fads, this one too will pass. But the REAL cops will go on forever.

I don't want to leave the impression that the media *always* distort our image. A recent example of a realistic presentation of police officers in action was the NBC production "Go With the 20," a 30-minute program about the 20 Pct., shown at 1230 hours on Saturday, September 8, 1973. This portrayal, which was viewed by 12–15 million people throughout the nation, captured the NYC police department as it really is. For those of you who didn't see it, I'm arranging to get a release so that the program can be shown on our own closed circuit TV.

I want to extend my warm thanks to NBC on behalf of all police officers in our department for a program that presents us so accurately. We appreciate the restoration of some balance to an otherwise steady diet of disparaging portrayals.

Pct. precinct
P.O. Police Officer
mm. millimeter
cal. caliber

Comparison

Questions

1 Would Wilson have had a stronger essay if he had given some actual examples of *reel* cops? Why, or why not?

2 Does the use of narration enhance or detract from the main rhetorical technique of the essay? Explain.

3 Would you change anything in this essay if you were writing for a different audience? If so, what and why? If not, why not?

4 Why is Wilson justified or unjustified in categorizing *reel* cops as "incompetent, violent, sadistic, and corrupt"?

ARGUMENT

A written *argument* attempts to convince the reader that some assertion or set of assertions is true. Usually it includes either or both of the two major processes of logical thought, *induction* and *deduction*. Induction is the process by which we gather evidence upon a specific subject and from that accumulated evidence arrive at a generalization. For example, your brother comes home one day and shouts at you to leave him alone—you have noticed that on his way into the house he kicked the cat. Before you can answer, you hear him slam the door to his room. On the basis of that evidence, you conclude that your brother is not in a good mood. In coming to this thought, you have moved from particular events to a generalization suggested by all those events—that is, you have arrived at an inductive conclusion. The formal use of induction requires the most indisputable evidence possible. In this regard, facts are always preferable to opinions or analogies, which are considered weak evidence. Also to be avoided is the hasty generalization—that is, the generalization arrived at on the basis of too few facts or unrepresentative ones.

Deduction is the process by which we move from generalizations to specific fact. If we generalize that all citrus fruit contains acid, and then we note that lemons are citrus fruit, we can deduce that lemons contain acid. This is a special kind of deductive reasoning called a *syllogism*. It is traditionally composed of a major premise that makes a general statement, a minor premise that mentions the specific case being related to the general statement, and a conclusion that follows logically from the combining of the major and minor premises. One problem with deductive reasoning, and with the syllogism in particular, is that it may yield valid but false conclusions if the premises involved are not true. Ideally, the premises should be true and the conclusion both true and valid. When that is the case, we can arrive at logically sound conclusions which are themselves true.

To reiterate, there are several major differences between induction and deduction. First, induction begins with specifics and moves to generalizations, whereas deduction begins with generalizations and develops specifics. Second, in an inductive argument the facts do not necessarily imply the conclusion, but in a deductive argument the premises provide conclusive evidence. Third, it is possible for the conditions of a properly developed inductive argument to be true and the conclusion false. In deduction, if the premises are true, it is impossible for the conclusion to be false.

People are often called upon to use argument. Lawyers and politicians use an informal kind of argument known as persuasion, and business executives and advertisers also need to persuade. Scientists often must construct formal arguments to get other scientists to seriously consider their theories. Argument is used to influence people in several ways. Sometimes it is used to change the denotative meaning of a word by introducing a set of connotations not previously attached to it: What is *moral?* What is *discrimination?* Argument can also be used to assess values; here it often treats fundamental oppositions: good and evil, right and wrong, practical and impractical. A third way to use argument is to examine consequences. This use of argument often assumes the form "If X, then Y." Finally argument can be used to influence policy. What should be done about inflation? How ought the government to control pollution? Occasionally, these uses of argument are intermingled.

As with most writing techniques, the purpose of argument depends largely upon audience. Is your argument directed at a friendly audience, one that is sympathetic to your views? If so, you may rely more upon emotional appeal and take a more informal approach. As the attitude of the audience shades off toward hostility to your views, you must become more and more precise and objective in your presentation of evidence.

The basic form of a formal argument has remained the same for centuries. This does not mean that you cannot deviate from it; however, you do so at some risk. It is probably best to follow the traditional form. First, you state your proposition. That is, you present a clear and concise introduction to a problem. This, of course, is analogous to the thesis statement that so often appears in introductory paragraphs. Second, you may elect to provide a clear and concisely phrased solution to the problem. Since this part is sometimes most effective in the conclusion, you must decide where it will best serve your purpose. Third, you should refute as nearly as possible all arguments against your position. If there are arguments against it that you cannot refute,

Argument

it is a good idea to grant them early in this part and then get on to other points. Fourth, you need to present evidence to support your position. Usually you will want to begin with your strongest evidence and work toward the weakest. However, if the points you are making are interdependent, one premise generated by the conclusion of another, you may effectively present them as a chain. Your final step is to sum up your points and offer a solution or restate the solution you proposed in the second step.

Capital Punishment

William F. Buckley

William F. Buckley, editor of the National Review *and host of the television program* Firing Line, *has long been identified with conservative issues. He is the author of books on politics, novels, and collections of essays, and he contributes articles to such magazines as* The Atlantic, Esquire, Harper's, *and* Yachting.

Buckley argues here against the abolition of capital punishment. His argument is formal in structure and makes great use of deductive logic. A clear and concise introduction to and analysis of the issue is presented in the first paragraph. The essay moves on to a step-by-step refutation of the arguments of those who would abolish capital punishment: it is not discriminatory, it is not unusual, it is not cruel, and we must choose the lesser of two evils in the absence of proof regarding the efficacy of capital punishment as a deterrent.

The summation presents Buckley's solution to the dilemma. Indeed, the deductive nature of the argument is clearest in the syllogistic reasoning Buckley offers in the last three paragraphs: since the deterrent capability of the death penalty is unknown, lives are at risk—those of convicted murderers, and/or those of potential victims—and thus it is reasonable to choose to protect the lives of the innocent until such time as proof can be found to support a change.

Buckley usually finds his audience among the well-educated. His essays are often witty and cleverly organized, but his language is just as often complex and convoluted. In this particular essay, his language is relatively clear; however, there are still sentences that can be unraveled only with great pain.

There is national suspense over whether capital punishment is about to be abolished, and the assumption is that when it comes it will come from the Supreme Court. Meanwhile, (a) the prestigious State Supreme Court of California has interrupted executions, giving constitutional reasons for doing so; (b) the death wings are overflowing with convicted prisoners; (c) executions are a remote memory; and—for the first time in years—(d) the opinion polls show that there is sentiment for what amounts to the restoration of capital punishment.

The case for abolition is popularly known. The other case less so, and (without wholeheartedly endorsing it) I give it as it was given recently to the Committee of the Judiciary of the House of Representatives by Professor Ernest van den Haag, under whose thinking cap groweth no moss. Mr. van den Haag, a professor of social philosophy at New York University, ambushed the most popular arguments of the abolitionists, taking no prisoners.

(1) The business about the poor and the black suffering excessively from capital punishment is no argument against capital punishment. It is an argument against the *administration* of justice, not against the penalty. Any punishment can be unfairly or unjustly applied. Go ahead and reform the processes by which capital punishment is inflicted, if you wish; but don't confuse maladministration with the merits of capital punishment.

(2) The argument that the death penalty is "unusual" is circular. Capital punishment continues on the books of a majority of states, the people continue to sanction the concept of capital punishment, and indeed capital sentences are routinely handed down. What has made capital punishment "unusual" is that the courts and, primarily, governors have intervened in the process so as to collaborate in the frustration of the execution of the law. To argue that capital punishment is unusual, when in fact it has been made unusual by extra-legislative authority, is an argument to expedite, not eliminate, executions.

(3) Capital punishment is cruel. That is a historical judgment. But the Constitution suggests that what must be proscribed as cruel is (a) a particularly painful way of inflicting death, or (b) a particularly undeserved death; and the death penalty, as such, offends neither of these criteria and cannot therefore be regarded as objectively "cruel."

Viewed the other way, the question is whether capital punishment can be regarded as useful, and the question of deterence arises.

(4) Those who believe that the death penalty does not intensify the disinclination to commit certain crimes need to wrestle with statistics that disclose that, in fact, it can't be proved that *any* punishment does that to any particular crime. One would rationally suppose that two years in jail would cut the commission of a crime if not exactly by 100 percent more than a penalty of one year in jail, at least that it would further discourage crime to a certain extent. The proof is unavailing. On the other hand, the statistics,

expedite perform quickly and efficiently
proscribed condemned, denounced
unavailing of no use

although ambiguous, do not show either (a) that capital punishment net discourages; or (b) that capital punishment fails net to discourage. "The absence of proof for the additional deterrent effect of the death penalty must not be confused with the presence of proof for the absence of this effect."

The argument that most capital crimes are crimes of passion committed by irrational persons is no argument against the death penalty, because it does not reveal how many crimes might, but for the death penalty, have been committed by rational persons who are now deterred.

And the clincher. (5) Since we do not know for certain whether or not the death penalty adds deterrence, we have in effect the choice of two risks.

Risk One: If we execute convicted murderers without thereby deterring prospective murderers beyond the deterrence that could have been achieved by life imprisonment, we may have vainly sacrificed the life of the convicted murderer.

Risk Two: If we fail to execute a convicted murderer whose execution might have deterred an indefinite number of prospective murderers, our failure sacrifices an indefinite number of victims of future murderers.

"If we had certainty, we would not have risks. We do not have certainty. If we have risks—and we do—better to risk the life of the convicted man than risk the life of an indefinite number of innocent victims who might survive if he were executed."

Questions

1 Examine each of the refutations carefully and explain the deductive process Buckley follows in each.
2 Explain the circularity of the argument that the death penalty is unusual.
3 Construct a syllogism from the information in the paragraph discussing cruelty.
4 Examine the fourth sentence in paragraph seven. What does the sentence mean? How does Buckley use the word *net*? Is the sentence well written? Why, or why not?

Smoking

Richard Selzer

Richard Selzer, an associate professor of surgery at Yale University Medical School, is the author of several outstanding articles on medicine. A contributor to such magazines as Esquire, Harper's, *and* Redbook, *he has also written a volume of short stories called* Rituals of Surgery.

In the following essay Selzer uses the rhetorical technique of argument in an unusual way. He does not make us aware, at first, that he is even attempting argument, but begins with what appears to be a pleasant meditation upon the desire of the average person to assert his or her own existence—as women do when they wear perfume, as whistlers do, and tuba players, and children. Selzer then confesses that his way of asserting his existence is to smoke.

That statement and the next serve to introduce the argument and to refute contradictory evidence: it does little good to tell a smoker about the danger or the cost of smoking; he will smoke anyway. In the rest of the essay, Selzer explains why the smoker smokes and argues for letting the smoker alone concerning his nasty habit. To support his argument Selzer presents evidence to prove why smoking is useful: it fills up an empty place, it allows the smoker to make his mark upon the environment; it makes him feel better emotionally.

The final paragraph of the essay describes in detail the physical process involved in smoking. In particular, Selzer describes how the smoker produces that beautiful and satisfying cloud that proves he exists because he produces it himself.

Selzer addresses himself to that legion of nonsmokers who attempt to save the smoker from himself. He tries to explain to such people what smoking really means and to convince them that it is not simply a nasty habit. He wants the reader—the nonsmoker, probably—to understand why, from the smoker's point of view, it is really necessary to smoke.

Good-natured, not overly technical, and somewhat tongue-in-cheek, the essay is certainly not an angry attempt to justify what many consider to be a dangerous habit. Selzer acknowledges smoking's deleterious aspects but lets us know that he is tired of hearing about them, tired of being pestered by nonsmokers.

hat some people will not do to assure themselves that they exist! A woman dabs her neck with perfume, then walks abroad. In the sensible cloud of droplets about her, she has created an extension of her corporeal self, and of her personality, too. With each inhalation, that which she may have but vaguely suspected, her *being,* is most indisputably confirmed. I am here, she sniffs happily. I am really here.

And whistlers. Even the air-hungriest asthmatic who has not the least idea where to place his pitch or tone, who plays blindman's buff with melodies no more intricate than *Mary Had a Little Lamb,* even such a one as will walk the earth, lips pursed to a fine aperture, an expression of distraction upon his face as though he had just seen a vision. All the while from his feeble reed there issues a toneless beeping, a sorry complaint. It does not matter that the music he makes will not enter the living repertoire. No special color identifies it as baroque, flamenco, or twelve-tone; it is all of these and none of these. All about his head the whistler draws his helmet of sound. It is a private affair. Blowing out, he directs his notes within. The whistler himself but half attends the noise he makes. It is enough. He listens, and knows beyond all evidence to the contrary that he is there. His presence cannot be denied.

Thus do tenors and tuba players alike take the deep breath, set the vocal cords just so, and blast forth the good news of their existence. So, too, the child who climbs to the top of the slide, sits down, and makes ready to plummet. At the last moment he pauses, calls out to his mother. "Watch me!" he cries. And in her face he reads the success of his advertisement: *Here I am.*

I myself do it by smoking. And let no meddlesome man caution me against the extravagance, the injuriousness, of tobacco. I am addicted in a way more fundamental than any mere physiological craving. To deny me my smoke is to extinguish me as utterly as would death itself. It is to butt me into cold ashes.

Consider the act of smoking. It is constituted, is it not, of inhalation and exhalation? To draw deeply upon a cigarette, to fill the tracheobronchial tree with smoke, is to feed an empty space deep within, a space that twenty times a day cries out for appeasement. As nature abhors a vacuum, so does that cavern yearn for repletion. Should it, by some unhappy circumstance (you have run out of cigarettes in the dead of night), remain empty for too long a time, then the yearning becomes palpable. There is discomfort. The hollowness becomes an ache. One may perish of it.

I am not so vain, nor so uniquely neurotic, as to believe that I am alone in the world with such a hungry hole, a pit in search of something to enclose.

tracheobronchial of the windpipe and branching passages associated with it
appeasement the act of soothing, placating
palpable capable of being touched or felt

Nor will mere fresh air suffice. For this interior sack is no mere biology, but an urbane bag for whom taste has been deliciously refined. It needs smoke. And smoke it shall have. Smoke is, after all, little enough. Time was when a man could, with the forthrightness of a child, enjoy a healthy expectoration, the passage of some audible flatus, or the scratching of his personals. But civilization has come to mean the narrowing down of what we are permitted to do in public. Little Bo-Peep has gone away, and in her place the Iron Maiden of Etiquette shepherds us toward good deportment.

Smoking is good for the dumpish heart; lights up the gloomies, don't you know? Let the innumerable sad circumstances of humiliations past, of stumbles yet to come, crowd in upon me; then, out of the night that covers me, I grope for that *thing* with which to tampon the leak in my soul. All at once there is the scratch of a match. A pretty flame breaks. It swings to the touch. Ignition! And there blows a very wind from paradise.

There are circuits in the brain and lung that are triggered by the shifting of gases in the blood. So goes our soughing: at the end of exhalation there is a small but measurable rise in the level of carbon dioxide. This is noted by the respiratory center of the brain. The order is issued to the lung: *inhale*. Oxygen is taken in, the carbon dioxide level falls. In a moment it will rise again. Now: *exhale*. The muscles of expiration, those strips of meat between and overlying the ribs, are commanded to contract. They close in upon the chest cage, compressing it. The leaves of the diaphragm billow upward, further encroaching upon the lungs, which twin sponges are squeezed toward the trunk of the windpipe.

The larynx, too, assumes a posture, its little muscles squeezing to hold open the glottic chink at the top of the trachea to let out the smoke. Aah . . . and out it comes, now a slow-blown wisp, now a fat cloud. It rises about the face. That which was a moment before deep within pours to the out-of-doors, the soul come punctually visible. See it diffuse, coiling fainter and fainter into the general atmosphere. Here is proof—one needs no more—you exist, are *here*, because smoke, that gaseous testimony, is *there*.

One *is*. This smoke is the ultimate assurance.

Here I am, I say to myself . . . and take another puff. It's me.

Questions

1 In what part of the essay does Selzer's statement of the proposition appear?
2 Is Selzer's appeal to logic or to emotion? How do you know?

expectoration the act of spitting
flatus intestinal gas
deportment conduct
tampon to plug or stop with absorbent material
soughing a soft murmuring sound

3 What is the purpose of Selzer's argument? Does it attempt to change behavior, arouse sympathy, refute a theory, stimulate concern, or win agreement?

4 Why does Selzer begin with the descriptions of the woman wearing perfume and the man whistling?

Two Aspects of Scientific Responsibility

John T. Edsall

John T. Edsall, a professor emeritus of biochemistry at Harvard University, has long been concerned with research into the physical chemistry of proteins and enzymes and the medical uses of blood plasma proteins. Editor-in-chief of the Journal of Biological Chemistry *from 1958 to 1968, he has also been a member, and for two years chairman, of the American Association for the Advancement of Science's Committee on Scientific Freedom and Responsibility.*

Edsall's argument here is two-pronged: it seeks to halt the trend against the traditional patterns of scientific reporting but also claims that, where public health and safety are concerned, the traditional patterns of scientific reporting may be ineffective and potentially dangerous. Edsall calls for clear policies regarding criticism and dissent within the scientific community and suggests that the overriding consideration should be a passion for getting at the truth.

The second focus of the argument is the more important one. The first concern actually functions here as a means of acquiring support for the second. By establishing himself as a conservative in the reporting of traditional kinds of scientific knowledge, Edsall seeks to gain the support of conservative scientists for his later argument. Even on the second matter, Edsall is careful to distinguish between those who are engaging in constructive criticism and those who are simply trying to raise controversy for its own sake. However, he does not find the scientific community without fault; some scientists he suggests, have undoubtedly based their decisions about publication and "whistle-blowing" on personal bias rather than on sound reasoning.

Edsall is careful to argue his points mainly on the basis of logic; only rarely does he attempt to support a point by means of emotional appeal. (That he does not always avoid the emotional appeal indicates a recognition of the emotional issues inherent in the subject.) His argument, while long, is graceful and carefully structured. Its departures from the traditional rhetorical model for argument are probably justified by its audience and purpose.

Edsall is arguing these volatile issues for a group of people who are notoriously "touchy" about such matters, research scientists. He must avoid alienating his audi-

ence if he is to command wide and serious attention to his proposal. His purpose is, of course, to get the scientific world to come to some kind of agreement on what constitutes ethical scientific reporting. He quite correctly realizes that many scientists will see no difference between the reporting that is frequent in basic science and the kind that is necessary in areas involving high levels of social responsibility. He is equally aware that some scientists, impatient with what must often seem an obstructionist tradition, may seek to circumvent that tradition. His argument attempts to forestall both extremes.

> Of all the traits which qualify a scientist for citizenship in the republic of science, I would put a sense of responsibility as a scientist at the very top. A scientist can be brilliant, imaginative, clever with his hands, profound, broad, narrow—but he is not much as a scientist unless he is responsible. The essence of scientific responsibility is the inner drive, the inner necessity to get to the bottom of things: to be discontented until one has done so; to express one's reservations fully and honestly; and to be prepared to admit error.
>
> —ALVIN WEINBERG (1)

I agree with this assessment of the central role of scientific responsibility but not in all respects concerning what constitutes responsible behavior in some difficult situations. There are two major kinds of scientific responsibility. There is the pattern of responsible behavior that is associated with basic research and the communication of the results. And there are the problems that arise when scientists deal with issues involving social responsibility—such matters as the control of nuclear and other weapons, the uses and hazards of toxic chemicals and radioactive materials, the choice among various modes of producing or conserving energy, or the criteria for deciding whether to dam a river or let it flow freely. These are very different problems from those involved in basic research; the decisions reached involve value judgments. They are, and indeed should and must be, political decisions. Nevertheless, applied scientific knowledge is an important element in the making of such decisions. Scientists who enter these disputed areas encounter problems of responsible behavior that are considerably more complex than those of the scientist who is working out basic problems in the laboratory, or in thought and calculation. However, the two areas also have much in common, and the problems of social responsibility cannot be considered properly without keeping in mind the general code of scientific behavior that has evolved over the last few centuries.

The pattern of conduct that has developed in basic research serves to maintain what Robert Merton called the ethos of science (2). It involves the acceptance or rejection of reported findings of other workers on the basis of what Merton terms "preestablished impersonal criteria," and the public pre-

ethos fundamental values or principles

sentation of scientific findings (usually, and preferably, after critical review by editors and referees) so that they are available to the whole community. It also involves the social system of "organized skepticism" that subjects reported findings to constant critical review, with no assurance of finality. Scientists are expected to point out the limits of uncertainty in their findings and the inferences they draw, and they are expected to acknowledge their debts to others whose work, both published and unpublished, has contributed to what they have achieved. Science is a communal enterprise; every contribution builds upon the work of others.

This is an idealized picture. Acknowledging the debt to other workers is indeed central in the ethos of science, yet it would be intolerable to cite a massive set of references for an ordinary paper. Aggressive scientists are sometimes skillful in getting credit for ideas that others may have published before, but they may also be genuinely ignorant of the earlier work. Even those who are quite scrupulous may pick up ideas from papers for which they serve as referees, or from serving on a panel that reviews grant applications, and they may remain quite unconscious of the source of their ideas. Since recognition of significant originality in discovery is the main road to scientific prestige and honor, most scientists are understandably sensitive to the failure of others to acknowledge their work. A few unusual people are dramatically different: they cast forth their ideas freely, and are happy to see others pick them up. This is what Jacques Monod (3) wrote about Leo Szilard:

> Most scientists of course do not formulate any significant new ideas of their own. The few that do are inordinately jealous of, and unduly faithful to, their own precious little ideas. Not so with Szilard: he was as generous with his ideas as a Maori chief with his wives. Indeed he loved ideas, especially his own. But he felt that these lovely objects only revealed all their virtues and charms by being tossed around, circulated, shared, and played with.

I am not an anthropologist and cannot claim knowledge of how Maori chieftains share their wives, but Monod's description certainly characterizes Szilard and other unusual individuals.

The pursuit of knowledge in basic science is inevitably full of rivalry and competition, especially in the fields that are most active, but it usually proceeds in an atmosphere in which there is a great deal of free communication of ideas and active discussion. When obvious major practical results begin to appear, a trend toward secretiveness usually sets in. The most dramatic example is the effect on physicists of the discovery of nuclear fission and the secrecy that followed. More than one distinguished physicist has recalled nostalgically the intellectual freedom of exchange in physics in the years before 1939. A somewhat similar change appears to be taking place among the molecular biologists today, as the techniques of gene cloning hold forth the promise of manufacturing substances of great biological importance, cheaply and on a large scale. Some of my younger colleagues have told me that they

scrupulous principled

find scientific meetings less interesting than they were, even 5 or 6 years ago; too many people, they say, are clearly holding back information, presumably with an eye to applying for patents on new processes. There have even been charges that some authors of reports are deliberately failing to cite relevant work of others in hopes of claiming a patent on some new biological process or product.

This competitive atmosphere has sometimes led to publicity of a sort previously not practiced among scientists. In a recent article entitled "Gene cloning by press conference," Spyros Andreopoulos (4) of the Stanford Medical Center News Bureau quotes a letter from Joshua Lederberg to Senator Gaylord Nelson of Wisconsin. "The possibility of profit—especially when other funding is so tight—will be a distorting influence on open communication and on the pursuit of basic scholarship," Lederberg wrote, although he noted that many, perhaps most, university scientists disagreed with his views. Andreopoulos showed that some new developments announced at press conferences receive wide publicity, before they appear in the scientific literature, while other work of at least equal significance passes through the regular channels of critical reviewing before it appears. Reports at press conferences can be misleading; for example, one new account of the production of human insulin by recombinant DNA techniques created the impression that the product was biologically active; the later publication of the data in a journal showed that this was not so (4).

The traditional patterns of scientific reporting and communication—the scientific ethos, in Merton's phrase—may be in danger of undergoing significant erosion. As a believer in the classical tradition of operation in basic science, I hope that the erosion may be halted.

INDEPENDENT SCIENTISTS AND ISSUES OF PUBLIC POLICY

A more difficult subject is the role of scientists in matters of public policy. Let me begin with a classic example from nearly 20 years ago: the publication of Rachel Carson's *Silent Spring* (5) with its vigorous attack on what she considered the gross misuse of pesticides. She was both a trained scientist and a gifted writer. The biological community had been concerned about the ecological damage from widespread use of pesticides such as DDT, but no authoritative body had made a critical study of the problem and publicized its conclusions. The book had an immense impact. It was also attacked by many agriculturists and nutritionists, who called it misinformed, fanatical, or even a hoax. The President's Science Advisory Committee, however, took Carson's charges seriously and set up a special panel of experts to investigate the problem. After 8 months of hearings they produced a report (6) that in large measure vindicated Carson's claims and also concluded that massive attempts

recombinant DNA techniques methods of forming, in an offspring, genetic combinations that its parents do not possess

Argument

to eradicate certain insects by pesticides were unrealistic and ecologically dangerous and that "elimination of the use of persistent toxic pesticides should be the goal." President Kennedy released the report in May 1963 and requested the responsible agencies to implement its recommendations.

The pattern of subsequent events is complex; but it would not please either the strong supporters or the fervent opponents of chemical pesticides. Some strong controls have indeed been imposed; DDT, which was the principal focus of Carson's attack, has been banned; but the general use of chemical pesticides in agriculture is probably as widespread as ever, if not more so. Many of the current pesticides are more toxic to humans than DDT. Other poisons, such as the polychlorinated biphenyls (PCB's), used in industry rather than in agriculture, have been recognized as serious environmental hazards. Highly specific pesticides for particular species of insects, such as the juvenile hormones, have been developed but as yet have found little practical use.

Mention of Carson's book can still rouse both enthusiasm and denunciation. Undoubtably in some respects she exaggerated the damage done by pesticides. My own view is that, on balance, she performed a great public service and deserves to be remembered with honor. Certainly the sense of responsibility for the environment that she inculcated is now implanted in a vast number of people.

This episode exemplifies many of the problems that scientists encounter when they become involved in issues of social responsibility. Carson was a trained scientist, but not in the field of agricultural ecology. She had much to learn, and she did learn, in the process of preparing to write the book. The agriculturists still did not regard her as a real professional in their field. However, many, if not most, of the agriculturists had financial and career ties to the use of pesticides and to the industries that produced them. The committees of the National Academy of Sciences that dealt with such matters in those days tended to be dominated by people who had similar biases. The Academy has changed and now examines systematically the industrial and other connections of the members of its committees. The aim is not to eliminate all people with possible bias—that would eliminate most of the experts, in some fields at least—but to obtain a balanced spectrum of people with different kinds of bias, together with some who might be genuinely dispassionate in considering the issues.

Since nearly all controversial issues of this sort involve technology, as well as basic science, the disputes cannot be resolved in terms of "preestablished impersonal criteria." Scientific facts and value judgments are so closely interwoven that it is exceedingly difficult to disentangle them, and the inferences to be drawn are inconclusive. Scientists can honestly disagree as to what inferences can legitimately be drawn from the facts.

juvenile hormones hormones, administered before an animal becomes an adult, that are intended to control population
inculcate to teach forcefully
dispassionate calm, impartial

Thus we are operating in a quite different domain from that of basic science. The Federation of American Scientists (FAS), which addressed this problem (7), accepted as inevitable ". . . that scientists involved in public debate will have to go beyond discussing what is scientifically known for certain," since public policy matters involve the making of decisions in the face of enormous uncertainties. At the same time, the FAS report said that scientists who take an active part in public debates should avoid dogmatic claims, be willing to admit and correct errors in their statements, and reason with those with whom they disagree. However, the report concluded that professional scientific societies are generally unqualified to monitor and pass judgment on the conduct of scientists involved in such debates. The societies are accustomed to dealing with more traditional patterns of conduct within the scientific community and are unequipped to deal with the far more unruly debates that arise when social and political questions are involved. It is the community of scientists who do take an active part in public debate on these controversial issues who must work out appropriate guidelines for responsible conduct. As the debate proceeds, it will become clear who the scientists are who are speaking responsibly and with due respect for the facts.

Weinberg (1) holds that the essential sense of responsibility is being eroded in the current debates on such matters as energy policy and environmental protection, with scientists making sweeping pronouncements on issues far outside their own fields of competence. He believes, for instance, that a scientist who thinks he has evidence that current standards of environmental protection are too lax should submit his findings to a refereed scientific journal before publicizing them. If the journal rejects the report, the author may honestly believe that the reviewers are biased. In that case he may be justified in bringing the matter before the public, while admitting that others disagree with him.

There are many cases in which such a procedure will help bring more rationality into the debate; but scientists discussing public issues are often involved in public discussions, or interviews on television, where the limited time makes it impossible to state all the reservations that a careful scientist might add to qualify his remarks. In the heat of debate there is also the tendency to overstate the case. Politicians and others would like simple answers to complex questions. Certainly scientists should be prepared to state publicly that they have made erroneous statements, and correct them; on this vital point there is no disagreement between Weinberg's position and that of the FAS.

Among the value judgments involved in these controversial issues, a fundamental difference of view is often present. If, for instance, the evidence is inconclusive about the toxicity of some industrial product, should it be banned until it is proved safe or used until it is proved dangerous? Until the last two or three decades, the latter policy was most commonly accepted. Recently the

dogmatic rigid, authoritarian
refereed scientific journal a journal whose articles are reviewed in advance by "referees"

more cautious policy has prevailed; the increasingly severe standards for the licensing of drugs by the Food and Drug Administration represent perhaps the most striking example. Such caution has its penalties as well as its merits; for example, Carl Djerassi (8) pointed out the difficulties in the development of new and better contraceptives that the strict rules of testing have imposed. Sometimes more is lost than gained by excessive zeal in testing before release. This is likely to be true for the selective pesticides that act by inhibiting the development of certain species of insects.

Decisions on such matters as building an airport or a power plant, or damming a river, inevitably involve value judgments as well as technical facts. They require estimates of future needs, which are often highly unreliable. For example, the estimates made a decade ago about future needs for electric power in the United States have been drastically scaled down in the light of experience. Expert testimony in such matters is likely to be colored, consciously or unconsciously, by the expert's system of values.

Cost-benefit analysis in such situations of conflict is a treacherous game; the costs and benefits are usually quite incommensurable; ultimately decisions are likely to be made by the political process in which the public perception of what is desirable counts for more than the cost-benefit calculations of experts. Lord Ashby (9) concluded that it is probably better so:

> All attempts to rely on quantification in such decisions as these, to create them out of computer scenarios, to deduce them from cost-benefit balance sheets, are likely to make the decision worse, not better; for in the process of getting hard data, the fragile values, the unquantified information, the emotive elements which nourish the public conscience, all run through the filter and are lost, and so the quantified information assumes an importance out of proportion to its real value.

WHISTLE-BLOWING AND PROFESSIONAL RESPONSIBILITY

Scientific and technical professional employees, in industry or government, on occasion have reason to sound warnings of dangers about process or products, or sometimes to call attention to opportunities for improvement that they believe are being neglected. Obviously employees should approach their superiors, point out the source of trouble, and urge correction. If the superiors fail to respond and the issue is really serious, the employee can bring it before the public. People who do this are commonly called whistle-blowers (10).

Whistle-blowing is obviously a high-risk occupation, and those who practice it must be prepared for trouble. A classic example arose during the building of the Bay Area Rapid Transit (BART) system in San Francisco (11). A major feature of the system was the automated train control, developed under a contract with the Westinghouse Corporation. Three engineers, Max

incommensurable lacking a common quality upon which to make a comparison

Blankenzee, Holger Hjortsvang, and Robert Bruder, concluded that the system design had grave defects, but their concerns were disregarded by the management. Finally, early in 1972, they went to BART's board of directors which, after a hearing, voted 10 to 2 with management. The three engineers were fired. Subsequent dangerous failures of the automated train control, which occurred after the system started to operate, fully vindicated the engineers. The California Society of Professional Engineers investigated the case and decided that the dissenting engineers "had acted in the best interest of the public welfare." The California legislature conducted an investigation that confirmed the validity of the engineers' warnings. The three then sued Westinghouse for $885,000 but eventually settled out of court for a relatively modest sum, which was probably quite inadequate compensation.

A more recent case involved Clifford Richter, a health physicist at a state hospital in Columbia, Missouri (12). He reported certain violations of safety regulations at the hospital to the Nuclear Regulatory Commission, as he was in duty bound to do by law. The hospital management retaliated by abolishing his job. A federal court eventually ordered his reinstatement, under the employee protection section of the Energy Reorganization Act, and the payment of back salary. The reinstatement has been challenged, however, and appealed to the U.S. Supreme Court.

In another case, Morris Baslow, a marine biologist, was fired after he presented evidence, in a court hearing on a U.S. Environmental Protection Agency inquiry, concerning the effects of cooling water from power plants on fish in the Hudson River (13). He urged his employers to present the evidence, but when they ignored his recommendations, he finally presented the data to the court directly. Eventually he reached an agreement with his former employers, but only after many months of delay, while he was out of work.

In these cases the whistle-blowers put their jobs and reputations in jeopardy. It is obviously in the interest of public health and safety that such people should be heard and fairly judged; and if their views are upheld after a hearing by a suitable body, they deserve commendation, and perhaps promotion, not discharge. Congress has passed several laws in recent years to protect the rights of employees who report to their employers matters that call for correction. The Nuclear Regulatory Commission is now formulating rules that should encourage employees to report matters of concern to higher officials, with guarantees against reprisals, whether or not the employee's recommendations are accepted. This represents an encouraging trend in the Executive Branch of the government. Rules to protect employees are still nonexistent in most private businesses, though a few firms have begun pioneer moves in this direction. David Ewing of the Harvard Business School has outlined detailed proposals for further reform (14).

Of course whistle-blowers are not always right. They might be motivated by personal malice, they may be cranks, or they may be honest, but mistaken.

reprisal repayment for an injury designed to inflict at least equal injury; retaliation

Both common sense, and a sense of loyalty to the employer, dictate an earnest effort to settle differences of opinion by working within the organization. However, if higher authorities fail to respond, and if the matter appears to involve serious issues of human safety and health, it may be necessary to bring the matter to public attention. The individual who takes such a risk obviously needs good legal advice and other kinds of help (15). Our complex society needs increasing input from those who perceive otherwise unnoted risks or opportunities and bring messages that may be unwelcome to established authorities. To use criticism and dissent constructively in dealing with both risks and opportunities, clear policies are needed, with definitions of procedures for due process in controversial cases and, if necessary, formal hearings and a possibility of appeal.

The polarization of opinions on some issues today is disturbing. The conflict between the advocates and enemies of nuclear power is one example; the dispute over the origins of cancer is becoming another. Richard Peto (16) described the distortions and untruths promoted by tobacco companies in their efforts to discredit the overwhelming evidence for the relation between smoking and lung cancer. At the same time he severely criticized some of the alleged evidence that would ascribe nearly all cancers to toxic substances introduced by man. S. S. Epstein, whom Peto sharply criticized, has responded vigorously (17). The gravity of the hazard from industrial carcinogens, to workers and others, is clear; but their relative role in the totality of human cancers is still hotly debated. In the bitterness of such controversies, either side may distort data. As Peto remarked, "Scientists on both sides of the environmentalist debate now have career interests at stake." But it is important above all that the passion for getting at the truth should be the dominant passion for scientific workers when they are trying to act as responsible scientist. That may appear sometimes to be an unattainable goal in the atmosphere of current debate, but it is worth striving for, both to maintain the confidence of the public and to keep confidence in ourselves.

References and Notes

1. A. Weinberg, *Minerva* **16**, 1 (1978).

2. R. K. Merton, in *The Sociology of Science* (Univ. of Chicago Press, Chicago, 1973), pp. 267–278; A. Cournaud and M. Meyer, *Minerva* **14**, 79 (1976).

3. J. Monod, in *Collected Works of Leo Szilard: Scientific Papers*, B. T. Feld and G. W. Szilard, Eds. (MIT Press, Cambridge, Mass, 1972), p. xvi.

4. S. Andreopoulos, *N. Engl. J. Med.* **302**, 743 (1980).

5. R. Carson, *Silent Spring* (Houghton Mifflin, Boston, 1962).

6. U.S. President's Science Advisory Committee, "Use of pesticides" (The White House, Washington, D.C., 1963); the report was reprinted in *Chem. Eng. News* **41** (No. 21), 102 (1963). J. Primack and F. von Hippel [*Advice and Dissent: Scientists in the Po-*

litical Arena (Basic Books, New York, 1974), pp. 41–46] provide a useful account of the effect of the report.

7. Federation of American Scientists, "To whom are public interest scientists responsible" (Public Interest Report 29, Washington, D.C., 1976).

8. C. Djerassi, *Science* **169**, 941 (1970); *Bull Am. Acad. Arts Sci.* **32**, 22 (1978).

9. E. Ashby, *Perspect. Biol. Med.* **23**, 7 (1979).

10. R. Chalk and F. von Hippel, *Technol. Rev.* **81**, 48 (1979).

11. J. T. Edsall, *Scientific Freedom and Responsibility* (AAAS, Washington, D.C., 1975).

12. L. J. Carter, *Science* **207**, 1057 (1980).

13. C. Holden, *ibid.* **210**, 749 (1980); J. L. Lawler, *ibid.* **211**, 875 (1981).

14. D. W. Ewing, *Freedom Inside the Organization: Bringing Civil Liberties to the Workplace* (Dutton, New York, 1977). See also A. F. Westin, Ed., *Whistle Blowing! Loyalty and Dissent in the Corporation* (McGraw-Hill, New York, 1981).

15. P. Raven-Hansen, *Technol. Rev.* **82**, 34 (1980).

16. R. Peto, *Nature (London)* **284**, 297 (1980).

17. S. S. Epstein, *Nature (London)* **289**, 115 (1981); ———and J. B. Swartz, *ibid.*, p. 127. Compare J. Cairns, *ibid.*, p. 353.

18. I am much indebted to my fellow members of the AAAS Committee on Scientific Freedom and Responsibility for our continued joint work relating to many of the problems discussed in this article. I am particularly indebted to R. Baum, F. von Hippel, J. Primack, and R. Chalk. This article is, however, an expression of my personal views. This work was supported by grant SOC7912543 from the National Science Foundation.

Questions

1 If Edsall had followed the traditional form for argument, what would an outline of his paper have looked like? Taking the information in this article, attempt to formulate an outline of that sort. What difficulties do you encounter? Why?
2 Could Edsall have left out the first argument and still have had an effective paper? Why, or why not?
3 What rhetorical techniques do you find in Edsall's article?
4 If you were rewriting this article for the average reader, what, if anything, would you change? Why? If you would not change anything, why not?

Pollution Control Strategies: Regulatory Problems?

John E. Blodgett

John E. Blodgett works for the Environment and Natural Resources Policy Division of the Congressional Research Service of the Library of Congress. His argument here for change in pollution control laws begins with a refutation of the assumptions underlying the controversy about environmental regulations. Blodgett disposes of the first four kinds of complaints by describing them as either a result of statutory rights (and thus unamenable to change) or a result of administrative practices for implementing statutes (and thus flexible only within the limits of the statutes themselves). Blodgett dismisses a final complaint concerning the difficulty of following the regulations by pointing out that the very nature of our government presupposes such complexity.

The rest of the argument explains what Congress has the power to do about environmental regulation, how Congress has established current practices, what problems have arisen in the last decade or two, and what suggestions have been offered to solve the problems. Blodgett then offers what he considers the most likely solution: he suggests that since Congress has been willing to make adjustments in the past, it will probably be willing to do so in the future. He then sets up some boundaries within which Congress will be likely to operate. He deals with three specific objections to congressional policy by pointing out that certain regulatory goals are legitimate, that some complexity is the result of attempts to accommodate special interest groups, and that technology must follow social change. In summation, Blodgett proposes that complaints be directed at real issues, and that those who complain learn what the real limits are for imposing environmental regulations.

Representing Blodgett's own personal views and not those of the Congressional Research Service, this speech was given before a meeting of the American Chemical Society. The members of that group can be assumed to be knowledgeable about the nature of chemicals and the difficulties of controlling them. Some members of the group can also be assumed to chafe under federal restrictions from time to time. The purpose of the speech was to enlighten the chemists about how public policy is formulated and how it can be reasonably expected to change.

Controversies surrounding environmental regulations have been heightened by perceptions that the nation's economic and energy problems have been exacerbated by enviornmental controls. Although environmental regulations have so far proved to be resistant to substantive change, pressure for procedural or substantive changes continues—most recently in the energy "fast track" proposals. Questionable cost-effectiveness, delays, confusion, and uncertain progress in environmental cleanup have all added legitimacy to the pressure for change. Yet it appears that many of the calls for revising environmental controls fail to consider underlying bases for the way current environmental programs are designed. Let us consider some of the basic points of contention about environmental regulations and explore briefly some of the underlying forces that must be taken into account if changes are to be made.

Five common points of contention about environmental regulations have been:

1. the regulatory approach;
2. the factors considered—or not considered—in making regulatory decisions;
3. the standards or requirements established;
4. the particulars of regulatory decisions; and
5. the regulatory maze.

The first two of these are basically statutory issues over which Congress has the final say. On these issues, the debates tend to concern efficiency and equity. The second two are basically administrative issues, in which the regulator is more or less guided and constrained by the statute. The last point of contention, the regulatory maze—in which a firm must run a seemingly endless path of ill-marked intersections with checkpoints requiring local, State, and Federal permits—reflects this nation's fragmented and decentralized political system, composed of many levels of government control and, at the national level, by disaggregated powers based on checks and balances.

Today I want to focus on Congress' role in constructing environmental statutes and on the implications of its choices. From this perspective, Congress is the definer of national goals and a mediator among conflicting claimants to the nation's resources. Thus, when the environment became a compelling national issue in the 1960s, Congress began a process of articulating the goal of what the nation's environment should be and of directing the nation toward that goal. But Congress cannot itself clean the environment as a janitor can clean a basement; it can only manipulate signals, provide incentives, and impose constraints within its constitutional powers. In short, Congress' role is to set in motion changes that will redirect the behavior of persons and firms which in the past have had little reason not to pollute—and usually good reason to do so. When the air, water, and land were cheap

exacerbate make worse, aggravate
substantive essential, having to do with the essence of
constrain to compel by physical, moral, or other force
disaggregated disjoined, separated

receptacles for wastes, it would have been folly not to use them. Indeed, a firm which went to extra expense to protect the environment would find itself at a competitive disadvantage. Congress, therefore, has set out to change the rules, and, consequently, this pattern of behavior.

In drawing up environmental protection statutes, Congress has considered four basic pollution control strategies:

1. ambient quality standards;
2. effluent discharge standards;
3. economic incentives and disincentives (pollution taxes); and
4. case-by-case analysis.

Each has advantages and disadvantages. And while they are often discussed separately—and sometimes as if they were mutually exclusive—they can be combined to gain at least some of the best of more than one approach. For example, the Clean Air Act is based on ambient air quality standards, but new sources of pollution are subject to technological capability-based standards. The Federal Water Pollution Control Act, while originally based on ambient quality standards, has since 1972 been based on technological capability-based effluent discharge standards (with the goal of zero discharge), but with ambient quality standards as backup. Case-by-case analysis is the basic strategy underlying the National Environmental Policy Act; the Federal Insecticide, Fungicide, and Rodenticide Act; and the Toxic Substances Control Act. Most pollution control statutes use economic incentives and disincentives through civil penalties, and noncompliance fees have been added to the water and air pollution control acts; but none is based on effluent taxes as the basic approach.

Several factors have determined the choice of approaches, of which the most basic has been the perception that the motive of potential polluters must be changed. The historical view of wastes and the environment has been that assimilative capacity is a free good up to a level at which the public health is threatened—this concept underlies ambient quality standards. The motivation implicit in this approach is for polluters to discharge wastes up to the limit, and he who gets there first with the biggest share of the assimilative capacity is best off. Moreover, given this motivation, the ultimate outcome will be that all air and water will be polluted to the limit set by public health considerations, at which point procedures for allowing growth in areas with no margin of clean air or water must be devised. This results in two regulatory complications, as we see in the Clean Air Act: provisions for allowing growth in areas which are polluted to or beyond the limit—nonattainment regulations; and provisions for allocating the assimilative capacity in clean areas—no significant deterioration requirements. Even without the no-significant-deterioration regulations, it would only be a matter of time until limits are reached, so the question is when and how regulations will be imposed, not whether.

Congress' clearest signal that this motivation must be changed came in

ambient encircling, surrounding

the 1972 amendments to the Federal Water Pollution Control Act: Public Law 92-500 shifted the basis of regulation to effluent discharge standards and set a national goal of zero discharge. The achievability of the goal is less the point than the signal it represents: pollution is no longer legal up to some level of potential hazard; rather, pollution is illegal. By making pollution illegal, the strategy is directed at motivating polluters to develop new techniques for eliminating water pollution, e.g., by recycling or process changes. The permit system in effect provides variances from zero discharge, and contingencies on permits can be used to foster innovation. A well-publicized shortcoming of the zero discharge goal is the inordinate cost of cleaning up the last increments of pollution—at least when traditional end-of-pipe cleanup is used. Of course, the underlying expectation is that innovation will replace this traditional view of how to clean up.

During the late 1960s–early 1970s, when the strategies underlying pollution control statutes were established, Congress explicitly considered effluent taxes. This approach was rejected for several reasons, partly political—which Congressional committees would have jurisdiction over taxes?—partly strategic—pollution taxes in effect legitimize pollution and shift motivations from reduction of pollutants to reduction in costs—and partly technical—how would it be done? Nevertheless, as I will note later, many economists contend that an economic approach would be more efficient and cost-effective than the regulatory approach.

For dealing with discharges, the case-by-case approach has had little attractiveness. It is cumbersome and requires an extensive decision-making apparatus, and it imposes significant time and dollar costs to generate information. Moreover, since existing procedures have the best information base, the approach tends to favor current practices. For problems arising when the polluting effects are intrinsically part of the benefits of an activity or substance, however, the approach permits the weighing of each case, and hence has been adopted in pesticide and toxic substance control. As might be expected, the regulatory problems associated with these acts have been primarily informational—e.g., data needs, validity, and confidentiality.

While one can second-guess the approaches adopted by Congress in the pollution control statutes, it cannot be denied that in one sense they have been successful: polluters have had to take notice. It's like the story of how to get a mule to move—first you hit him on the head with a two-by-four to get his attention. At the same time, no one could deny that problems have emerged. In part these were not unexpected: the legislation has in a sense been experimental, and change therefore anticipated. But this has meant regulatory change and uncertainty, the bane of corporate planning. Moreover, since the environmental statutes were designed to force change, both in behavior and in technology, it is not surprising that difficult problems and stresses have emerged.

Three factors have highlighted these difficulties and stresses. First, the

contingency a possibility; something that may occur but is not likely

lack of information about pollution, its effects, and the implications of various approaches to controlling it. When Congress established the environmental programs, adequate information on the nature of the problem and on what to do about it was often lacking. Congress was pressed from two sides: one philosophy says that when in doubt, discretion and a limited approach is best, while the other says that safety must be the overriding concern. This is ultimately a political problem, and the appropriate decision is likely to change as more information becomes available. For example, the standard for nitrogen oxide emissions from autos has been adjusted as the result of new data; the emergence of chronic toxicity has introduced new concerns and regulatory problems.

Second, the implementation of pollution controls has raised substantial problems of equity, which Congress has established as a principle of pollution control. Equity means that no controller of pollution should be at a competitive disadvantage because of pollution control expenses—nor should any facility enjoy a competitive advantage because it has failed to install pollution controls. When problems of equity arise, Congress' usual response has been twofold: first, to build equalizers into the statute. For example, the Clean Air Act imposes controls on utilities which might most efficiently be met by some eastern power plants burning western low-sulfur coal; but to protect local economies, the Act includes a provision by which such plants can be compelled to contract for and burn local coal. The need to ameliorate the local economic impacts of the pollution controls has in this case been judged more important than efficiency. Second, Congress has built into the statutes a complex set of mechanisms by which standards can be subjected to administrative and judicial review. These provisions, designed to ensure equity, add substantially to the regulatory complexity. And at times, since Congress is responding to diverse pressures from all segments of the nation (including industry), some of these provisions appear inconsistent. Thus the pollution control statutes are rife with various kinds of accommodations, some specific, some generic—exceptions, variances, extensions of deadlines, requirements to consider economic or other impacts, opportunities for public input, judicial reviews, and so on. All of these are intended to ensure that the burdens of pollution control do not fall unreasonably and disproportionately on anyone, and that any interested party has an opportunity to challenge the propriety of the foreclosing of a formerly free public good. But the cost of these accommodations is usually to be found in further layers of regulatory requirements and a sacrifice in efficiency.

The third force highlighting problems in pollution control is the change underway in the world at large. All this process of trying to redirect behavior and to accommodate resulting inequities has been going on in a world of change. The economy, so stable during the 1960s, has changed in puzzling and unpredicted ways. And energy prices and availability, taken for granted

ameliorate to improve, make better
rife with full of

in the 1960s, have become major uncertainties. The concern for the national goals of economic stability and low-priced, assured supplies of energy has led to questions about the tradeoffs between these goals and environmental controls.

Many economists, in particular, have suggested that allowing the marketplace to allocate pollution control costs would be more efficient and cost-effective than regulation. Congress, however, has been reluctant to rely on economic incentives and disincentives as a basis for pollution control, although it has provided disincentives in the form of civil penalties and it has introduced noncompliance penalties as a way of ensuring equity among competitors. Besides the strategic considerations noted earlier, Congress' increasing attention to toxics has blunted the arguments for an economic approach, for nearly everyone agrees that effluent taxes have limited utility in controlling toxic hazards. Moreover, it is not clear that the economic approach would be simpler. The example of the income tax code is not reassuring. Indeed the recognition that regulatory complexity reflects procedural safeguards and the multiplicity of legitimate viewpoints suggests that whatever the approach, the maze of controls will remain. Nevertheless, the Environmental Protection Agency has been experimenting with various innovations, such as "bubbles" and offsets.

At this point, let us note that the regulatory costs and the complexity imposed by each pollution control statute are in large part inherent in its Congressional evolution—first, because of the decision that new motivations must be engendered, and second because of the adoption of the principle of equity.

To the problems that each act imposes on those affected must be added the problems that emerge as a result of the fact that Congress has enacted a series of pollution control laws piecemeal, at different times and with different approaches. Thus the emergence of what many call the regulatory maze. One law says you can't dump your wastes in the water, then another comes along and says you can't dump it on land either. What to do?

The answer lies in the fact that the pollution control statutes are not set in concrete. Congress has been willing to make adjustments: for example, it has several times delayed the auto emission standards and it has adjusted the requirements of the water pollution control act. But these adjustments have been marginal; not fundamental. This is not surprising, since the basic goal, improved environmental quality, has not lost any of its legitimacy. The question is, what changes in particular requirements may be justified without unduly sacrificing progress in abating pollution? And this is where the kicker comes in: The success of attempts to modify environmental regulations will depend significantly on the extent to which the underlying strategic needs are taken into account.

Objectors to the zero discharge goal of the water act on the ground that removing final increments of pollution is too expensive often overlook its

abate to lessen, reduce in amount or in degree

strategic goal of encouraging new concepts of water recycling and process change. Thus proposals for changing the approach should show how this goal would be met under the alternative.

Objectors to the regulatory complexity which they face often forget that many (though certainly not all) of these complexities reflect procedural opportunities for diverse parties to protect their interests. Thus proposals for simplifying regulatory requirements should show how alternatives will provide any concerned party opportunity to protect his interests.

Objectors to pollution control requirements on the grounds they are technically unachievable often forget that the law is not a cleanup mechanism itself; rather, it is a social rulebook designed to instill patterns of behavior. Thus proposals to limit requirements to what is technically achievable or scientifically defensible are often subject to the criticism that they reflect a business-as-usual approach when new social requirements dictate change.

It should be clear that I am not saying one cannot object to environmental laws as written. On the contrary, I am saying that environmental laws are dynamic and interactive. They can, and must, change. What I am saying is, first, that complaints about pollution control regulations must be directed at the real issue; blaming the Environmental Protection Agency for statutory requirements is rarely helpful—and vice versa. And second, it is important to understand the forces underlying the pollution control statutes and to take them into account when proposing alternatives.

Questions

1 Although the speech is an argument, Blodgett employs another rhetorical technique to provide background and support his purpose. What is that technique? Discuss its use in detail.

2. Is Blodgett's point made strongly enough? Would organizing the speech differently make that point clearer? Why do you think Blodgett chose to organize the speech the way he did?

3 Blodgett makes use of two levels of discourse, formal and informal. Examine the speech to see where each level is used and attempt to justify its use there.

4 How would Blodgett's speech be received by members of a conservation group? Would the group be likely to accept Blodgett's arguments? Why, or why not?

EXEMPLIFICATION

Exemplification is the process of explaining ideas or generalizations by using examples. It is, therefore, a process of making abstractions or generalities concrete. For instance, if we say, "Government has assumed too much control of private business," we have stated an opinion about the function of the government. We could have stated a fact, "Government's control of private businesss has increased 60 percent since 1937." Or we could have stated an inference, "The proliferation of regulatory agencies suggests that government is rapidly stepping up its control of private business." When we are asked what we mean, we are actually being asked to support the generalization. Generalization is a process of induction by which we observe specific cases and draw conclusions about the common element forming a relationship among them. Those conclusions are stated as generalizations and usually contain at least one general term such as *all, some, many, most.* We must be careful, however, not to make the generalization too broad; often we must acknowledge that a generalization is not universally true and avoid using *all* or *none* or *never.* The classic case of an overly broad generalization is one we have all used in some form or other: "Everyone else does it." Of course, in very few instances is that true. What we mean is either that most of our friends do it or that most people in general do it.

The use of examples is one way to make general statements more interesting, more concrete, more convincing, and clearer. Anything offered as an example should be pertinent—that is, relevant to the main qualities of the generalization. It is also wise to choose an example that relates to all those main qualities rather than to a few. This choice of one case to represent many cases depends greatly upon a firm grasp of purpose and audience as well as a clear and well-phrased thesis.

Many different kinds of experiences can serve as examples: parables and fables as well as anecdotes and analogies. But examples taken from personal experience can be particularly useful. Writing that uses personal experience is likely to be more vivid and concrete than writing that uses fictitious examples. A great many relevant details are always stored in memory. As a result, examples drawn from personal experience tend to be more interesting than those imagined by many writers, not only because of the concreteness of detail but also because there is an element of intimacy. Writing that is concrete and interesting is more likely to convince.

Examples can indeed bring clarity and concreteness to writing, but increased confusion can easily result if the examples used are not to the point. A good precaution is to write an introductory paragraph that includes a clear statement of a generalization. Your first series of examples should follow that paragraph and illustrate the points made by the generalization.

The Peter Principle

Raymond Hull

Raymond Hull, co-author with Laurence J. Peter of The Peter Principle *(1969), was born in England and has lived in Canada since 1947. A professional playwright, he has written many dramas for television and the stage and has contributed articles to several prestigious British, Canadian, and American magazines, including* Punch, Macleans, *and* Esquire.

Hull makes excellent use of example in his essay "The Peter Principle." His opening statement is a broad generalization, which, although most of us would agree with it, still needs support. For instance, what does Hull mean by "bunglers"? Hull explains the word by giving four examples. And his next generalization—that we accept incompetence as a necessary feature of civilization—is supported by a rapid barrage of eight examples.

Hull introduces us to Laurence Peter by listing six or seven examples of Peter's competence. Having explained that Peter founded the science of hierarchiology, *Hull quotes from Peter's book to define, by example, what hierarchiology really is. Within that example is a set of examples to explain the concept in more detail. The essay continues by stating generalizations and then quoting passages as examples in support of these generalizations. Frequently, the example itself contains other examples.*

Two unusual uses of example can be found in the article. The first occurs in the paragraph beginning "An employee may, like Mr. Cube, reach. . . ." Hull refers the reader to a previous example that can do double duty by illustrating an additional point. The other, occurring toward the end of the article, is an example that makes a negative point. Having stated the ultimate sensibleness of the Peter Principle, Hull cites the academic world's skepticism, supposedly to support the idea that the principle is in fact really a theory. But he phrases the example so as to imply that the academic world is not very sensible and that most academics have reached their level of incompetence.

Written shortly before Peter and Hull's book was published, the article no doubt served to advertise the coming book among Esquire's *readers and to tease them into purchasing a copy. The audience was exceptionally well chosen. The readers of* Esquire *can be fairly described as upwardly mobile, intelligent, and ambitious. Both the subject of the book and the manner in which Hull discusses it involve just enough irony to appeal to the intelligent reader and enough truth to appeal to the ambitious reader.*

Bunglers are always with us and always have been. Winston Churchill tells us, in his history of World War II, that in August 1940, he had to take charge personally of the Armed Forces' Joint Planning Committee because, after almost twelve months of war, the Committee had not originated a single plan.

In the 1948 Presidential election, the advance public-opinion polls awarded an easy victory to Thomas E. Dewey. In the Fifties, there was the Edsel bungle. In 1965, Houston's domed baseball stadium opened and was so ill-suited to baseball that on sunny days, fielders could not see fly balls against the blinding glare from the skylight.

We have come to expect incompetence as a necessary feature of civilization. We may be irked, but we are no longer amazed, when our bosses make idiotic decisions, when automobile makers take back thousands of new cars for repairs, when store clerks are insolent, when law reforms fail to check crime, when moon rockets can't get off the ground, when widely used medicines are found to be poisons, when universities must teach freshmen to read, or when a hundred-ton airliner is brought down by a duck.

We see these malpractices and mishaps as unconnected accidents, inevitable results of human fallibility.

But one man says, "These occurrences are not accidents; they are simply the fruits of a system which, as I have shown, *develops, perpetuates and rewards incompetence.*"

The Newton of incompetence theory is a burly, black-haired, slow-spoken Canadian philosopher and iconoclast, Dr. Laurence J. Peter, who made his living as Assistant Professor of Education at the University of British Columbia until recently, when he moved down the coast to become a Professor of Education at the University of Southern California.

There is nothing incompetent about Dr. Peter. He is a successful author: his *Prescriptive Teaching* is a widely used text on the education of problem children. He built a house with his own hands, makes his own wine, is an expert cook, a skilled woodcarver, and an inventor (He created a new tool rack for schoolwork shops and perfected an apparatus for marking fifty exam papers at once.) Yet his chief claim to fame may be his founding of the science of hierarchiology.

> Hierarchiology [he says,] is the study of hierarchies. "Hierarchy" originally meant "church government by clergy graded into ranks." The term now includes any organization whose members or employees are arranged by rank or grade.
>
> Early in life, I faced the problem of occupational incompetence. As a young schoolteacher I was shocked, baffled, to see so many knotheads as principals, inspectors and superintendents.
>
> I questioned older teachers. All I could find was that the knotheads, earlier in their career, had been capable, and that was why they had been promoted.
>
> Eventually I realized that the same phenomenon occurs in all trades and professions, because the same basic rule governs the climb through every hi-

Exemplification

erarchy. A competent employee is eligible for promotion, but incompetence is a bar to promotion. So an employee's final position must be one for which he is incompetent!

Suppose you own a drug-manufacturing firm, Perfect Pill Incorporated. Your foreman pill-roller dies of a perforated ulcer; you seek a replacement among the rank-and-file pill-rollers. Miss Cylinder, Mrs. Ellipse and Mr. Cube are variously incompetent and so don't qualify. You pick the best pill-roller, Mr. Sphere, and promote him to foreman.

Suppose Sphere proves highly competent in this new job: later, when deputy-works-manager Legree moves up one step, Sphere will take his place.

But if Sphere is incompetent as foreman, he won't be promoted again. He has reached what I call his *level of incompetence* and there he will stay till he retires.

An employee may, like Mr. Cube, reach his level of incompetence at the lowest rank: he is never promoted. It may take one promotion to place him at his level of incompetence; it may take a dozen. But, sooner or later, he does attain it.

Dr. Peter cites the case of the late General A. Jacks.* His hearty manner, informal dress, scorn for petty regulations and disregard for personal safety made him the idol of his men. He led them from victory to victory.

Had the war ended sooner, Jacks might have retired, covered in glory. But he was promoted to the rank of field marshal. Now he had to deal, not with fighting men, but with politicians of his own country, and with two punctilious Allied field marshals.

He quarreled with them all and took to spending whole days drunk, sulking in his trailer. The conduct of the war slipped out of his hands and into those of his subordinates.

The final promotion had brought him from doing what he *could* do, to attempting what he could not do. He had reached his level of incompetence.

The Jacks' case exemplifies the Peter Principle, the basic theorem of hierarchiology. *In a hierarchy each employee tends to rise to his level of incompetence: every post tends to be occupied by an employee incompetent to execute its duties.*

How is it, then, that any work is done at all? Peter says, "Work is done by people who have not yet attained final placement at their level of incompetence."

And how is it that we occasionally see a competent person at the very top of the hierarchy? "Simply because there are not enough ranks for him to have reached his level of incompetence: in other words, *in that hierarchy* there is no task beyond his abilities."

As a rule, such a prodigy of competence eventually sidesteps into another hierarchy—say from the Armed Forces into industry, from law to politics,

* It is Dr. Peter's usual practice to employ fictitious names in his case histories.

from business to government—and there finds his level of incompetence. A well-known example is Macbeth, a successful general, but an incompetent king.

In an unpublished monograph, *The Pathology of Success: Morbidity and Mortality at the Level of Incompetence,* Peter expands his theory to take in matters of health.

Certain physical conditions are associated with the final placement: peptic ulcers, high blood pressure, nervous disorders, migraine headaches, alcoholism, insomnia, obesity and cardiovascular complaints. Obviously such symptoms indicate the patient's constitutional incompetence for his level of responsibility.

Edgar Allan Poe, a highly competent writer, proved incompetent when raised to the rank of editor. He became "nervous in a very unusual degree," took to drink and then to drugs in a vain search for relief.

Such ailments, usually appearing two or more together, constitute the Final Placement Syndrome.

Medication and surgery are often prescribed for F.P.S. patients, but they miss the root cause of the condition. Psychoanalysis fails for the same reason. The analyst is probing into the patient's subconscious for Oedipus complex, castration-complex, penis-envy or whatnot, when the trouble really lies outside, in the patient's hierarchal placement.

Is there no escape? Must every worker reach his level of incompetence, suffer the miseries of Final Placement Syndrome and become a laughing stock for his behavioral or temperamental symptoms?

Peter describes two escape routes. The first is for a man who realizes that he has reached his level of incompetence, yet still wants to preserve health, self-respect and sanity.

Many an employee adjusts to final placement by the process of Substitution. Instead of executing his proper duties, he substitutes a set of irrelevant duties, and these self-imposed tasks he carries out to perfection.

A. L. Tredwell, assistant principal of a secondary school, was intellectually competent and maintained good relationships with teachers, students, and parents. He was promoted to principal. Soon it became clear that he lacked the finesse to deal with newspaper reporters, school-board members, and the district superintendent. He fell out of favor with the officials, and his school lost community support. Realizing consciously or subconsciously—it doesn't matter which—that he was incompetent for the proper duties of a principal, Tredwell *Substituted.* He developed an obsessive concern with the movement of students and staff about the school.

He drew complex plans of traffic-flow, had white lines painted on floors and arrows on walls, spent hours prowling the building looking for violations of his rules, and bombarded professional journals with articles about his scheme.

Tredwell's Substitution is a great success. He is active and contented now, and shows no sign of the Final Placement Syndrome.

Exemplification

Peter's alternate escape route is for the employee who is capably and happily doing his work and who wants to avoid ever reaching his level of incompetence.

Merely to *refuse* promotion seldom leads to happiness. It annoys one's superiors, rouses suspicion among one's peers, and shames one's wife and children. Few people can endure all that. So one must contrive never to be offered promotion.

The first step is to avoid asking, or seeming to ask, for it. The oft-heard complaint, "My job lacks challenge," is usually understood as showing desire for promotion. So don't give voice to such complaints!

The second step is described by Peter in his lecture, Creative Incompetence: "I have found some employees who are contented in their work, and who seem to be using effective means of maintaining their position."

Adam Greenaway, a gardener, happily tends the landscaped grounds of the Ideal Trivet Company. He is competent in all aspects of his work but one: He keeps losing delivery slips for goods received. He gives vague explanations such as "I must have planted the papers with the shrubs." Most important, he concealed the fact that he wanted to avoid promotion.

Lack of delivery slips so upset the accounting department that, when a new maintenance foreman was needed, Greenaway was not considered for the post.

Thus he could stay indefinitely at a level of competence and enjoy the keen personal satisfaction of regularly accomplishing useful work. Surely this offers as great a challenge as the traditional drive for higher ranks!

By his Darwinian Extension Theorem, Peter applies his Principle to the whole human race. Man may go the way of the dinosaur and the sabre-tooth tiger. Those beasts were destroyed by excessive development of the qualities—bulk and fangs—that had originally favored their survival. Man's cleverness was originally a survival characteristic, but now he has become clever enough to destroy himself. If he takes that step, he will achieve his ultimate level of incompetence, in proving himself unfit to live.

"Man's one hope," says Peter, "lies in hierarchiology. I feel that it will soon be recognized as the supreme science. Earlier sociological studies have insufficiently recognized man's hierarchal nature."

A knowledge of the Peter Principle becomes more and more important as hierarchal systems becomes stronger. Government and education are prime examples. Both already swollen, both expanding their demands for money and manpower, both extending their influence as more people stay longer in school, and as government controls more functions of life. Even industry, once a stronghold of individualism, is largely an aggregation of hierarchies. My point is that man ought to be using the hierarchal system for his benefit. But he can't possibly use it unless he understands it, and to do that he must understand the Peter Principle. Failing such understanding, the system will destroy the individuals who comprise it.

The Peter Principle 253

Many people accept the Peter Principle on first hearing. It sounds so obvious, so like common sense; it explains so aptly a group of hitherto mystifying phenomena.

In academic circles, however, the Principle has made little impression. A few of Peter's subordinates when he was at the University of British Columbia grasped it, but none of his superiors. Some of them saw it as a humorous trifle, others as sociological heresy. Said Peter at the time: "I'm neither primarily funny or unfunny. I study society scientifically because I must live in it. I present my findings to you because they describe the world you live in."

> Anyway, I'm too busy to worry much about what others think of me. I teach future schoolteachers how to work with handicapped and disturbed children. I'm pursuing two fascinating lines of research: into autism, a profound emotional disorder in which children have no sense of self, and no ability to learn by experience; and into developmental dyslexia, an inability to recognize printed words that often, tragically, pins a "mentally retarded" label on a genuinely intelligent child. It's all deeply satisfying: I'm about as happy in my work as anyone I know.

The thought then occurred that Peter's hierarchiology might, just might, be *his* form of Creative Incompetence—a means of making himself slightly suspect, and so avoiding an unwanted academic promotion.

"No, no! Of course not!" said the doctor. "But even if it were, of course I wouldn't admit it!"

Questions

1 Would Hull's article appeal to a general audience? Why, or why not?

2 Does the passage of time since the publication of the article (1967) reduce its appeal? Why, or why not?

3 Is the inclusion of many excerpts from the book an effective use of example? Explain.

4 What rhetorical techniques other than exemplification are used in the article?

Truth and Consequences

Nora Ephron

Nora Ephron is a professional journalist who lives in New York. She has written for many of the country's major publications, including Esquire, Ms., New York, The New York Times Book Review, The New Yorker, *and* Rolling Stone.

Ephron begins her "Truth and Consequences" with an example meant to establish a principle she will defend throughout the essay; this example does not carry the highly charged political and emotional connotations that the examples she will use later do. The principle it helps to establish is that writers should be objective, observe clearly, and tell the truth about what they see; they should not color the truth by omission of facts or events they have observed, even at the expense of a cause they believe in. Ephron's cause is feminism, and her essay illustrates, primarily through examples drawn from personal experience, how difficult the principle is to adhere to. Each example is a situation in which Ephron was forced to make a choice between protecting the image of the women's movement and telling the bald truth.

The first example shows how, in the early days of "the movement," when various issues were still relatively undefined, some rather amusing non sequiturs occurred. Ephron's point here is not that the movement was ridiculous, but that it could be made to appear so if as an objective observer, she reported every conversation, every incident she witnessed.

The next example relates a problem that arose when the movement tried to get Shirley Chisholm nominated for Vice President. The leaders had given the wrong date as the deadline for submitting petitions in support of Chisholm's candidacy. Ephron, as a feminist, found herself in conflict with her own principle of objectivity, and she explains how she failed to restrain her impulse to correct the error.

The third example works in a somewhat different way. Ephron finds that ideas she admires as a feminist are so poorly presented that she must again confront the choice: should she tell the truth? How can she really tell the whole truth? Her final example is the most clear-cut. A fellow reporter, a feminist, deliberately withheld information because it would hurt the movement. Ephron is critical, and properly so.

These examples are lengthy, and at first appear to have little purpose beyond simple support. When we reach the final example, however, we recognize the parallel to the introductory example, the critical factor being the attitude of the reporter in each case. That recognition leads us to look at the examples cumulatively and to see that, indeed, Ephron is telling the reader something important, not only about the journalistic profession but about the women's movement. Each institution is strong enough not to be coddled.

Ephron writes in this essay primarily for women, but the issue she confronts has relevance for any reader. Her purpose is to explore the often paradoxical relationship between truth and falsehood.

I read something in a reporting piece years ago that made a profound impression on me. The way I remember the incident (which probably has almost nothing to do with what actually happened) is this: a group of pathetically naïve out-of-towners are in New York for a week and want very much to go to Coney Island. They go to Times Square to take the subway, but instead of taking the train to Brooklyn, they take an uptown train to the Bronx. And what knocked me out about that incident was that the reporter involved had been cool enough and detached enough and professional enough and (I could not help thinking) cruel enough to let this hopeless group take the wrong train. I could never have done it. And when I read the article, I was disturbed and sorry that I could not: the story is a whole lot better when they take the wrong train.

When I first read that, I was a newspaper reporter, and I still had some illusions about objectivity—and certainly about that thing that has come to be known as participatory journalism; I believed that reporters had no business getting really involved in what they were writing about. Which did not seem to me to be a problem at the time. A good part of the reason I became a newspaper reporter was that I was much too cynical and detached to become involved in anything; I was temperamentally suited to be a witness to events. Or so I told myself.

And now things have changed. I would still hate to be described as a participatory journalist; but I am a writer and I am a feminist, and the two seem to be constantly in conflict.

The problem, I'm afraid, is that as a writer my commitment is to something that, God help me, I think of as The Truth, and as a feminist my commitment is to the women's movement. And ever since I became loosely involved with it, it has seemed to me one of the recurring ironies of this movement that there is no way to tell the truth about it without, in some small way, seeming to hurt it. The first dim awareness I had of this was during an episode that has become known as the *Ladies' Home Journal* action. A couple of years ago, as you may remember, a group of feminists sat in at the offices of *Journal* editor John Mack Carter to protest the antediluvian editorial content of his magazine; to their shock, Carter acceded to their main demand, and gave them ten pages of their own in the *Journal,* and $10,000. Shortly thereafter, I was asked if I would help "edit" the articles

antediluvian literally, before the flood; thus, something hopelessly outdated

that were being written for the section—I put edit in quotes, because what we were really doing was rewriting them—and I began to sit in on a series of meetings with movement leaders that I found alternatingly fascinating, horrifying, and hilarious. The moment I treasured most occurred when the first draft of the article on sex was read aloud. The article was a conversation by five feminists. The first woman to speak began, I thought, quite reasonably. "I find," she said, "that as I have grown more aware of who I am, I have grown more in touch with my sexuality." The second woman—and you must remember that this was supposed to be a conversation—then said, "I have never had any sensitivity in my vagina." It seemed to me that the only possible remark a third person might contribute was "Coffee, tea, or milk?"— there was no other way to turn it into a sensible exchange. Anyway, when the incident happened, I told it to several friends, who all laughed and loved the story as much as I did. But the difference was that they thought I was telling the story in order to make the movement sound silly, whereas I was telling the story simply in order to describe what was going on.

Years pass, and it is 1972 and I am at the Democratic Convention in Miami attending a rump, half-secret meeting: a group of Betty Friedan's followers are trying to organize a drive to make Shirley Chisholm Vice-President. Friedan is not here, but Jacqui Ceballos, a leader in N.O.W., *is,* and it is instantly apparent to the journalists in the room that she does not know what she is talking about. It is Monday afternoon and she is telling the group of partisans assembled in this dingy hotel room that petitions supporting Chisholm's Vice-Presidential candidacy must be in at the National Committee by Tuesday afternoon. But the President won't be nominated until Wednesday night; clearly the Vice-Presidential petitions do not have to be filed until the next day. I am supposed to be a reporter here and let things happen. I am supposed to let them take the wrong train. But I can't, and my hand is up, and I am saying that they must be wrong, they must have gotten the wrong information, there's no need to rush the petitions, they can't be due until Thursday. Afterward, I walk out onto Collins Avenue with a fellow journalist/feminist who has managed to keep her mouth shut. "I guess I got a little carried away in there," I say guiltily. "I guess you did," she replies. (The next night, at the convention debate on abortion, there are women reporters so passionately involved in the issue that they are lobbying the delegates. I feel slightly less guilty. But not much.)

To give you another example, a book comes in for review. I am on the list now, The Woman List, and the books come in all the time. Novels by women. Nonfiction books about women and the women's movement. The apparently endless number of movement-oriented and movement-inspired anthologies on feminism; the even more endless number of anthologies on the role of the family or the future of the family or the decline of the family. I take up a book, a book I think might make a column. It is *Women and Madness,* by Phyllis Chesler. I agree with the book politically. What Chesler is saying is that the psychological profession has always applied a double standard when dealing with women; that psychological definitions of madness have been dictated by what men believe women's role ought to be; and this is wrong. Right on, Phyllis. But here is the book: it is badly written and self-indulgent, and the research seems to me to be full of holes. If I say this, though, I will hurt the book politically, provide a way for people who want to dismiss Chesler's conclusions to ignore them entirely. On the other hand, if I fail to say that there are problems with the book, I'm applying a double standard of my own, treating works that are important to the movement differently from others: babying them, tending to gloss over their faults, gentling the author as if she and her book were somehow incapable of withstanding a single carping clause. *Her heart is in the right place; why knock her when there are so many truly evil books around?* This is what is known in the women's movement as sisterhood, and it is good politics, I suppose, but it doesn't make for good criticism. Or honesty. Or the truth. (Furthermore, it is every bit as condescending as the sort of criticism men apply to books about women these days—that unconsciously patronizing tone that treats books by and about women as some sort of sub-genre of literature, outside the mainstream, not quite relevant, interesting really, how-these-women-do-go-on-and-we-really-must-try-to-understand-what-they-are-getting-at-whatever-it-is.)

I will tell you one more story to the point—though this one is not about me. A year and a half ago, some women from the Los Angeles Self-Help Clinic came to New York to demonstrate do-it-yourself gynecology and performed an abortion onstage using a controversial device called the Karman cannula. Subsequently, the woman on whom the abortion had been performed developed a serious infection and had to go into the hospital for a D and C. One of the reporters covering the story, a feminist, found out about the infection, but she decided not to make the fact public, because she thought that to do so might hurt the self-help movement. When I heard about it, I was appalled; I was more appalled when I realized that I understood why she had done it.

But I cannot excuse that kind of self-censorship, either in that reporter or in myself. I think that many of us in this awkward position worry too much about what the movement will think and how what we write will affect the movement. In fact, the movement is nothing more than an amorphous blob of individual women and groups, most of whom disagree with each other. In fact, no amount of criticism of the movement will stop its forward momentum. In fact, I am intelligent enough to know that nothing I write really matters in any significant way to any of it. And knowing all this, I worry. I am a writer. I am a feminist. When I manage, from time to time, to overcome my political leanings and get at the truth, I feel a little better. And then I worry some more.

258   *Exemplification*

Questions

1 Explain the relationship between the first example and the last. What is the rhetorical effect of the parallel between these examples?

2 What is the rhetorical purpose of the examples Ephron uses? How do you know?

3 Try to differentiate the essay's effects on several different audiences. Would it appeal to readers of *Ms.?* of *Esquire?* of *The New Yorker?* Would it appeal to Phyllis Schlaffley's adherents?

4 What rhetorical techniques does Ephron use besides exemplification?

Complexity and Pomposity— Mostly Complexity

John O'Hayre

John O'Hayre was an employee of the Department of the Interior's Bureau of Land Management in Denver, Colorado, during the 1960s. He wrote the pamphlet Gobbledygook Has Gotta Go *as a manual to help BLM employees write more clearly.*

O'Hayre's entertaining essay uses example as its principal method of development. The majority of the essay is devoted to an analysis of examples of complexity and pomposity occurring in BLM reports, memos, and news releases. For each example of gobbledygook O'Hayre provides a revision which states the idea in clear, simple, and direct language.

O'Hayre's main point is to show that clear communication is more important than showing off with big words. Big words are not evil in themselves; they become a problem only when they are too often or improperly used. Each of the examples O'Hayre cites represents a particularly awful abuse of language. Some of the errors result from a failure to keep the relationships between words, clauses, and phrases simple and logical; some from repetition; and some from the tying together of ideas that are not really related.

The essay is addressed to employees of the Bureau of Land Management, who could be expected to be familiar with the ideas the writers of the examples were attempting to express. But this special background is not essential to the reader. We can all benefit from the essay's focus on the tendency of people to try to impress with their vocabulary and from its reminder that simple writing is usually the most effective kind.

One thing is clear about BLM writing: It's neither clear nor simple; most of it is complex and pompous. This shouldn't upset anyone. It's an indisputable fact. And all we have to do to know it is to read critically what BLM writes normally.

But BLM is not alone with its complexity and pomposity. These same gobbledygook factors bother other government agencies, businesses, and industries every day. What, exactly, do these two, two-syllable words mean in writing?

They mean:

(1) Complex:—NOT simple . . . . knotty, tangled.

(2) Pompous:—NOT natural . . . . . stilted, stuffy.

And here are a few of the terms used by experts to describe complex and pompous prose:

. . . . falsely formalistic . . . . cluttered with officialese . . . . written to impress, not express . . . . ostentatious . . . . bookish . . . . priggish . . . . unnatural . . . bearing complexity as the badge of wisdom . . . . stuffed with language of incredible specific gravity.

If we are complex and pompous in our writing, and we are, why are we? There are many reasons, of course—poor training in college, bad thinking habits, slavish imitation of other bad writing, wrong ideas about readers, lack of hard work, a confusion between dignity and pomposity, and a failure to understand that wisdom goes arm-in-arm with simplicity.

Professor E. A. Stauffen, who agreed that complexity and pomposity are the biggest killers of the prose cat, put his chalk on two basic errors that too many people make. They believe:

(1) That an educated man automatically learns how to write well as he works his way through college;

(2) That good writing is easy.

As for *Error No. 1,* he said:

"To prove that 95 percent of the college graduates don't know how to write is easy. All you have to do is read them. If that doesn't prove to you they can't write, then it proves to me you can't read!"

Of *Error No. 2,* he said:

"If you think good writing comes easy, then you either don't write, or if you do, you don't know how yet. Good writing is plain, hard, sweaty work."

As you go through our BLM writing samples, ask yourself if they sound like:

Reading made *easy* by HARD work? Or—

Reading made *hard* by EASY work?

And ask yourself this, too: Are these BLM samples clear and simple writing? Or are they complex and pompous?

But before we get into our samples, let's make a point:

Complexity and pomposity are two of the biggest fog factors we have in our writing. They kill quick and they kill dead, and they are usually found together. In fact, trying to separate complexity from pomposity is almost impossible, for in a sense, one is the other. But for our purposes, we'll look at them separately.

Complexity is primarily, but not exclusively, a mechanical failure. It results from not keeping the relationship between words, phrases and clauses simple and logical. It usually comes about when we pack too many facts and ideas into a single sentence; when we thread together too many related objects or effects.

The following sentence from a BLM news release shows this kind of complexity at work:

> This land exchange is mutually beneficial through elimination of problems connected with the administration of scattered tracts by consolidating larger blocks of land for each agency (BLM and the State).

On the surface this sentence doesn't look too bad, but, like it or not—it reads hard—and there's no reason why it should. It's one simple sentence, 26 words, 6 hard words, several near hard words, and a writer's grade of 60.

If you break this sentence down, you'll find that what really fogs it up are its numerous polysyllabic prepositional phrases—seven in all—tacked on to and piled high after its opening independent clause. Like this:

> This land exchange is mutually beneficial . . . through . . . of . . . with . . . of . . . by . . . of . . . for. . . .

And there, in this threading together of too many related objects lies the complexity. And that means gobbledygook!

How much simpler it would have been this way:

> This exchange makes it easier for both agencies (BLM and the State) to manage their own lands. In trading their hard-to-manage scattered tracts, they were able to block up their own larger holdings.

We now have 2 sentences (up from 1), 30 words (up from 26), 1 hard word (down from 6), and a writer's grade of 73 (up from 60).

Now here's another example of complexity that is caused primarily by mechanical failure. This time the fog is not so much a result of threading together related objects as of fumbling together logically unrelated objects. Once again, notice the big words; these cause complexity and show pomposity.

> Area mineral classification will be completed to provide availability of currently valuable mineral resources, as well as presently unfavorable mineral occurrences for expanding demands as these occurrences become potentially valuable.

One sentence, 30 words, 14 hard words, and a writer's grade of 43. This would be far too low—even if it made sense!

Eight different BLM'ers read this sentence three times, and not one thought it made sense. Each agreed it was all right, though stuffy, through the 14th word. But not a person could untangle the final 16.

Here's how we untangled, through context, this slough of illogical and illogically placed modifiers:

> Mineral classifications will be made by areas; and these will show resources that are valuable now and those that might become valuable in the future.

We submitted our version to the same eight people and said, "We think this may be what the writer meant."

They agreed: "It probably is; at least it makes sense now."

However, we still wouldn't swear to what we think the writer was saying when he wrote:

> . . . . as well as (to show) presently unfavorable mineral occurrences for expanding demands as these occurrences become potentially valuable.

Maybe we can see what happened. The writer decided he needed to use "unfavorable" and "potential" to make his meaning clear and had these words running around in his head. But when he got them down on paper, he got them down wrong, in the wrong place and modifying the wrong words.

First he made "presently unfavorable" modify "mineral occurrences for expanding demands." We simply couldn't understand what an "unfavorable mineral occurrence" was, or what "for expanding demands" meant. We finally decided that what the writer really meant to do was tie in "unfavorable" with "today's market," not with "mineral occurrences."

Second, the writer didn't mean "as these occurrences become *potentially* valuable." They're that already. What he meant was "as these *potentially* valuable occurrences" become *actually* valuable on *"the expanding market."*

And the difference between what he meant to say and what he did say is as great as the difference between an atom and an atom bomb. That's where the complexity lies. The sentence is complex from the point of view of mechanical structure, big word use, and wrong word use.

Here's another sample of complexity at its amazing best. It was brought to us by someone who honestly didn't think it was for real. It was booked as a digest of BLM directives on JCC camps, but it is neither a digest nor a directive!

> Section 103 authorizes the Director of the Office of Economic Opportunity to:
>
> (a) enter into agreement with any Federal, State, or local agency or private organization for the establishment and operation, in rural and urban areas, of conservation camps and training centers, and for the provision of necessary facilities and services, including agreements with agencies charged

with the responsibility of conserving, developing, and managing the public natural resources of the nation and with protecting the public recreational areas, whereby the Corps enrollees may be utilized by such agencies in carrying out, under the immediate supervision of such agencies, programs planned by such agencies to carry out such responsibilities.

All the things that can go into making fog this sentence has in abundance. It is one complex sentence, 95 words, 28 hard words, and a ridiculous writer's grade of 40. See what the writer forced the reader to go through if meaning was to be unscrambled. Remember: When we read a sentence, we must keep suspended in our head ALL its ideas and ALL the various shades of meaning that modifiers give these ideas. Then when the end is reached, we must gather them together and drop them as ONE into our mind to get proper and precise meaning.

Unfortunately, the human mind—even a finely honed and disciplined one—can handle only so many things at one time before it has to stop, assemble, and conclude. Our writer threw two main ideas at us, which was all right, but then he modified—gave different shades of meaning to these 2 ideas a total of 21 different times, in 18 prepositional phrases, 7 of which were compound, and 3 participle phrases. This is a total of 30 separate distinctions we were supposed to keep suspended in proper order before our minds assembled them into an orderly conclusion.

If the real meanness of such a sentence is not yet apparent, put it on a balance board—diagram it. Assign a weight of 1 pound to each sentence element. You'll find that you have 29 pounds on the right side of the teeter-totter and 1 pound on the left. And to add to the confusion, the 29 elements on the right side are mixed together with about as much order as a can of worms.

Nor are these all the fog factors in this sentence. One more that's serious enough to isolate is the curious batch of careless repetition that ferments around the words "such" and "agencies" and "responsibilities." This all takes place in the latter half of the sentence and there is no excuse for it.

Let's strip the last part of the sentence down to point up the gluey repetition:

. . . (authorized to make agreements) . . .
. . . including agreements with agencies charged with the (conservation) responsibility . . . whereby Corps enrollees may be utilized by such agencies in carrying out . . . under supervision of such agencies . . . the programs planned by such agencies . . . to carry out such responsibilities.

What can anyone say about such a sentence fragment as this—such variant repetition? . . . such complex structure? There's no defense of it . . . none.

What our writer meant to tell his readers in this latter half-sentence was this:

. . . make agreements with conservation agencies . . . to supervise and use JCC enrollees . . . on projects these agencies have on public lands.

We went back through this whole sentence to see what could be done with a blue pencil. This helped some, but it was a little like getting a sick man's fever down from 114 to 110—it's still going to kill him! So we rewrote the sentence:

Section 103 authorizes the OEO Director to:
    (a)make agreements with any government agency or private group to set up and operate JCC camps and training centers; and make agreements with conservation agencies to use and supervise Corps enrollees on projects these agencies have on public lands.

And that's really all he tried to say—or need to.

And now let's look at one more sample of complexity caused primarily by ridiculous repetition:

Programing for 3 years beyond the program is required in the preparation of the Range Conservation and Development Programs and may be required for other programs for selected items of information. If the programing is needed for years subsequent to the program year, this requirement, along with the specific program elements to be programed, will be stated in the Program Advice.

In this we have two sentences, 61 words, 9 hard words, and a writer's grade of 46. Of course the thing that really makes this sentence complex and fog-filled is the insipid repetition of the word "program" nine times. This shows lack of consideration for the reader and a lack of work by the writer.

Can you imagine anybody giving directions like that to anyone on how to prepare anything? And please don't say—"But samples like these are exceptions!" They aren't! And we've been telling each other they are far too long—as we puddle through one another's gruely gobbledygook day after day.

Compare the original directive to this rewrite:

When you prepare your RC&D program for the year, you'll have to make projections for three additional years. You may also have to do the same for certain parts of other programs. If so, we'll tell you what these are in our Program Advice.

Now it reads easily and naturally. This is because of what we call a "loose and personal style," which we'll get around to some other time. Right now we don't even want to mention being warm and friendly and human. Somehow, the thought of writing that way scares some "dignified" people half to death!

And now we come to a sample of that kind of writing in which it is impossible to draw the line between complexity and pomposity:

insipid flavorless, uninteresting

           Exemplification

The adopted measure will broaden the exchange provisions of the Taylor Grazing Act and make them a flexible, efficient, and economical instrument facilitating the consolidating and management of the public domain lands.

There's simply no sense in writing like that unless you're purposely trying to be misunderstood. See if our rewrite doesn't say the same thing simply and without the pretentious puff and pomp:

This change in the regulations will make it easier for BLM to consolidate and manage the public lands under its care.

Here's another sample in which complexity and pomposity struggle to stay even. It's short, that's true. Which proves that some of us don't even have to work long or hard to be complex and pompous. We've done it so long it's now natural—like smoking a cigarette with our after-dinner coffee.

This sample was taken from a BLM report that had 64 pages and thousands of words, most of which carried the same credentials as our sample—complexity and pomposity. Read it and see:

Endemic insect populations cause little-realized amounts of damage to forage and timber.

This sentence actually contains a wrong but common use of understatement, but we won't bother with that right now. What primarily concerns us here is stuffiness, which is pomposity, which is gobbledygook. See how the atmosphere of this short sentence is changed by rewriting it this way:

Native insects do more damage to trees and grass than we realize.

It's true we cut down by only one little word, but there is a very big difference between the two sentences, even if we don't count the error in the original. This difference deals with tone and naturalness—atmosphere.

Which one sounds easy and natural—like a forester-friend of yours telling you what the bugs are doing to the trees and grass? And which one sounds stuffy and pompous—like a superior of yours launching into an academic lecture on the barkiverous proclivities of facinorous endemic insect populations and what the infestations of these populations are resulting in the currently available forage and timber species that are not being administered by appropriate silvicultural practices or under adequate range protective procedures?

Ridiculous? You said it! But not uncommon. In fact, the opposite—very common.

For more proof, if anybody needs it, try this actual BLM sentence on for size:

Much of an organization's effectiveness depends upon the adequacy of the data and information with which its employees work. The multifarious overlapping planning units have produced fragmented data, oriented toward single uses of land, and as these data were used by employees organized into single use office groupings, the problem was exacerbated.

Do you like that better?

Questions

1 What is the tone of the essay? How does the tone help the reader understand the points O'Hayre is making?
2 Do you think O'Hayre's essay is clear and understandable? Why, or why not?
3 What rhetorical techniques does O'Hayre use besides exemplification?
4 Could O'Hayre's essay have been written for different audiences? If so, name two. What would have to be done to the essay to make it suitable for each audience?

Nursing Communication: Nurse's Notes And Accurate Diagnosis

Carolyn M. Bell

Carolyn M. Bell, a graduate of the University of Texas and the Catholic University of America, is an assistant professor of nursing at Texas Woman's University; she is also working toward a doctorate in nursing.

In the following selection, Bell uses example in a traditional way to reinforce points she has introduced in generalizations. Her examples are of several kinds: an appositive construction in the second paragraph explains what she means by "learned nurses"; in the sixth paragraph there is a direct illustration of what an old-fashioned nursing entry probably looked like; in the next, a typical present-day entry; and in paragraphs ten, eleven, and twelve, examples of the type of notational system Bell is describing in each paragraph.

Bell expected her reader to be a freshman-level nursing student, and the purpose of her essay is two-fold: she wants to let this student know that, while nursing is a scientific occupation, it nevertheless involves controversy; she also wants to show that the way nurses communicate information about a patient is dictated to a large extent by both their positions on controversial matters and the position of the institutions for which they work.

When I chose to enroll in rhetoric as a minor during my doctoral program in nursing, I had presumed that I would learn the techniques to unravel a continuing debate in nursing. The nursing profession is divided on what the basic educational preparation of a professional nurse should be, what is included in the professional practice of nursing, and what nonprofessional levels of personnel should work under the supervision of the professional nurse for optimal patient care. (In one arena now patients are not called patients but are called clients.) A closely allied question concerns the impact of advances in medical technology and of the increasing training of nurses in medical specialties upon the relationship of the nurse to the doctor in view of changes in the legal responsibility of professional nurses. Imagine my surprise when I found that there has been similar debate among rhetoricians and philosophers for centuries.

The learned nurses, those who are principally teachers and administrators of nursing departments of health care facilities, opine that professional nurses must be educated in a college or university. These are typically called generic baccalaureate programs. Nurses who are trained in either junior colleges with an associate degree or in a hospital school with a diploma are called technical or bedside nurses, and must complete lower-division and varying upper-division requirements for the professional degree. All three types of nurses presently sit the same registration exam for licensure.

Interestingly, hospitals, where the majority of practicing nurses are employed, prefer to have the technically trained nurses as employees. During their training, there is a greater emphasis on the technical or psychomotor skills which a nurse commonly performs and thus less on liberal arts and the theoretical basis for professional nursing practice.

This difference of opinion is called the "entry into practice issue." Other issues that are debated by the learned include the feasibility and necessity of mandatory continuing education for all levels of nurses, the methods and utility of developing theories of nursing, the terminology for a taxonomy of nursing diagnoses, the preferable method of credentialing for the various levels of nursing practice, and the roles and functions of beginning and advanced levels of nursing practitioners.

The majority of nurses practicing in hospitals or other institutional settings are often removed from active concern for these issues. Communication is more functional, relating information about the patients in the nurse's care and about the nurse's activities; in fact, its very functionality makes it prime grist for the legal mills. At a recent mock trial presented to make practicing nurses aware of the current legal issues related to the practice of nursing, the attorneys stressed the legality of nurse's notes on patient's charts. The nurse should document in the nurse's notes promptly, thoroughly, and accurately the assessment of the patient's condition and any activities performed by the nurse for the patient. During the last few years, the responsibility of nurses has been increasing and increase in legal liability has paralleled that increase in responsibility. The "captain of the ship" status of the physician as responsible for the nurse has been overturned as a legal defense for the nurse.

In the past, traditional nursing training focused on the nurse's documentation of the nurse's activities and on the patient's responses to therapy. Any direct expression of a judgment about the patient's symptoms was to be avoided. It might be construed that the nurse was diagnosing the patient's illness, and diagnosing was what physicians did. The entry in the nurse's notes of "Urine appears red" would have been used when the urine was actually, and obviously to the nurse, bloody. The nurse could not state that the urine contained blood. Today, one would certainly question the nurse's competence if such an entry was made. Nurses trained in the old school often have difficulty in adjusting to the present expectations, not only of documenting but also of performance of some activities.

A typical entry in the nurse's notes for a patient in a general ward or unit of a hospital might be "Ate well. Up to BSC. Assisted c̄ AM care. No % SOB." Translated into common English, the entry means that the patient ate most of the food that was served on the meal trays while the nurse was on duty, got out of bed to use a bedside commode chair, was assisted in bathing and personal hygiene, and expressed no feelings of being short of breath. In nurse's notes, complete sentences are rarely used. The implied subject of all sentences is *the patient*. When some other person is intended, the entry will be different, as in "MD notified of chest pain," which actually means that the nurse who wrote the entry called the physician to discuss the chest pain that the patient was experiencing. Interestingly, the statement of the patient of any symptom is called a *complaint*. The use of "no %" means that the patient had no complaints of—sometimes the expression is used with no object for the preposition *of*, which I suppose means that *anything* should be inserted.

Acronyms and other forms of verbal and written shorthand are in frequent use. Most hospitals publish lists of accepted abbreviations for use in patient's charts. Some come from the Latin, like NPO, *nil per os*, for "nothing by mouth" and PRN, *pro re nata*, for "as the patient needs the treatment or medication." Others come from the acronyms for symptoms or machinery, like SOB for "shortness of breath" and IPPB for "intermittent positive pressure breathing machine." Being creative people, nurses make up their own terms in various units, depending on the types of illness the patients have who are usually admitted to that unit, making the uninitiated incapable of reading most nurse's notes without some translation.

Since the national accrediting agency (JCAH, of course) has decreed that a patient assessment statement be included in nurse's notes, there has been some controversy over the style(s) that should be used. Two are patterned after the "medical model" or the way that physicians write their notes. These are called either the systems model or the Problem-Oriented System. The third style is based on the nursing diagnosis.

In the systems model, the patient is considered as a composite of seven to ten physical systems, like the respiratory (breathing), cardiovascular (heart), etc., and psychological, sociocultural, and patient education systems. The nurse's notes are then entered under the headings describing the patient's symptoms and reactions in each of the systems. One might see: *"Neurological:* Awake, alert and oriented X3." (The patient is awake and answers questions which show that he knows who he is, where he is, and the approximate time.)

The Problem-Oriented System (POS) includes the determination of patient problems. Problems can be symptoms, diseases, and psychological or social conditions. Each entry in the nurse's notes is under a specific problem heading and includes the subjective and objective data about the patient, a statement of assessment, and a plan for assisting the patient to recover from or deal with the problem—obviously called SOAPing the problem. For example:

> #1 N & V (nausea and vomiting)
>   S "I can't keep anything in my stomach."
>   O Abdomen tender. BS increased. Vomited X2. Remains NPO. Medicated X2.
>   A Persistent vomiting, unrelieved by (medicine name)
>   P 1. Keep NPO
>   2. IV replacement of fluid lost. . . .

This means that the patient has not been relieved of vomiting, that he has a tender abdomen with an increased frequency of bowel sounds, that the nurse has given him a medicine two times during the shift, and that the nurse plans to continue replacing the volume of fluid lost by intravenous infusion that the doctor has ordered, while giving the patient nothing by mouth.

As I mentioned previously, nursing diagnosis is a controversial issue. Should the medical diagnosis be utilized? Should the nursing diagnosis include only those conditions that can be managed by nursing measures—without prescribing medications? Or should nurses prescribe medicines for commonly occurring, uncomplicated illnesses? Typically the nursing diagnosis includes some disturbance in normal activities of daily living and some specification of the presumed cause (etiology). Using the example of the problem above, the nursing diagnosis might be stated as "increased fluid loss related to increased gastrointestinal motility." Here the nurse denotes the major element of the patient's condition as fluid balance, not the vomiting. The entries in the nurse's notes could be related to the diagnosis, and the format is determined by each institution.

Nurses in each institution—hospital, college, or other type—select one of the styles or some combination of them for use. There is in-service training to be sure that all the nurses understand the method and the intent of the style selected. Then the rhetoric continues and the individual nurses often adapt the style to make minimal changes from whichever style was their original indoctrination in school.

Questions

1 What elements of Bell's essay would you like to see explained in greater detail? Why?

2 What other kinds of examples might Bell have used in this essay? For instance, can you find a place where an anecdote might have been useful? Where? Why?

3 What rhetorical techniques does Bell use besides exemplification?

Copyrights and Acknowledgments

Judy Syfers, for permission to reprint "Why I Want a Wife," by Judy Syfers, from *Ms.* magazine, Spring 1972.

Viking Penguin Inc., for "Computers," from *Lives of a Cell* by Lewis Thomas. Copyright © 1973 by the Massachusetts Medical Society. Originally appeared in the *New England Journal of Medicine.* Reprinted by permission of Viking Penguin Inc. And for "Work, Labor, and Play," from *A Certain World,* by W. H. Auden. Copyright © 1970 by W. H. Auden. Reprinted by permission of Viking Penguin Inc.

Sergeant Joseph Wilson, for permission to reprint "Real Cops, Not 'Reel' Cops," by Joseph Wilson.

Woman's Day, for "How to Get Your Money's Worth from Your Doctor," by Mike Oppenheim, M.D., from *Woman's Day,* March 10, 1981. Reprinted by permission of *Woman's Day* magazine. Copyright © 1981 by CBS Publications, the Consumer Publishing Division of CBS Inc.

Copyrights and Acknowledgments

NATIVE ❖ LATIN ❖ AMERICAN ❖ CULTURES

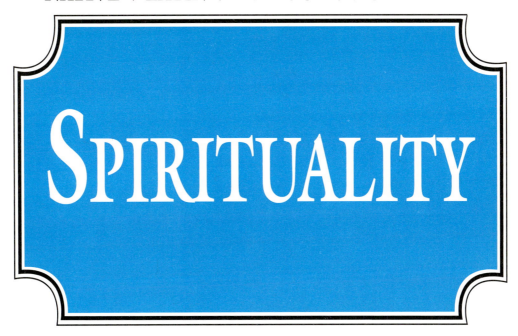

SPIRITUALITY

Victoria Sherrow

Series Editor
Robert Pickering, Ph.D.

ROURKE PUBLICATIONS, INC.
Vero Beach, Florida 32964

Printed in the United States of America.

A Blackbirch Graphics book.

Senior Editor: Tanya Lee Stone
Assistant Editor: Elizabeth Taylor
Design Director: Sonja Kalter

Library of Congress Cataloging-in-Publication Data

Sherrow, Victoria.
Spirituality/by Victoria Sherrow.
     p. cm. — (Native Latin American cultures)
     Includes bibliographical references and index.
     ISBN 0-86625-557-5
     1. Indians—Religion—Juvenile literature. 2. Latin America—Religious life and customs—Juvenile literature. I. Title. II. Series.
E59.R38S54   1995
299'.792—dc20   95-8490
                                        CIP
                                        AC

Contents

Introduction   *4*

Chapter 1   ❖   Northwestern Mexico   *7*

Chapter 2   ❖   The Central Valley of Mexico   *17*

Chapter 3   ❖   Southern Mexico and Central America   *29*

Chapter 4   ❖   The Caribbean   *37*

Chapter 5   ❖   South America   *45*

Chapter 6   ❖   The Amazon   *55*

Glossary   *61*

Further Reading   *62*

Index   *63*

Introduction

The towering temples and fierce warriors of the Aztecs, the sophisticated lords of the Maya, and the vast empire of the Inca that extended along the Andes are all images that come to mind when the native cultures of Mexico, Central America, and South America are mentioned. While these images are real, they are only a small part of the story of the indigenous peoples of the Americas. More important, there are hundreds of other cultures that are not as well known, but just as interesting. To explore the cultures of this huge area is to examine the great diversity and richness of humanity in the Americas.

This series on *Native Latin American Cultures* presents six books, each with a major theme: the arts, daily customs, spirituality, trade, tribal rules, and the invasion by Europeans. It focuses mainly on pre-Columbian times (before the arrival of Columbus in the New World) through about 1800. These books illustrate the ingenuity, resourcefulness, and unique characters of many cultures. While a variety of tribes share similarities, many are extremely different from one another.

It is important to remember that the Americas were home to people long before Europeans arrived. Archaeologists have uncovered sites as old as 12,000 years. Over the years, human cultures in every part of the Americas developed and evolved. Some native cultures died out, other peoples survived as hunter-gatherers, and still others grew to

❖

5

create huge empires. Many native languages were not recorded and, in some instances, they have been forgotten.

But other groups, such as the Maya, did record their
languages. Scientists are just now learning to read the
Mayan language. Mayan stories tell of the power and glory
of great rulers, heroic battles between city-states, and other
important events. Massive stone temples and ruins of cities
have survived from several cultures, giving us insight into
the past.

Many native cultures of the Americas exist today. Some
have blended with the modern cultures of their countries
while maintaining their traditional ways. Other, more remote groups exist much as they did several hundred years
ago. The books in the *Native Latin American Cultures*
series capture the richness of indigenous cultures of the
Americas, bringing past cultures alive and exploring those
that have survived.

Robert Pickering, Ph.D.
Department of Anthropology
Denver Museum of Natural History

Northwestern Mexico

Like other groups of indigenous (native) peoples through-out the Americas, each tribe in northwestern Mexico had its own special customs. All of the tribes, however, shared certain spiritual beliefs and had similar ceremonies. Their religions included numerous gods. Much of the land was dry, so many ceremonies aimed to "bring down the clouds," or make the rain come. In lands that were less dry, people still held ceremonies to ensure a good harvest.

Northwestern Mexico contains hot lowlands, dry deserts, and highlands with variable temperatures. In the western highlands are rivers that drain into the Gulf of California. Highland tribes included the Cahita, Cora, Huichol, Tepehuan, and Tarahumara peoples. Like most tribes in the region, these groups spoke languages from the Uto-Aztecan root. Uto-Aztecan languages were also spoken by tribes that lived in what is now the southwestern United States.

Opposite:
Saguaro cacti populate
the Sonoran Desert in
northwestern Mexico.
The Pima was one
tribe that made its
home in this region.

A Pima woman kneels in front of her home in a photograph that was taken by Edward Curtis in 1907.

In the hot lowlands lived the Pima, the Yaqui, and other tribes. The Pima lived in the Sonoran region that includes northwestern Mexico and parts of the United States—California, New Mexico, and Arizona. These tribes had contact with others living to the north of them.

The Cochimi and the Seri lived on the deserts of Baja (Lower) California and on the Sonoran coast. Unlike most of the tribes around them, the Seri spoke a Hokan language.

Supernatural Beings

The peoples of this region recognized more than a hundred deities. Many deities took the forms of animals. Others took part in creating the world. The Tarahumara believed that animals and human beings were made from clay and that, at the beginning, the earth was too close to the sun. In order to move the sun away, six spirit beings performed a special dance. Some regional creation stories also claimed that the world was once destroyed by a flood.

Deities in this region were usually linked to rain or to the health and needs of the people. The Cora believed that ancient spirits in the rocks and the hills controlled the rain clouds. Huichol rain gods appeared as snakes and lived in caves. Other serpent spirits were involved with springs and various other water sources. The Cora also believed that the "Aunt of Mother" controlled the fertility of the earth and brought rain. Fertility and rain deities were known as "Grandmothers" among the Huichol.

The sun god was very important. The Cora and Huichol believed that this god lived under the earth. The Tepehuan had a "Father Ruling Spirit" associated with the sun. This hero, or ruling man, fell from grace and goodness. He had to prove himself during a long journey to heaven. This ruling figure resembled an important Aztec deity, Quetzalcoatl. Because of this similarity, it is thought that ancient Tepehuan and Aztec peoples may have had contact with each other at some point.

Other male and female supernatural beings were connected with the heavenly bodies in the sky. There were also animal spirits. As in other parts of North America, a coyote spirit often had the role of a trickster. Deer and certain flowers were revered. The northern Tepehuan worshiped a spirit symbolized by the deer, a spirit that made the winds, and another that appeared as a light shining in the sky after someone's death.

Certain spirits were feared as evil forces. The Tarahumara, who lived in the highlands and canyons of what is present-day Chihuahua, believed in invisible devilish creatures, witches, and sorcerers. Some evil spirits were small, birdlike beings. Another evil being was fat and resembled a pig. It

This present-day Tarahumara home is situated in that tribe's ancestral homeland—the highlands of northwestern Mexico.

lived in a whirlpool inside a deep cave and tried to steal souls by causing great sickness and other troubles. The Tarahumara saw wind as a good spirit and whirlwinds as evil. Rainbows were thought to come from evil spirits in the underworld; shooting stars were thought to be flying sorcerers who wanted to steal souls.

Spiritual Leaders and Healers

People called shamans were the spiritual leaders of their tribes. Shamans sought to connect humans and the spirit world. They prophesied, or foretold, the future and led ceremonies. Sometimes they were asked to find lost objects or to choose names for newborns. Names might be linked to the seasons or to a deity with a special interest in a child. Names might also come to shamans in dreams. Shamans had a key role among the Seri and the Cochimi of the Sonoran coast. They received their power through dreams and visions.

A family seeking help would call a shaman to their home, where they would offer gifts to the gods. The shaman's ceremony would include chanting and shaking a special gourd in order to bring helpful spirits to the roof of the house.

Shamans were also healers. Diseases were thought to have spiritual causes. Illnesses were sent, perhaps, by gods who felt ignored or by dead relatives who wanted the company of the living. Illnesses might also arise from poor relationships with animals or because people had neglected their tribal customs. The Tepehuan and others thought that disease was caused by sorcery and witchcraft. The Tarahumara believed that the loss of one's soul or contact with evil animals or people could make one sick. Pima and Tarahumara shamans (who were male or female) often focused on one kind of disease, but would still attempt to cure several.

To treat disease, shamans chanted. Sometimes, other men and women of a tribe sang special songs and performed ritual dances, which might last all night. Treatment included blowing smoke on the sick person or sucking on the person's skin to remove bad spirits. Some shamans used herbs, but in certain tribes, people other than the shamans were experts in herb use. Most treatments lasted five days. (Many northwest tribes attached special importance to the number five.)

Some shamans ate peyote, a kind of cactus plant, during treatment rituals. Eating the dried top part of the plant can produce a dreamy or trancelike state. People of this region and the southwestern United States have used peyote in different ceremonies for thousands of years. Shamans used it in order to receive messages from the spirits and to understand and learn from their dreams.

If healing did not occur, members of a tribe might make a pilgrimage to the place where the angry god was thought to dwell, in order to make an offering. People also traveled to shrines, or holy places, at certain times of the year. Numerous caves and cliffs dot this region, and many were revered as dwelling places of the deities. Huichol shrines were located in certain caves.

Rites and Ceremonies

The native peoples of this region held ceremonies in order to praise, ask for help from, or thank the spirits. Ceremonies were less frequent during the busy seasons of planting and tending crops. After September, people had more time for religious events. At harvest time, from October to November, food and peyote were available for offerings and use in rituals. Ceremonial drinks were made from maize (also known as corn) and cactus fruits.

Some important ceremonies for fertility and thanksgiving, called *mitotes*, lasted for five days. The Cora held three all-night *mitotes* for the entire community, each of which related to a part of the growth cycle of maize, their main food. Prayers and fasting took place during the *mitotes*, and special dances were performed on the fifth night. At sunrise, people broke the fast. The southern Tepehuan ended their *mitotes* by eating a variety of foods that had been placed on an altar to the east of their dancing platform.

Some ceremonies, such as those celebrating the harvest, were joyful ones. The Green Corn Festival marked the ripening of the main crop. Children holding gourd rattles took part in the Huichol Squash Ceremony. Deer antlers were used to represent the deer deity, who was a messenger to other gods and sometimes a trickster. Offerings of green squash were made. At the Roasting Ears Ceremony, purple ears of maize were offered to the sun. The Parched Corn Ceremony included the ritual use of peyote.

At one Huichol ritual, shamans invited their deities to appear. Then they chanted a series of sacred stories that told the origins and purposes of the deities. The chants might last for days. The Tarahumara held rain dances to help crops grow. Music was played on flutes and drums. The Cora prayed to their Morning Star deity for bountiful crops.

Certain ceremonies, such as those for the dead, were quite solemn. Huichol rituals addressed the problems the people experienced, such as sickness and crop failure. Some Cahita ceremonies were associated with war. They held victory dances and a scalp-pole dance. Sometimes, objects made for these ceremonies were discarded afterward.

Ceremonies were often held to achieve particular goals, such as to bring rain. Here, a Tarahumara dancer uses ankle rattles made of moth cocoons, the sound of which could symbolize falling rain.

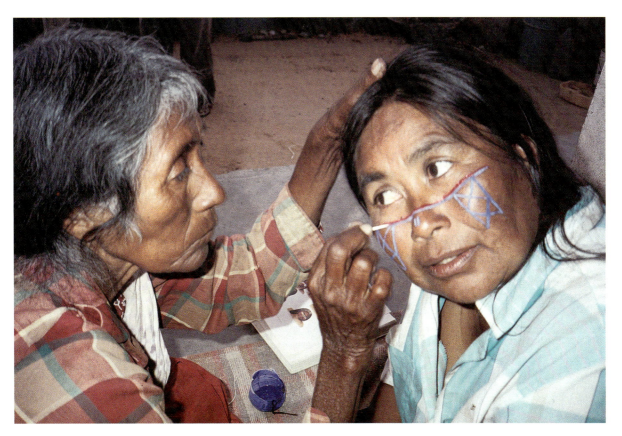

Two Seri women engage in a sacred face-painting ceremony in Sonora, Mexico.

The Yaqui had many ceremonies, mostly to honor the spirits. They focused less on the issues of rain or crops than many other tribes did. This was probably because they had more food in their region. Rainfall was sufficient to raise crops, many edible plants grew in the wild, and fish and shellfish were abundant. During the year, the Yaqui honored their ancestors during the Days of the Dead. Yaqui families kept their ancestors' names in a book that was placed on altars during ceremonies.

A number of ceremonies aimed to strengthen ties among people in the community. The Cora usually assembled large groups at their ceremonies. Often, their prayers were said, "for all of us, for all the Cora, for all people in the world."

During some of the ceremonies, people pledged to devote their lives to spiritual activities or to spend a certain amount of time as religious dancers or singers. This was believed to bring good fortune on the group. By neglecting the ceremonies, a person or a family could bring disaster on themselves or the whole community.

Sacred Objects

Ceremonial objects were made from reeds, bamboo, gourds, cotton fibers, wool yarn, and beads. A person might attach an object that represented a desired thing to a prayer arrow painted with a deity's personal symbol. Diamond-shaped figures were used to prevent a departed spirit from entering the world of the living by an unwanted path.

The images of deities were found on many objects. Rectangular figures made of sticks and yarn represented different gods. Their images were also sculpted from stone, and stone tablets were carved with religious symbols. Gourd bowls were decorated and used to carry certain requests to the gods they symbolized.

The Cora and Huichol gave their deities symbolic offerings made of sticks and yarn, prayer arrows, and gourd bowls. Food and drink were also offered to the gods. Shamans shook hawk plumes during chants and prayers. Seri and Cochimi shamans used small fetishes, or charms, to bring good fortune and ward off evil.

Many ceremonies made use of masks. Since animals were important spiritual figures, images of them frequently appeared in masks. Deer and other woodland animals were also portrayed in traditional dances.

Music was important. Among the Cora, it was reserved for ceremonies. Huichol instruments included log drums with deerskin tops, which shamans beat while they chanted.

Death and the Afterlife

Like many other people around the world, the native peoples of northwestern Mexico thought that human existence continued after death.

Certain rites were performed at the time of death to help the deceased move into the spirit world. Others were done to keep the spirit of the dead person from doing evil.

❖

15

The Huichol and the Cora held burial ceremonies five days after death. A shaman chanted during the ceremony. The Huichol asked their deer messenger spirit to be present. They believed that the soul went first to the spirits' dancing ground. On its return, it was cleansed in five hot pools of water. To pay for any misdeeds that the person may have committed while alive, his or her spirit was then obliged to eat rotten fruit and drink stale water.

At the Huichol burial ceremony, a shaman made offerings to the spirits and revealed how the deceased person's property would be distributed. The shaman gave the new spirit the choice of going again to the spirits' dancing ground or accompanying the sun. It was thought that most spirits would choose to go with the sun.

The Tarahumara believed that after death, a person's soul went to a heavenly place if he or she had lived a good life. The Tarahumara both feared and respected the souls of their dead. Certain animals were used to represent these souls: the owl for men, the fox for women, and the bird for children.

The Cora were buried in caves, with their heads facing west. At the burial ceremonies, a shaman summoned the spirit, which was thought to linger in the house. The spirit was sent off with the shaman's prayers and the family's farewells. The shaman then cleansed the house with holy water and a prayer stick. The Cora believed that souls went to a round hill full of caves, far to the northwest. There the dead lived and danced. However, evil souls went to a fiery place of punishment under the earth or sea.

The Tepehuan believed that a dead person's soul stayed in the house for a month, after which it went to a place in the sky. It left during a special good-bye party, when the deceased's finest clothing was laid out, along with food for the trip to the afterworld. People then vacated the house, lest the soul return to do harm.

Chapter

2

The Central Valley of Mexico

The Aztecs, who built their empire in the central valley of Mexico, had complex ideas about the universe and their place in it. Their spiritual life was elaborate, with rich ceremonies held in grand buildings. They believed in more than 1,600 deities.

Cultural roots of the Aztecs grew over a period of many centuries, starting with the Olmecs in about 1500 B.C. until the Spanish invaders arrived in the valley of Mexico in 1519. The customs of the groups of people who had lived in the region formed the basis of Aztec spiritual life.

Opposite:
In this Toltec sculpture, the god Quetzalcoatl rises from the jaws of the earth, as represented by the coyote.

Ancient Roots

In 1500 B.C., people called the Olmecs lived in southeastern Mexico. They built a great culture that eventually influenced the Aztecs. The Olmec believed in many deities.

They built flat-topped pyramids as temples for their gods and goddesses, as well as ceremonial centers that people visited for spiritual reasons.

The warlike Toltecs came to power from A.D. 750 to 900. They constructed fine pyramids to the gods in their capital city, Tula. Tula was overcome in 1168, but many Toltecs remained. Toltec legends speak of the power of nature. Many of their gods were animals or were associated with other things in nature.

Their most important god was Quetzalcoatl, or the Plumed Serpent. He may have been based on a real-life Toltec leader. Quetzalcoatl had charge of the wind, maize, and the morning star. Thrones for him were made of gold, silver, and precious stones. High priests paid him homage. The largest building in Tula, the Temple of the Morning Star, was a religious pyramid. The eagle was another important Toltec spiritual symbol and was associated with the sun.

There are signs that the Toltecs made animal and human sacrifices to their gods. Scientists have excavated Toltec sites and have found stones with pictures of men holding up the hearts of human sacrificial victims.

After the Aztec people settled in the valley of Mexico around 1325, they gradually became more powerful than other neighboring groups, such as the Tepanec and the Totonac. After conquering a tribe, the Aztecs would often take statues of that tribe's deities back to their own temples and incorporate these gods into their spiritual customs.

Aztec Creation Stories

In the Aztec version of creation, a god and a goddess worked together to create the earth. They were the Lord of Duality (Ometecuhtli) and the Lady of Duality (Omecihautl). Two of their four sons went on to create other gods and human beings, animals, fish, birds, and other things of the earth and sky.

The Aztecs believed that the process of creation took place four times. Each time the world was created, it was then destroyed by a flood, a hurricane, or another calamity. Then a fifth world began, ruled by the sun god, Tonatiuh. In order to keep the fifth world and its sun from being destroyed, the Aztecs held a New Fire Ceremony every fifty-two years. Without this ceremony, they believed, the fifth sun and the fifth world would be destroyed. (As it did for the tribes of northwestern Mexico, the number five had special meaning for the Aztecs.)

The Aztecs viewed life as unpredictable and difficult. Many of their legends, stories, and poems describe the misfortunes and suffering of life.

The Afterlife

The Aztecs believed that people had invisible souls that lived on after death. They visualized the world as flat, with thirteen heavens in the sky above and nine hells in the underworld below. After death, people's souls wandered until they reached the place in which they deserved to remain. The highest heaven was thought to be located close to the sun.

The Aztecs believed that one's fate after death depended greatly on how a person had died. Those who had died in childbirth or battle, and those who had served as sacrifices to the gods, were believed to reach the highest heaven.

Supernatural Forces

The Aztecs felt that supernatural beings were responsible for events that occurred in nature. Deities brought the sunlight and the rain that produced crops. These beings also brought the floods, droughts, and earthquakes that could destroy all things. When a disaster occurred, the Aztecs feared it was a sign that the gods were very upset. They tried even harder to please them, with more sacrifices and ceremonies.

The goddess of maize, Xilonen, is represented in this Aztec stone sculpture.

One of their chief gods was Huitzilopochtli (Hummingbird on the Left, or Blue Hummingbird). Priests hoped to see this god in visions and to hear his answers to their questions. Legend said that it was Huitzilopochtli who had told the wandering Aztec people where they should settle in the valley of Mexico.

Certain gods ruled the crops, flowers, fire, and other areas of Aztec life. Various trades and professions had particular gods as patrons. The sun god was considered to be superior to the moon god. Often, gods had more than one role and could appear in different forms.

People kept stone images of gods in their homes. One of the female deities—Xilonen, the young goddess of maize—had a friendly face. People often chose to put a clay image of Xilonen in the corner of the home reserved for the gods. Around such images, they might place flowers or leaves.

Some gods were viewed as cruel and fearsome. Smoking Mirror had jaguar claws and a threatening expression. Tlaloc, the god of rain and fertility, had the fangs and tongue of a serpent. His mouth was formed by two entwined snakes. Also intimidating was the god of death, Mictlantecuhtli, who ruled over the deep pits of the underworld.

The Aztecs believed that their gods were easily angered. If the deities were displeased, they would not send the right kind of weather. They might cause famine, earthquakes, or diseases, and might even end the world. To soothe the gods, the Aztecs made many sacrifices to them, including human sacrifices. The Aztecs thought that their gods needed human blood and hearts to live. An Aztec poem expresses their ideas about the power of the god of darkness:

> He mocks us
> As he wishes, so he wills.
> He places us in the palm of his hand,
> He rolls us about;
> Like pebbles we roll, we spin . . .
> We make him laugh.
> He mocks us.

Religious Leaders

At the peak of the Aztec Empire, there were tens of thousands of priests, priestesses, and astrologers. These religious leaders held high places in society and were treated as nobles. After years of studying and giving up personal pleasures, priests assumed their duties. Some of them studied the heavens, tracking the movements of stars and other celestial bodies. These movements helped them to predict the future and to create calendars that told them when to hold ceremonies for the gods. They also used these calendars to set dates for major events, such as the day and time a new ruler should take office.

The priests spent much of their time praying and making offerings to the gods at the many Aztec temples that existed. They watched over the sacred fires, which were never allowed to go out. They organized and led ceremonies for the Aztec people throughout the year. Priests were also asked to answer important questions, to solve problems, and to find lost objects.

The so-called calendar stone of the Aztecs shows the sun god emerging from the symbol "4 Earthquake," the date the Aztecs believed that the world would come to an end in a catastrophic earthquake.

Religious specialists dealt with illness, too. Like other native peoples, the Aztecs thought that most diseases were caused by the gods or by someone who wanted to hurt another person. Through witchcraft, a person could send a dart or a stone into another's body. Certain gods were blamed for certain kinds of illnesses. For example, the Aztecs believed that the god of night caused people to become blind.

To cure an illness, a shaman was called in. By rubbing the sick person's body, the shaman hoped to bring up the dart or stone that was causing the disease. The shaman also used medicines made of herbs or plants after consulting a special book that contained paintings of herbs and described their healing powers. Herbs were made into powders and blown into a person's nose or brewed in hot water to make medicinal teas.

Magic was also used to identify and treat illnesses. To figure out what was wrong with somebody, a shaman might throw maize kernels and beans onto a cloak. The shaman would then look at the pattern they made. Different patterns had different meanings.

If someone was dying, special priests called *tonalpouqui* might be summoned. They would blow smoke on the person and examine a sacred book to find out whether he or she was dying under a lucky sign. Dying people were given a chance to confess any misdeeds they may have committed. The evil could then be washed away in order to prevent bad luck in the community.

The Great Temple of Tenochtitlán

The Aztecs built a vast stone pyramid, about ninety feet high, in their capital city of Tenochtitlán. This four-tiered temple had ornate carvings and paintings on its walls. It was the site of many important ceremonies.

High on top of the pyramid stood shrines to the two most important gods: Tlaloc and Huitzilopochtli. Paintings and wood carvings adorned their altars. The statue of Huitzilopochtli was covered with gold, pearls, and precious stones. Its eyes were two mirrors set inside a golden mask. The figure wore a necklace of gold human hearts around its neck. The other god, Tlaloc, was depicted as half human, half alligator in the Tenochtitlán temple.

The Spanish conqueror, Hernando Cortés, described the great temple this way:

It has the appearance of a four cornered pyramid of four tremendous stairways. At the summit of the wide platform, which is reached by a wide exterior stairway, there stand two tower temples made of polished stone and carved woodwork in which the huge idols are enthroned. The walls around them are richly decorated and painted with all manner of monsters and singular figures. Here too are the graves of the Kings.

Aztec Ceremonies

This Aztec mosaic mask of turquoise and pearl shells is thought to represent the god Quetzalcoatl.

The Aztecs held numerous ceremonies, both public and private. Curing an illness was usually done at home. Public ceremonies were often lavish, with music, feasting, and many torches. A variety of musical instruments—wooden gongs, bone rattles, drums made from hollowed logs, and clay

During the New Fire Ceremony, people discarded their possessions. These figures of gods and temples came from household shrines.

flutes—was played. Priests wore costumes embellished with feathers, gems, and animal skins so that they would resemble certain gods, or to demonstrate their power to the people.

Different groups participated in different parts of a ceremony. Hundreds of people might serve as musicians, singers, and dancers. Warriors who belonged to the Knights of the Eagle and the Knights of the Jaguar often performed ceremonial dances, accompanied by drums and horns. They wore ornate costumes decorated with feathers and animal skins, as well as masks to make them look like eagles or jaguars. Masks for religious rituals were often studded with pieces of mother-of-pearl and turquoise, obsidian, and other stones. Mosaic designs were common. Some masks were made with real human skulls.

Many ceremonies aimed to bring good health, bountiful harvests, or rain. There were, however, seasons in which the priests tried to prevent rain. If it came at the wrong time, rain could damage the crops.

The New Fire Ceremony was of foremost importance. At the start of the ceremony, the Aztecs put out every fire already burning. They discarded their household goods and belongings, including old statues of the gods. People cleaned their homes. At twilight, they climbed onto roofs or atop walls. Children and pregnant women wore face masks to avoid being turned into mice.

At midnight, the priests sacrificed a man and offered his heart to the gods. They started a fire, called the "new fire," inside his open chest. This fire was a sign that the world would go on for the next fifty-two years. From this new fire, priests lit torches, which were carried away by swift runners first to the main temples and then the lesser ones, then to the palace of the ruler, then to the nobles, and finally to the common people. The sight of these fires reassured the Aztecs that the world would go on.

Sacrifices to the Gods

The Aztecs believed that their gods demanded sacrifices. It was thought that the gods would keep the sun and the world going only if they were fed enough human blood and hearts. Prisoners of war were used as human sacrifices. Other sacrifices were Aztecs who offered to give up their lives. They believed that by doing so, they would go straight to the highest afterworld.

Sometimes, people who were to be sacrificed wore the costumes of a god or a goddess and ornate jewelry. They may have spent a period of time acting out the role of that deity and being waited on by servants before the day of the sacrifice.

Human sacrifices were a part of most public ceremonies held at the Great Temple of Tenochtitlán. A victim climbed 114 steps to reach a large altar in front of the shrines. There, priests used a special obsidian knife with a mosaic handle to cut the chest open and pull out the beating heart. The heart was put into a *chacmool*, a stone carving of a reclining man holding a bowl.

After the person had been sacrificed, his or her body was pushed down the temple steps. It is said that these steps were covered with bloodstains. The skulls of honored sacrificial victims were put on a skull rack (Tzompantli) on a platform near the sacred ball court.

A Prophecy Unfolds

Ancient legends said that in the year 1519, the Smoking God (the god of war) would fight a pale-skinned god from the east, Quetzalcoatl. Another myth said that Quetzalcoatl had left Aztec lands but would someday return. During the early 1500s, many Aztecs told their astrologers about dreams in which the people faced fires and other disasters.

In 1519, Hernando Cortés and his troops reached the eastern coast of Mexico. The Aztecs thought that this fair-skinned stranger must be Quetzalcoatl. They gave him gifts and clothing suitable for a god and treated the Spanish as honored guests. When the Aztec ruler Moctezuma took Cortés to see the Great Temple of Tenochtitlán, however, Cortés ordered his men to push the stone figures of the gods down the steps. The Spaniards also stole gold and treasure from the royal palace, where they were staying as guests of the Aztecs.

Soon the Spanish troops were at war with the Aztec armies. Within a few months, the Spaniards, with their native allies, horses, and superior weapons, had won. New diseases brought to the area by the Spaniards, in part, helped to weaken the Aztecs. Now the Aztecs were captives. It was as if the battle that the spiritual leaders had foretold so long ago had come to pass.

Chapter

3

Southern Mexico and Central America

Evidence of an amazing civilization dating back to about A.D. 200 can be seen in Central America. Throughout some 125,000 square miles of southern Mexico and what is present-day Guatemala, the Maya built rich cities and impressive ceremonial centers. Their pyramids rose among the trees in the lush jungles of the Yucatán Peninsula. Like other tribes in the Americas, the Maya believed that they had to treat the gods correctly and live as directed or they would perish.

Olmec Roots

The Olmecs began the first civilization in Central America. They eventually influenced the Maya, as they had the Aztecs. From around 1500 to 100 B.C., the Olmecs lived in southeastern Mexico. Among their numerous religious shrines are those devoted to hills and water, two things many native peoples held sacred.

Opposite:
A Mayan chacmool on the coast of Cancun, Mexico.

The Olmecs created religious monuments. This Olmec altar shows a figure of a person emerging from the earth.

The Olmecs also held ritual sacrifices, a tradition that lived on with their descendants. They offered blood to the jaguar spirit in exchange for rain they needed for their crops. Jaguar gods were important in Central American cultures perhaps because jaguars were the fiercest animals in the jungle. Many religious figures were depicted as part human and part jaguar.

The Olmecs believed in many supernatural beings. There were gods of the sun, fire, earth, water, and various animals. Some dwarflike spirits played tricks on people and lived in waterfalls. They were said to leave their footprints on stones.

The Olmecs were among the first Americans to construct religious centers. Their most elaborate monument was built at San Lorenzo. Workers brought millions of cubic feet of earth to a hilltop they had flattened. With this earth, they made finger-shaped ridges along the sides of the monument. Craftsmen then carved enormous stone heads on platforms that still other workers had built on the hill. The Olmecs of Tres Zapotes made stone heads that stood more than five feet tall and weighed about eight tons each. These heads may represent Olmec rulers. Most spiritual monuments were probably made of stone, but scientists have also excavated wooden ones.

In Olmec cities, scientists have found rubber balls dating back more than 3,000 years. Pictures carved on stones show masked men playing a ceremonial ball game. Versions of this game were later played by the Aztecs, the Maya, and the Inca. Soccer is a modern form of the ancient ball game.

The Temples of Teotihuacán

The city of Teotihuacán flourished from around A.D. 1 to 750, when it was home to some 125,000 people. By about A.D. 125, people there had built two massive religious buildings, the Pyramid of the Sun, which stands about 216 feet high, and the Pyramid of the Moon. Atop the Pyramid of the Sun was the Temple of the Plumed Serpent. It featured dazzling stone carvings of feathered serpents and a figure resembling the Aztec god Tlaloc.

The Pyramid of the Sun had broad stairways leading to four platforms, with a temple at the top. The temple was decorated with wood, straw, flowers, and bright green quetzal feathers. Green was sacred—green stones and green feathers represented Tlaloc and his power. Quetzal birds were prized. These jungle birds were kept in a special place so that their feathers could be collected as they fell off. Killing a quetzal bird was punishable by death.

Stone tablets and wall paintings from Teotihuacán show images of the Fire God and the Goddess of the Waters. There are also pictures showing spirits in paradise. In one scene, figures representing the souls of the dead are shown playing ball near a river and eating plenty of maize.

Classic Mayan Spirituality

The Maya in the lowland areas of the Yucatán built what is called the classic Mayan culture from A.D. 250 to 900. Their religion became more complex as they built cities and ceremonial centers at Tikal, Palenque, Copán, and other places.

The Maya developed a system of picture writing that was more advanced than any other in their region. They recorded their history, beliefs, prophecies, and way of life in a sacred book called the *Popul Vuh*. This book includes stories about the creation of the world and its people.

According to the *Popul Vuh*, the first humans were made of earth, but they were destroyed because they had no minds. Humans were then made of wood, but they had no hearts, so a flood carried them away. Finally, humans were created from kernels of maize. These people were allowed to remain on the earth and were the first Maya. From the beginning, then, maize has been viewed as sacred.

Many gods ruled over the Maya. Among them were the chief god, Itzamna (Lord of Life); his wife, Ix Chel, goddess of weaving, medicine, and childbirth; Ah Kin, the sun god; the Hero Twins; and Puch, chief god of the dead. The Chacs, or rain gods, were highly respected: Without rain, there would be no harvest of maize, which was called the "sunbeams of the gods" by the Maya. Lightning was the "spears of Chac." The Maya also worshiped Kukulcan, who resembled Quetzalcoatl.

Like the Aztecs, the Maya thought that their gods required human blood and sacrifices. During special ceremonies, they offered the heads or the beating hearts of these human sacrifices to the gods. Victims included prisoners of war, peasants, and those Maya who volunteered to be sacrificed.

People would also cut themselves because they believed that this pleased the gods. Priests sometimes pierced their tongues with thorns and offered the blood as a sacrifice. Blood would be offered to the gods at planting time, during building dedications, at burials, and on other occasions. Blood was allowed to drip onto special paper, which was then burned so that the smoke could rise up to the spirits.

Mayan priests had many duties. Some were experts in the movements of the stars and other heavenly bodies. They used star charts and other books to predict events and to

This detail of a vase dating from approximately A.D. 750 illustrates a Mayan priest.

choose names for babies. Priests determined which god or goddess governed the day on which a person was born. The person then devoted himself or herself to that deity throughout his or her life. The Maya asked their religious leaders for help when they were ill or had a problem. They also asked the priests to interpret their dreams.

Priests sometimes called all citizens to public meetings. People stood in the plaza, the central square of the city, and heard prophecies or other important messages during these meetings. A priest might then ask the citizens to say special prayers or to try harder to follow the Mayan rules for a good life.

The word *chac* was also used for assistants to the priests. *Chacs* were usually older men who had been trained to help the priests prepare and carry out ceremonies. They also prepared the rituals for people who planned to marry. The *chacs* knew how to read the sacred books and were experts on chants and Mayan history. Children were also supposed to learn the many chants and songs that told about Mayan history and their gods.

All Mayan festivals had spiritual meaning. Festivals were held for special gods who were the patrons of hunters, fishermen, farmers, artisans, and other types of workers. There were festivals to honor the bee and various other animals and crops. Since all animals were viewed as beings that had souls, they were respected. During parts of the festivals, priests chanted and people sang and danced. Professional musicians played drums, trumpets, flutes, bells, and gourd rattles.

The classic Maya of Tikal, a city located in the Petén jungle of northern Guatemala, built large, ornate temples and shrines for their gods. One of the most impressive buildings was the Temple of the Giant Jaguar. Inside is a tomb that held the body and the jewels of a ruler named Ah Cacau. As other Maya were, Ah Cacau was buried with belongings and food to take on his trip to the afterworld.

Human sacrifices might also be made during the burial services of rulers and nobles. Commoners were buried with their belongings and tools under the mud floor of their houses. A dead person's belongings were not touched. After a generation of people was buried under a house, the house was abandoned.

Life After Death

The Maya regarded the ceiba tree (which they called *yaxche*) as sacred. These rainforest trees reach heights of 150 feet. An important Mayan myth said that the earth was square and that the ceiba tree stood at the center of the universe. Its branches stretched into the Upperworld, its trunk stood level with the Middleworld, and its roots were in the Underworld. After death, it was said, a person's soul moved among these worlds by means of the tree.

A dead person had to overcome a number of trials in the Underworld, or "place of fright," before moving to higher levels. People's souls entered the Underworld through a cave or a body of water. In the Underworld, they encountered cruel, hideous spirits wearing trinkets made from the eyes of dead Maya.

The Toltec-Maya

During the 900s, the classic Mayan centers lost their influence and the period that was dominated by the Toltec-Maya began. Maya from the northern Yucatán and the southern highlands (present-day Guatemala) merged with Toltec peoples from Mexico to build new capitals—Chichén Itzá and Mayapan—both in the Yucatán.

As these two cultures blended, the god Quetzalcoatl became part of Mayan spirituality. Quetzalcoatl was thought to have invented agriculture, the calendar, and writing. Images of feathered serpents appeared on various Mayan buildings and in paintings, sculpture, and pottery. At Chichén Itzá, the entry to the Temple of the Warriors has columns in the form of feathered serpents with large, open mouths. There are many symbols of war and human sacrifice, which reveal a strong military influence.

The Great Ball Court, one of seven courts in Chichén Itzá, stood opposite this temple. There, men played a game that had a spiritual significance. Although nobody is sure exactly what the rules of this game were, it appears that some of the players were sacrificed after the game. Pictures of the ball court show players holding knives and the heads of other participants. It may be that this event was offered to the fertility gods.

Many offerings were made to the rain gods or water gods. The sacrifices were thrown into a well that the Maya considered to be a shrine. Both human beings and valuables—gold objects, pieces of jade, textiles, ornate knives, pottery, seashells—were thrown into this well. When rain was scarce, the priests held ceremonies during which they chanted, burned incense, and made offerings.

Kneeling on one leg, a Mayan ball player throws a ball in a game that symbolized the war of the Heavenly Twins against the rulers of the Underworld.

Chapter

4

The Caribbean

Different groups of native peoples have lived on Caribbean islands and the coasts of present-day northeastern Nicaragua and Colombia. The Tairona lived in the rainforest and the semi-desert lands of Colombia between the Atlantic Ocean and the Sierra Nevada de Santa María Mountains. Other groups of Caribbean peoples lived in Panama—on the San Blas Islands, along the nearby coast, on the shores of the Tuira River, and in central Panama. These included the Cuna and the San Blas. They shared common beliefs and spiritual practices similar to those of other people in Central and South America. Because they were often isolated from one another by forests or mountains, individual tribes also developed unique customs.

These peoples believed in many deities and worshiped the sun and other things found in nature. They thought that supernatural forces ruled the universe and that all things in nature had invisible and eternal spirits, or souls.

Opposite:
The Caribbean was home to many different tribal groups, including the Tairona, Cuna, and Taino.

This gold Tairona artifact depicts a human figure as a mythical bird.

Ceremonies

At many Caribbean ceremonies, people often played drums made from the hollowed-out trunks of trees and covered with tight animal hides. The native peoples of Panama made many ceremonial instruments from animal bones and the large seashells they found along the shores.

Tairona ceremonial objects included gold pieces and double-headed animals. Ceremonial dancers wore masks that were sometimes decorated with feathers and gold charms or objects. The jaguar symbol represented the sun. That symbol seems also to have portrayed the dual nature of humans, who are capable of both good and evil acts. Crystals, too, were important spiritual objects. It was thought that they had certain powers and might bring new knowledge or even cure diseases. The Tairona used stones in their natural form and also made them into necklace beads.

Shamans and Healers

As they did in other native cultures, shamans served as intermediaries between the human and spirit worlds. Illness was considered to have a spiritual or a magic cause. Shamans who were healers or medicine men were called upon in times of illness.

Cuna healers were called *neles* or *innatuledis*. They performed their treatments inside a special house set aside for that purpose. Before beginning a curing ritual, *neles* put medicine dolls, called *nuchus*, next to a patient. These dolls were carved into human shapes from balsa wood. Blue pins were used for the eyes. Besides having curative powers, the dolls were thought to bring good luck.

Tairona religious leaders also served as astronomers and keepers of the calendars, as well as healers and diviners. Since the Tairona believed that crystals held special powers, they sometimes ground them up and used them to cure specific illnesses.

Burial Customs

The tribes in this region shared a belief in a life after death. People were buried with possessions they might need to take with them into the afterworld. Among the funeral offerings of the Sinu of Colombia were ceramic pieces, gold objects, carved shells, and cloth. Many of the carved wooden religious figures found in ancient Sinu graves were coated with gold.

Some tribes burned the corpses of their dead, then put the bones inside special containers, or urns. Certain tribes, such as the Sinu, sometimes ground the bones of their dead into a powder. They did this because they believed that human bones were a source of fertility and power and a link with the afterlife. One Caribbean tribe called the Makiritare was among those that used human bones in their rituals. They added some of the bone powder to an alcoholic drink made from maize and drank some of the mixture in order to absorb the power and wisdom of the deceased.

The Elder Brothers

A group of Tairona called the Kogi have some especially interesting customs. The Kogi call themselves the Elder Brothers of Humanity, and they have held on to their ancient ways of life for thousands of years. Scientists have called the Kogi the most complete indigenous culture to have survived since the 1400s.

❖

40

Kogi legends claim that they are the guardians of life on the earth. Their spiritual beliefs include a great respect for all forms of life. They believe that they are responsible for looking after the earth and its creatures. Their teachings stress harmony and balance between humans and the physical and spiritual worlds. The earth is considered sacred.

Kogi creation stories are complex and take more than ninety days to tell in detail. The Kogi believe that the earth arises from eight lower worlds, making it the ninth world. Above it are nine upper worlds. Humans live between the upper and lower worlds, between life and death.

In Kogi legends, the seas were created first, before the sun and the moon. The Mother was a symbol of an eternal force sometimes referred to as That Which Was to Be; this force existed amid darkness. The Mother's son, Serankua, fertilized the world.

While living among the Kogi and learning about their ways, writer Alan Ereira recorded some Kogi chants. These words reveal some of their beliefs about creation and the purpose of humankind:

> Serankua tells us
> that he created us
> that he created the earth
> that he made the sky.
> He is called Serankua.
> He made us to care for the creatures, flowers, nature.
> Thus it was.
> The Elder Brother was there to protect the earth,
> because the earth
> it is our Mother, earth.
> Without earth we cannot live.

The ceremonial house has long been the center of Kogi life. It is circular. The floor, with its four fires—one in each quarter—symbolizes the earth. A cone-shaped roof represents the top half of the universe. Only men use these houses, where they sit around the fires or lie in hammocks. Kogi legends say that the original ceremonial houses were in the mountains.

Kogi priests are called Mamas. They are both male and female and also serve as judges. The Mamas have spent time studying the Law of the Mother so that they can help others to know the right way to live. All Mamas study certain basic things, then go on to learn other, special things on their own. Perhaps they study Kogi history or certain birds and animals in great depth. Mamas are the only Kogis allowed to wear pointed hats—symbols of a house.

The Mamas appoint *comisarios*, or "town leaders," to ensure that towns and roads are well maintained and to keep the public order. These town leaders are all men. The Mamas also serve as advisers and healers in the community. Illness is said to occur when someone is out of balance with the world. When people are in pain, have bad dreams, or are ill, they ask a Mama for help. They may spend several days talking with the Mama about what has been happening in their lives. The Mama listens, and tries to figure out what has gone wrong.

When the Mamas want to solve a problem in the community or make an important decision, they talk together. They may also go to higher ground—a hill or a mountain— to think and seek spiritual guidance. They try to divine, or interpret, signs that will help them. This is a way to receive messages from the gods or their own ancestors. Men are required to attend sessions, held by the Mamas, on Kogi law. The men make decisions for the community, but women can influence the decisions and express their views. Women are respected as being signs of the Mother, who gave people all things of the earth.

The leaves of the coca plant, from which cocaine is obtained, were used by many different indigenous peoples, both in the Caribbean and South America.

As other tribes in the region do, the Kogi chew the small green leaves of the coca plant. The dry, bitter leaves are used during certain ceremonies. Chewing a small amount acts as a mild stimulant. Coca leaves are also used as medicine and to stop hunger pains.

The Kogi do not place much emphasis on material goods or possessions. They focus, instead, on the *aluna*, the world of thought and spirit. For the Kogi, *aluna* shapes everything—it is more real than the material world. The stones, water, trees, and everything else in the world have an invisible spirit form. The Kogi concentrate and meditate often in order to enter this world of spiritual awareness.

The Taino

The Taino were a very peaceable tribe. They fought only if forced to repel an attack from a fierce neighboring tribe called the Caribs, or if required to enforce tribal laws. The Taino lived on the present-day islands of Hispaniola and Puerto Rico.

The Taino had strong class distinctions. Their social structure was much like that first developed by the Olmecs. The nobility was at the top. The village chiefs and their families were members of this class. They lived in the largest homes and made decisions for the community about constructing new buildings, greeting visitors, and organizing festivals. The chiefs knew all the words to their traditional tribal songs. They were also the song leaders.

Taino villages were grouped first into districts and then into provinces. District and province leaders were also members of the nobility. Although they ruled over larger areas, these leaders were not as powerful as the individual village chiefs, because they could not make decisions that would have a direct impact on the lives of the people, as village chiefs could. In Taino society, priests were considered part of the nobility. It was their responsibility to lead the community in religious ceremonies and sacred rituals.

In the Caguana Ceremonial Park in Puerto Rico, standing stones of the Taino tribe are marked with petroglyphs.

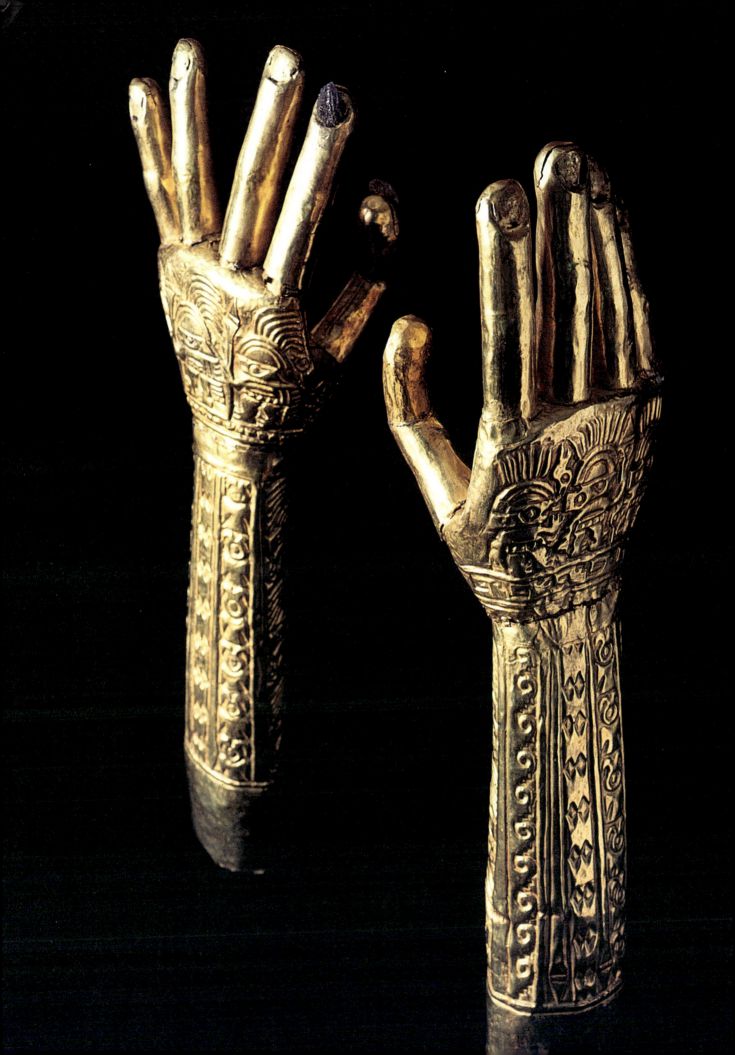

Chapter

5

South America

The Inca of South America built upon the customs of their ancestors to create a complex spiritual life. Incan culture was rich in ceremonial buildings and objects. Living in and around what is present-day Peru in the Andes Mountains, these people honored the sun and other deities. Their spirituality was woven into their daily life, uniting communities and the entire empire.

Earlier Customs

Long before the Inca there were the Chavin, who lived near Peru's northern highlands around the year 1000 B.C. Figures that resemble a jaguar or a puma have been found among the ancient remains of Chavin settlements. Some of these figures are half man, half cat. Like other native peoples of the Americas, the Chavin seem to have given the fierce jaguar a role similar to that of the Christian devil.

Opposite:
These gold arms, from the Chimu culture in Peru, were used in funeral rites.

46

The Chavin produced beautiful works of art and textiles. They wove and embroidered robes for the dead. Bodies dating from 250 B.C. have been found wrapped in cloths decorated with fancy needlework and in hundreds of different colors. Such elaborate cloths may have taken years to make. The Chavin sent off the dead with some of the finest robes and other belongings of this life.

The details of Chavin spiritual life are unclear. It appears, however, that religious customs were a strong force that united the Chavin people. With the people united and following the same religious customs, it was easier for their rulers to maintain a strong influence. This would be true for the Inca as well.

The Moche developed a remarkable culture in a valley on the northern coast of Peru from about 200 B.C. to A.D. 800. Among their finest pyramids were the 135-foot-high Shrine of the Sun (Huaca del Sol), which was probably a religious building, and the Shrine of the Moon (Huaca de la Luna), which may have been a palace. The Shrine of the Sun may contain 130 to 140 million mud bricks. Experts have estimated that it weighs more than 4 million tons.

Moche healers included men and women. They used magic, herbal juices, and massage to treat illnesses. The Moche hunted sea lions off the coast and removed stones from their stomachs. These stones were thought to have healing powers. Priests drank a ceremonial beverage made from fermented maize. They chewed coca leaves to reach a trancelike state that made them feel closer to the gods.

The Moche buried their dead with numerous possessions, including jewelry and clay pots filled with funeral offerings to the gods. Offerings were also placed in gourd bowls. They included corn, peanuts, fish, and birds.

By A.D. 900, Moche society had disappeared. The Chimu culture that followed was located near the great

Moche temples. The Chimu also built pyramids as temples to their gods. Many ceremonial objects were made of gold, and the sun was their chief god.

During these years, another group, the Aymara, lived around Lake Titicaca on the border of present-day Peru and Bolivia. From about A.D. 900 to 1200, these mountain people built the Tiahuanaco culture. They seem to have studied astronomy intensely. They used the word *huaca* to refer to a holy or magical thing. A *huaca* took the form of a mountain, lake, cave, stone, or other feature in nature.

The most famous Tiahuanaco building is the Gateway of the Sun, which may have been a pilgrimage site. This great stone ceremonial center is located 12,500 feet above sea level. It shows a god surrounded by beautiful carvings, with mythical creatures running toward him.

Life-size carvings of people have been excavated near here. An Incan legend says that the god Viracocha once turned humans into stone because they had thrown rocks at a stranger. Viracocha had come from the waters of Lake Titicaca to create a dark world peopled by giants. After these giants angered him, Viracocha created a new world in which people were of normal size.

The Tiahuanacans put their trust in a variety of magicians, prophets, and herbal healers. They honored a god who was part human and part animal. These people believed not only in a Sun God but also in a Weeping God. Sometimes this god wept tears in the form of snakes or animal heads.

When the Inca conquered the people of Tiahuanaco, they chose to allow Tiahuanaco religious customs. The Inca continued to respect other religious ideas as they went on to conquer various other groups throughout the region. People were permitted to keep some of the old ways as long as they adopted the main Incan customs and accepted the sun as their chief deity.

❖

49

People of the Sun

By around A.D. 1200, the Inca had amassed much land and power in the fertile Cuzco Valley. These Quechua-speaking people called themselves "children of the sun" and worshiped the sun as a deity. The Inca believed that their ruler, the Lord Inca, was part god, the son of the sun.

The Incan creation story said that the first two Inca were Manco Capac and his sister-wife, Mama Ocla. After their father, the sun, had created them and they rose up from Lake Titicaca, the sun gave them a rod of gold and told them to carry it across the land and look for a place where it would sink deep into the ground.

The golden rod sank into the fertile land of the Cuzco valley. There, Manco Capac and Mama Ocla settled and began the Kingdom of the Sun. The sun agreed to give the world light and warmth, allowing the crops to grow. He commanded humans to live properly by treating one another with justice and fairness and avoiding the misdeeds of dishonesty, theft, and laziness.

A Golden Capital

The Inca saw their capital city, Cuzco, as the body of a puma (a large, powerful jungle cat). The puma's body was the city, which lay between two rivers; its head was their fortress, Sacsahuaman. Cuzco gleamed with gold—on the walls, on the roofs of buildings and temples, and on numerous objects. Millions of ounces of gold may have been brought there each year, and its use was controlled by the government. Gold was regarded as having a religious meaning, being "the sweat of the sun." Silver was "the tears of the moon."

The walls of the fabulous Coricancha, the Temple of the Sun, were lined with golden plaques. A huge disk shaped like the sun hung above the main altar. Another room was devoted to the moon and was paneled in silver. On display

Opposite:
An Incan textile shows the god Viracocha holding symbols of power.

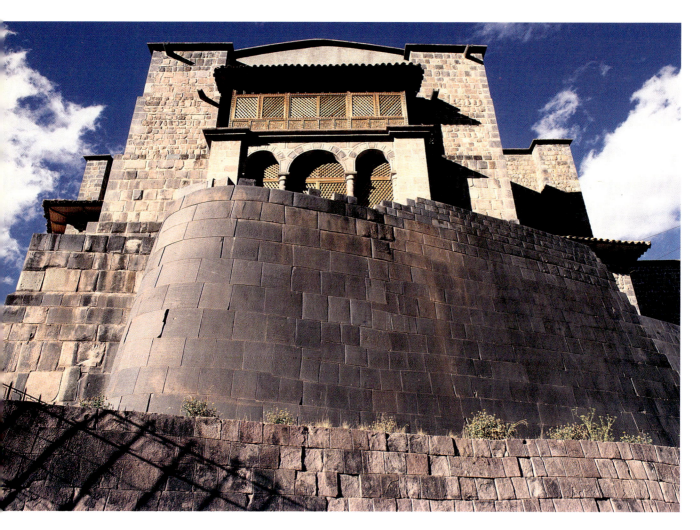

The curved walls of the Incan Temple of the Sun still stand in Cuzco, Peru. The Santo Domingo Church, above the Incan temple, was built with some of the original stones of the Temple of the Sun.

was a large, silver moon with a woman's face. Other rooms honored the stars, lightning and thunder, and the rainbow. A garden outside glittered with golden llamas, shepherds, snakes, animals, butterflies, cornstalks, and birds.

Feasts and Festivals

The Inca held at least one religious festival a month. Some lasted a week or more. The first Incan festival of the year was devoted to Ilapu, or Thunupa, the Storm God. In August, the month of plowing, came the festival of Pachamama (Mother Earth). A ceremony for the Thunder God was held if there was no rain in December. People dressed in black and marched, weeping, through their villages. Musicians played tambourines and shell rattles, and dancers wore arm and ankle bands adorned with copper and silver bells.

❖

51

For the Inca, the Sun King Festival was the most important event of the year. It took place during the summer solstice, which in Peru occurs in December. People from all over the Incan Empire came to Cuzco for this event. In preparation, all the Inca fasted for three days. On December 21, they spent the night kneeling as they faced the east and prayed for the sun to rise. The next day, they watched as the Lord Inca lifted up a golden cup of *chicha* (a sacred beverage to them), which had been blessed by the priests. As sunlight glowed on the cup, the Lord Inca drank. People rejoiced that the sun would shine for another year.

As the festival went on, the Lord Inca offered certain people golden cups of *chicha*. This was a way to honor them for their achievements and their services. Later, animal sacrifices were offered to the gods. Musicians played special songs. Commoners who were not involved in any activities with the Lord Inca joined the ritual dancing, to the music of drums, flutes, and trumpets.

Incan dancing was performed for religious purposes and was made up of slow, carefully planned steps. Certain occasions called for the snake dance, the rope dance, or the heron dance. During the rope dance, people performed slow movements that showed their loyalty to the Incan laws and way of life. Other ritual dances were done at planting and harvest times. Incan dancing and music reflected their social behavior—serious and quiet rather than lively and enthusiastic.

In contrast with the Aztecs and the Maya, few Incan ceremonies involved human sacrifice. At times, a llama would be offered to the gods. In extreme situations (for instance, if the Lord Inca was gravely ill), the priests might ask one of the Chosen Women to serve as a human sacrifice. These were women of special beauty who were educated to serve their ruler and the nobility, or serve in the temples. As the Aztecs and Maya did, the Inca believed that those who died as sacrifices were guaranteed a happy existence in the afterlife.

During days of public festivals, the Inca wore their best clothing and did not work. Often, they drank *chicha* and chewed coca leaves. Priests gave out small amounts of coca to help people reach a trancelike state that would bring them closer to the spirits.

Spiritual Leaders

The Inca looked to their spiritual leaders to connect them with the strong and unpredictable forces of nature. The Incan high priest was the brother or uncle of the Lord Inca. He lived in Cuzco, where he was in charge of the Temple of the Sun. Under his authority were ten bishops, who helped to direct numerous priests in various Incan communities.

Several kinds of priests lived among the Inca. Some were in charge of the calendar. They told people the best days to plant and harvest crops or conduct spiritual activities. There were also priests who made predictions and tried to read signs that would help them make decisions about important events. Other priests served as investigators. They made sure that the temples were well tended and that spiritual events were carried out properly.

Other priests heard confessions of wrongdoing. During a special ritual held near a river, a priest would listen as a person admitted misdeeds. Depending on what he or she had done, the priest might hit the person with a stone or give another punishment. People guilty of grievous misdeeds might be banished—sent to live by themselves in the wilderness—for a long period of time.

Healing priests used chants, herbs, and ritual touching. Another treatment was trepanation, in which holes were drilled into a person's skull. It was thought that this would release demons from people who were possessed or bewitched.

Death and Dying

The Inca believed that their souls were immortal but that their bodies had to be preserved and buried properly after death in order to ensure eternal life. The bodies of Incan rulers were mummified. Many were kept in the Temple of the Sun or in splendid tombs within their palaces. Servants and family members looked after them and continued to serve them meals. Commoners were buried in special mounds with other relatives. Family members cared for these mounds.

For the Inca, spiritual customs gave life a clearer pattern and meaning. By following the rules, they felt that their souls would live in peace after death.

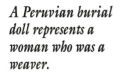

A Peruvian burial doll represents a woman who was a weaver.

6

The Amazon

Amazon tribes have lived, and continue to live, in a region of lush, plant-filled forests and many rivers. Along these rivers, groups have built villages, gathered and raised food, and reared their children for thousands of years. Many of the tribes are isolated from other people and have kept their ancient customs and beliefs to this day.

The spiritual life of the Amazonian peoples includes a belief in the balance of nature and the need to show respect for plants and animals—or else risk illness or other misfortune. They believe that not only animals in the forest but also rocks, plants, and stars may once have been people. These things may be housing the souls of dead ancestors and must therefore be treated with care.

Creation Stories

Opposite:
Many tribes made
masks that represented
the birds of the region,
such as these macaws.

Amazonian peoples tell the old legends, often at night around a fire. Elders pass on the stories that were told to them by their elders. The Matsigenka of southeastern Peru believe that they were created from young trees. Their creative spirit, Makineri, shaped and breathed life into the wood.

55

They also believe that their main foods—manioc, potatoes, yams, and maize—came from the moon. The moon showed people how to use these gifts.

The Yanomami live in the remote forests of southern Venezuela and northern Brazil and have many myths and legends. The stories have some basic elements in common, but are told a bit differently in the various villages. This use of imagination is approved of by the people.

The Yanomami creation story says that the world is made up of four levels, one on top of the other. Humans and other living things came from the highest layer, through the spirit layer above the earth, and down to the third layer, earth. The earth is seen as a vast jungle. The lowest layer, below the earth, holds evil spirit people who struggle with the people on earth.

Among the first Yanomami on earth was a man named Bore. He is said to have been the first person to eat plantains, a fruit that is a main food among the Yanomami. Other tales explain how people first used fire, plants, and animals.

This Kaipo village is organized within a circle, which represents the round universe.

A legend from the Kaipo of eastern Brazil says that the first man came down from the sky on ropes. The Kaipo see the universe as round and build their villages and fields in a circle to stay in harmony with it.

Supernatural Beings

Most Amazonians worship not one supreme being or god, but many supernatural beings. Some tribes believe that animals and plants have invisible souls, or spirits. Animals can change their forms to become something else.

Many tribes, however, point to a supreme spirit or to one that created the world. Some Orinoco River tribes view the sun as the leading god, while other tribes give this higher role to the moon. Twin myths are common. In some stories, twins teach the people of the earth how to use fire. The Xingu, a southeastern Amazon tribe, speak of twins called The Sun and The Moon. They have water spirits, tree spirits, and land spirits, and they wear masks during ceremonies that represent these beings. Birds are also represented—the Amazon region contains many colorful types, including parrots, macaws, toucans, and hummingbirds.

Religious Leaders

Amazonian peoples have shamans, usually men, who know much about the spirits and healing. Some shamans eat or drink substances that cause visions and enable them to dream about the spirit world. They might be asked to find lost items, detect sorcerers, conduct ceremonies, counsel people about war, predict the future, name infants, uphold traditions, and heal people. Their daily lives and their appearance are usually like those of other people in the village.

Shamans may carry certain items as signs of their position: quartz crystals, gourd rattles, feathered sticks, or a special doll to take along when visiting patients. Those who misuse their powers may be punished. Tribes often deal severely with those who use magic or invoke the spirits with the intent of harming their enemies.

Yanomami shamans sing and dance. They pose in ways that symbolize the idea of flight toward the sun or the moon. They try to cure the sick by drawing bad objects out of the body. Since some illnesses are thought to arise when people lose their souls, shamans might lead close relatives in a hunt to find the soul. Or they might try to drive away the enemy spirit that is causing an illness.

The Tukano people, who form part of the Desano group, have *payes* who conduct rituals at important times in the life cycle—birth, initiation into adulthood, and burial. The *paye* also has special duties associated with hunting.

Payes use special substances to induce trancelike states. One is a powder called *viho*, which is sniffed through the nose with small, tube-shaped bones. They also drink *gahpi* and *chicha* on certain occasions. These religious men use gourd rattles and wear ornaments made of polished white or yellowish quartz around their necks.

Ceremonies

Many Amazonian ceremonies are tied to events in the life cycle—birth, becoming an adult, and death. Harvest ceremonies and festivals are held to give thanks for food or to ask for success in hunting and fishing. A number of tribes conduct five-day mourning ceremonies. The number five also has significance in other activities, such as fasting.

The Kaipo hold ceremonies during which they give ancestral names to young tribal members. They also have ceremonies to ensure good crops. An immense tree trunk serves as a centerpiece for some of the ceremonial dances. The Kaipo also use black and red body and face paint, and chiefs and other leaders wear elaborate ceremonial headdresses.

These present-day Kaipo people wear the traditional black and red body paint of their ancestors.

One type features a design made of feathers that shows the sun, with rays of gold and red. Music may be played on gourd instruments.

The Wayana people hold special ceremonies in a communal hut called a *tukusipan*. A painful ritual that initiates young people into adulthood is called *marake*, the ant test. At this ceremony, there is dancing and a retelling of important Wayana legends. The young initiate must then try to stand still and remain quiet while a frame filled with stinging black ants is pressed against all parts of his or her body. Afterward, if the initiate is a girl, her hair is cut off. It is thought that the ant test unites the Wayana and prepares their young people for the hardships that they will face later on in life by giving them spiritual strength.

Death and Dying

Amazonian peoples believe in an afterlife. Kaipo legends say that souls go to the Village of the Dead. There, men sleep during the day and hunt at night while they grow younger. Children who die go there and grow older. The Desano believe that the dead who are deserving go to paradise. If they are not deserving, they change from one animal to another, depending on how they have behaved during life.

The dead are buried with their belongings, such as tobacco and earrings. During the mourning ceremony, the men bathe in the river, then gather around the grave. They smoke while a relative of the dead person describes his or her life and character, especially the good traits. Only friends are invited to this gathering. Afterward, the dead person's name is not mentioned again.

Body paint and adornment holds spiritual meaning for the Yanomami people, as seen on this young member of the tribe.

The Yanomami burn their dead, then collect the bones and grind them to dust. The dead person's relatives eat this bone powder mixed with banana. It is supposed to bring peace to the soul of the deceased. Pregnant women are not allowed to collect the bones of the dead for this ceremony. It is thought that doing so might cause the child to be born weak, with sore eyes.

When a Yanomami man dies away from his settlement, the others hang his body from a tree in the forest. After the flesh has fallen from the bones, the bones are taken back to the settlement, to be burned in the proper place. If the body does not burn properly, it is considered a sign that the person did misdeeds during his life.

The spirituality of Amazonian peoples is rich and vivid, often in contrast with a simple way of life that includes few material goods. Like other American tribes, they have developed belief systems that explain how humankind came to be, the meaning of life on earth, the struggle between good and evil, and the fate of human beings after death.

Glossary

aluna The world of spirit and intellect.

chac A rain god; also, an assistant to a priest.

chacmool A stone carved in the shape of a reclining man holding a bowl; used to hold the hearts of human sacrifices during rituals.

comisario A Kogi town leader.

huaca A holy or magical thing that may take the form of a mountain, lake, cave, stone, or other feature in nature.

initiation A ceremony that signifies entry into a group or a stage of life. Initiation rites are performed when young men and women move into adulthood.

innatuledis A Cuna healer.

marake A Wayana ritual, used to initiate young people into adulthood, that involves their being stung by ants.

mitotes Important fertility and thanksgiving ceremonies that last for five days.

nele A Cuna healer.

nuchus Cuna medicine dolls carved from balsa wood.

paye Tukano holy men who conduct rituals and give advice, among other duties.

Quetzalcoatl A god, also called the Plumed Serpent, thought to have invented agriculture, the calendar, and writing.

shaman A person who is wise in the ways of the spirits and religion; may act as a healer; also called a priest or a medicine man.

tonalpouqui Special Aztec priests called in when someone is dying.

tukusipan A communal hut used by the Wayana of the Amazon for ceremonies.

❖

62

Further Reading

Berdan, Frances F. *The Aztecs of Central Mexico: An Imperial Society.* New York: Holt, Rinehart, & Winston, 1982.

Clay, Rebecca. *The Arts: Native Latin American Cultures.* Vero Beach, FL: Rourke Publications, Inc., 1995.

Fagan, Brian M. *The Aztecs.* New York: Freeman, 1984.

Lewington, Anna. *Threatened Cultures: Rain Forest Amerindians.* Austin, TX: Raintree/Steck-Vaughn, 1993.

Mangurian, David. *Children of the Incas.* New York: Four Winds, 1979.

Millard, Annie. *The Incas.* New York: Franklin Watts, 1980.

Morrison, Marion. *Original Peoples: Indians of the Andes.* Vero Beach, FL: Rourke Publications, Inc., 1987.

Sherrow, Victoria. *Spiritual Life: Native American Culture.* Vero Beach, FL: Rourke Publications, Inc., 1994.

_____. *Daily Customs: Native Latin American Cultures.* Vero Beach, FL: Rourke Publications, 1995.

Wood, Tim. *The Aztecs.* New York: Viking, 1992.

Index

A

Afterlife, 14–15, 19, 34, 53, 59–60
Aymara tribe, 47
Aztecs, 9, 17, 18–27

B

Ball games, ritual, 30–31, 35
Burial rites, 14–15, 39, 34, 44 (photo), 59–60

C

Cahita tribe, 7, 12
Chacmools, 28 (photo)
Chavin tribe, 45–46
Chimu tribe, 44 (photo), 46–47
Chosen Women, 51
Coca plant, 42 (photo)
Cochimi tribe, 8, 10
Cora tribe, 7, 8, 9, 11–12, 13, 14–15
Cortés, Hernando, 23–24, 27
Cuna tribe, 37, 38–39

D

Desano tribe, 58, 59

G

Great Temple of Tenochtitlán, 23–24, 26–27

H

Huaca, 47
Huichol tribe, 7, 8, 12, 14–15
Huizilopochtli, 20, 23

I

Inca, 45, 47, 49–53

J

Jaguars, 30, 45

K

Kaipo tribe, 56 (photo), 58, 59 (photo)
Kogi tribe, 39–42

L

Lord Inca, 51

M

Macaws, 54 (photo), 57
Maize goddesses, 20 (photo)
Makineri, 55
Mamas, 41
Manco Capac, 49
Marake, 59
Matsigenka tribe, 55–56
Maya, 5, 28 (photo), 29, 31–35
Mitotes, 11–12
Moche tribe, 46
Moctezuma, 27
Moon gods, 56, 57

N

New Fire Ceremony, 19, 25 (photo), 26

O

Olmecs, 17–18, 29–31
Orinoco tribe, 57

P

Payes, 58

Peyote, 10
Pima tribe, 6 (photo), 7 (photo), 10
Popul Vuh, 32
Priests
    Aztec, 21, 23
    Incan, 51, 52
    Kogi, 41
    Mayan, 32, 33 (photo)
Pyramid of the Sun, 31

Q

Quetzalcoatl, 9, 16 (photo), 18, 24 (photo), 27, 35

R

Rain ceremonies, 7, 12

S

Sacrifices
    Aztec, 19, 26–27
    Incan, 51–52
    Mayan, 32
    Toltec, 18
Seri tribe, 8, 10
Shamans, 10–11, 22–23, 38–39, 57–58
Sun gods, 9, 19, 47, 57

T

Taino tribe, 42–43

Tairona tribe, 37, 38, 39
    Kogi, 39–42
Tarahumara tribe, 7, 8, 9 (photo), 10, 12 (photo), 15
Temple of the Sun, 49–50 (photo)
Tepehuan tribe, 7, 9, 10, 15
Tlaloc, 20, 23
Toltecs, 16 (photo), 17, 34–35
Tonalpouqui, 23
Tukano tribe, 58
Twin myths, 57

V

Viracocha, 47, 48 (photo)

W

Wayana tribe, 59
Writing, Mayan, 31–32

X

Xilonen, 20 (photo)
Xingu tribe, 57

Y

Yanomami tribe, 56, 57, 60 (photo)
Yaqui tribe, 8, 13

Photo Credits

Cover: ©Denver Museum of Natural History/Department of Anthropology; p. 6: ©Jay W. Sharp/DDB Stock Photo; p. 8: Library of Congress; p. 9: ©Robert B. Pickering; pp. 12, 20, 22, 30, 33, 38, 43, 44, 48, 50, 53: ©Robert Frerck/Odyssey Productions/Chicago; p. 13: ©Dirk Weisheit/DDB Stock Photo; pp. 18, 24, 25: ©Werner Forman Archive/Art Resource, NY; p. 28: ©D. Aubry/Odyssey Productions/Chicago; p. 35: ©Erich Lessing/Art Resource, NY; p. 36: ©Suzanne L. Murphy/DDB Stock Photo; p. 42: ©Gregory G. Dimijian/Photo Researchers, Inc.; p. 54: ©R. Perron/DDB Stock Photo; p. 56: ©Saulo Petean/DDB Stock Photo; p. 59: ©Nair Benedicto/DDB Stock Photo; p. 60: ©Claudia Andujar/Photo Researchers, Inc.

J Snow, C.O. trained in Orthoptics at St. Louis Children's Hospital where he became Certified in 2001. He currently practices Orthoptics at the Penn State Hershey Eye Center in Hershey, PA.

For more info, visit:
pennstatehershey.org/eyecenter

Sheena Hisiro has been drawing since she could hold a pencil. She currently lives in Astoria, NY, where she is still drawing and loving every minute of it. Sheena has a BFA in Communications Design from Pratt Institute. She has illustrated 11 other books including *The Boy Who Cried Wolf!*, *My Glasses*, *Josiah and Julia Go to Church*, and *My Pal Needs a Root Canal*.

For more info, visit:
oodlesofdoodles.tumblr.com

ISBN 978-0-97185980-7

The Adventures of Patch Cat and Strabismouse

A Detective Duo Out to Uncover the Mystery of Strabismus and Amblyopia

written by
J. Snow, C.O.

illustrated by
Sheena Hisiro

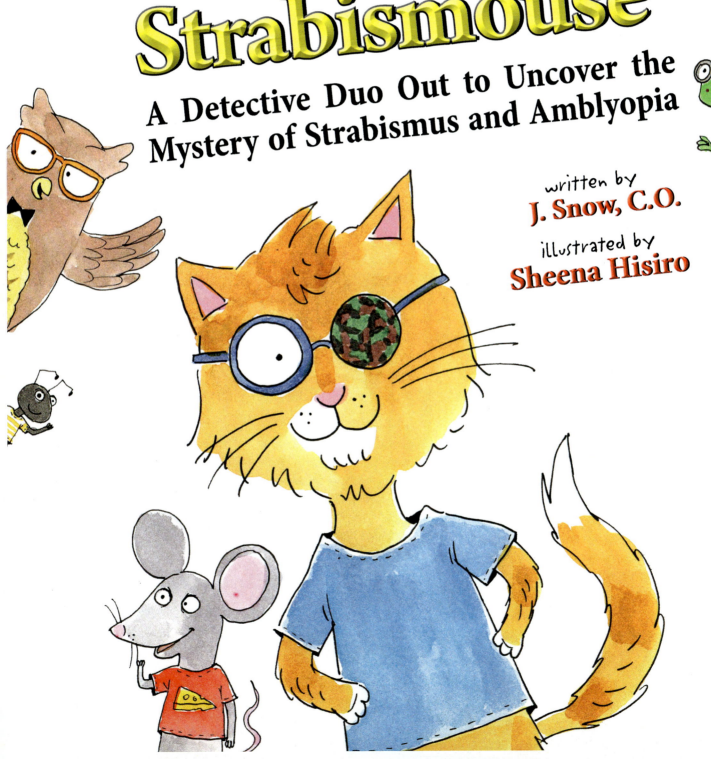

Amblyopia (pronounced AM-BLEE-O-PEE-UH)– a condition in which a healthy eye does not develop to its full visual potential due to some interruption during the period of normal visual development – birth to around the age of 7 to 9 years old.

Strabismus (pronounced STRAH-BISS-MUSS) – a condition where the eyes are not straight.

Strabismouse – a mouse with strabismus.

**T**his book is dedicated to all the children who complied with their amblyopia treatment as directed by their Eye Doctor and recovered useful and meaningful vision which they will be able to enjoy for the rest of their lives - and to the parents who helped them achieve it.

A special thanks to Dr. Joel Weinstein, Dr. Amanda Ely, and Amy Crockett for their assistance in completing this book.
--j.s.

For Liz.
--s.h.

Publication of:
Richmond Products, Inc.
4400 Silver Ave.
Albuquerque, NM 87109
www.richmondproducts.com

ISBN 0-9718598-0-9
ISBN-13: 978-0-9718598-0-9

Text copyright © 2012 by J Snow, C.O.
Illustrations copyright © 2012 by Sheena Hisiro.
Graphic Design by Sheena Hisiro.
First Edition, 2012. All rights reserved.

NOTICE

Richmond Products, Inc.

Strabismouse

eam Up?" asked Strabismouse. "Yeah," replied Patch Cat, "by teaming up we can share what we know about our eyes with each other, and then look for others to share what they know about their eyes."

"O.K.," Strabismouse said as he pulled up a small rock and sat down, "I'll go first." Patch Cat then sat down upon the grass in the warm sun to make himself comfortable.

Taking a deep breath of the fresh country air Strabismouse began to share with Patch Cat how his eyes work. "I have strabismus. Strabismus is when both eyes are not straight. One eye will point at what you want to see, but the other

eye may drift up, down, in, or out. Sometimes the eye is never straight. But in other cases the eye is straight part of the time, and then drifts away part of the time. Sometimes it is only one eye that drifts, while other times the eyes take turns – sometimes the left eye drifts while the right eye is straight and other times the right eye drifts while the left eye remains straight."

"Wow!" Patch Cat exclaimed. "That is a lot of information. I do have a few questions. If your eyes are pointing at two different things, do you see both things at the same time?"

"No," replied Strabismouse. "Over time your brain learns to ignore the image from the eye that is drifting because it learns that you are not trying to look at that image."

"Hmmm…" thought Patch Cat. "How long does the brain take to learn this?"

"Well, when you are born with strabismus like I was, the brain learns it very quickly and you are never really aware of seeing two different images or seeing the same image in two different places. It is your brain's way of helping you see the world as it appears."

"That makes sense" Patch Cat said. "Now you mentioned different types of strabismus, which type do you have?"

"Well," Strabismouse started, "my eyes take turns crossing in, so that is called an alternating strabismus."

"Why do the eyes take turns drifting in some people and in other people only one eye drifts? Is one way better than the other?" Patch Cat asked.

"Well it's up to the brain. Sometimes the brain chooses to always use one eye and let the other drift and sometimes the brain chooses to take turns with the eyes. There is no telling which way the brain will choose. I do know if your brain takes turns using one eye and then the other, each eye

may likely develop normally. So it may be less troublesome if your strabismus is alternating. But in both cases the ability of your brain to learn how to use both eyes together can be greatly decreased. Now, if the brain only uses one eye and lets the other eye drift, the eye that the brain uses may develop normally but the eye that always drifts may not develop normally. So the drifting eye often times does not see as well as the other eye. I think this is called amblyopia or lazy eye."

"It is!" exclaimed Patch Cat, who has a lazy eye himself and wears a patch to treat it. He then asked "And, can I assume

that you do not have amblyopia since your brain takes turns using one eye and then the other?"

"That is correct! My brain takes turns using one eye and then the other eye so both of my eyes have developed normally and see fine."

Then Strabismouse proceeded to tell Patch Cat that lazy eye refers to a situation where one eye does not see as well as the other eye. It does not refer to a condition where an eye drifts – as many people think.

"What causes an eye to drift?" asked Patch Cat.

"Well, there are different reasons why an eye can drift. Each eye has six muscles that help move the eyes into all the different positions we use to look at things. They work together to make sure the eyes move together. Sometimes one of these muscles may be stronger or weaker than the other muscles so it does not pull as much, or pulls too much, and it causes the eye to drift away from the other eye. Also, sometimes a person needs glasses and when he is not wearing them he has to focus really hard to see clearly. When you focus really hard on something it may cause your eyes to cross."

"What are some of the other reasons?" Patch Cat asked.

"Let's see, it does not happen as much but if one of your eyes is not healthy it may drift because the brain is not getting a good image from it. After all, the brain has to do work to keep an eye straight. If it is not getting a good image from an eye why should it do the work to keep it straight? And sometimes something may block the eye from seeing an image, like a droopy eyelid and the eye may drift because it does not have anything to look at or any reason to stay straight."

"If your eye drifts can it be made straight again?" asked Patch Cat.

"Yes!" Strabismouse replied. "If your eyes drift because you need glasses your Eye Doctor will give you glasses. If they drift because an eye muscle is too strong or too weak your Eye Doctor can operate on the muscles to make them equal to each other. If something is blocking an image from getting to your eye, like a droopy eye lid, your Eye Doctor can do surgery to move whatever is blocking the image. If your eye drifted because it is not healthy, your Eye Doctor may be able to operate on the eye muscles to get your eye straight again, even if he cannot correct the problem that made it unhealthy."

"Wow! Now that sure was a lot of information," Patch Cat said. "It is time to give my brain a rest and enjoy this warm sun and fresh air." Strabismouse agreed. And with that Patch Cat curled up into a ball and fell fast asleep for a nice summer's nap. Strabismouse thought that was a great idea and hopped down from his rock and snuggled up in the tall grass. He listened to sounds of the birds singing off in the distance as he too fell fast asleep.

Patch Cat

he wind was blowing slightly when Patch Cat awoke. Fresh from his nap he stood up and stretched as hard as he could and let out a big yawn. He could hear the brook gently babbling in the distance and settled back down. He was content in enjoying his beautiful surroundings as Strabismouse was still asleep. Strabismouse awoke a few minutes later and also stood up and stretched feeling quite good and well rested.

"We sure did cover a lot." Patch Cat said.

Strabismouse agreed. "And now it is your turn my friend to share with me what you know about eyes. I see you are

wearing glasses and a patch on your left eye. Do you also have strabismus?"

"No" replied Patch Cat. "My eyes are purrrrfectly straight" he joked as Strabismouse laughed.

"Then why do you need the patch and glasses?"

"I do not have strabismus like you do," Patch Cat continued. "But I do have amblyopia. My right eye does not see as well as my left eye. Some people call my right eye a lazy eye."

"So why do you wear a patch on your left eye if your right eye is lazy?"

"When you have a lazy eye the goal is to improve the vision in that eye. The only way you can do this is to make the brain use it. To do this you must somehow penalize the good eye. By patching my left eye my brain has no choice but to use the right eye. Hopefully as it keeps using it, the vision in that eye will improve."

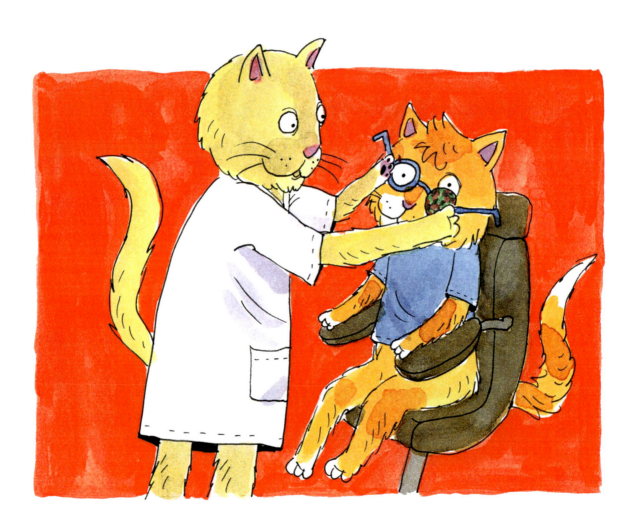

"How long does it take to improve the vision in the lazy eye?"

"It depends on a few things. First, the younger you start the easier it is to get the brain to develop the weak eye. Also by starting early you have more time to work on it before your vision is complete. Patching is more successful the earlier the problem is found and the younger the patching is started."

"What do you mean when you say – before your vision is complete?"

"Your vision develops from birth until around the age of seven to nine years old. After that your vision is pretty much completely developed and any improvement that may occur after that will be small. But some Eye Doctors will try to patch someone even after they are ten years old in the hope that there is still a chance for some improvement. The later you start to treat lazy eye the longer you have to wear a patch to improve the vision in that eye."

"How long do you have to wear the patch?"

"Again it depends on how old you are, when you start, and

how much amblyopia is present. But, in my case, I was told to patch my left eye two hours a day. Treatment can vary from a couple of months to over a year, again according to the situation."

"When we were taking our nap did that count as part of your two hours of patching?"

"No. The purpose of patching is to get your brain to use the lazy eye. When you sleep your brain is not using either eye. You need the lazy eye to be visually stimulated to improve."

"How do you do that?"

"Almost anything is visual stimulation. Walking in the woods, watching TV, playing video games, board games, coloring, and stuff like that. As long as you are not staring at the same scenery that does not change for two hours you should be helping that lazy eye."

"If you don't have strabismus how did you get amblyopia?" asked Strabismouse.

"Amblyopia, or lazy eye, occurs when for some reason a

healthy eye does not develop as well as the other eye during the time when vision develops, again from birth until around the age of seven to nine. This results in one eye not seeing as well as the other eye. There are various things that can cause it. The most common causes are needing glasses, strabismus, and something blocking the image from the eye."

Patch Cat continued, "If you need glasses that means you are either farsighted or nearsighted and your eye needs a lens in order to see clearly. Sometimes the eyes need the same power lens to see clearly. When this is the case both eyes see equal images without glasses, even if those images

may not be perfectly clear. The brain does not notice one eye as having a clearer image than the other, so it should develop both eyes equally. But glasses will still be needed to ensure that the development is complete. If the brain receives blurry images from the eyes, it may not develop them to the point where they can see 20/20 - which would be normal for healthy eyes. This is because the crisp detail of a clear image is needed for complete development. That detail is lacking in a blurry image."

"But in some cases a person may have one eye that receives an image that is blurrier than the image the other eye receives. It may go unnoticed by that person and he may not be wearing glasses to correct it. The brain may fully develop more the eye with the clearer image and develop less the eye with the blurry image.

"It would be like the brain would be saying:

'This eye is giving me a better image, so I am going to spend more time developing this eye. This other eye is giving me a blurry image so I am not going to spend as much time on it.'

Because of this the final vision will not be as good as the other eye."

Patch Cat continued, "Now, if a person has strabismus and has one eye that does not point at what the brain wants to see, the brain may choose not to develop it as well because it is not pointed at what the brain wants to see. Also, if something blocks the image from the eye, like a droopy eyelid, the brain will likely not develop the pathway to that eye because it is not getting any image from it. No visual stimulation means no visual development."

"Hmm…" Strabismouse responded. "By comparing the two lists it shows that some of the things that cause strabismus can also cause amblyopia. Likewise, strabismus can cause amblyopia and amblyopia can cause strabismus."

Patch Cat agreed. "That is correct."

"Now," Strabismouse started, "If you correct the problem that caused the amblyopia, for example, give glasses or do surgery, why do you still have to wear a patch?"

"Well," Patch Cat responded. "While you must fix the problem that caused the amblyopia that does not mean the brain will automatically start using that eye and develop it. In my case, when I received my glasses it gave both of my eyes equal images, but by that time my left eye had a head start and was more developed. My brain was in the habit

of developing the left eye much more than the right. So, despite the fact that each eye now had an equal image my brain decided to continue the habit of developing the left eye more than the right. The patch forced my brain to break that habit."

"I am confused," Strabismouse said. "If your glasses give each of your eyes an equal image how can one of your eyes see better?"

"Because it is more developed," replied Patch Cat. "What does that mean?"

"You got me Strabismouse, I am not sure I can explain it better than that. We should write that down on our list of things to find out."

"Well that is it then," Strabismouse replied, "it is time we gather our things and travel the field in search of the answers to our remaining questions about our eyes."

"I do believe you are right."

And with that Patch Cat and Strabismouse gathered everything they would need for their journey. Strabismouse found a pencil and some paper to write down what they

hope to learn. They both filled their pockets with small pieces of dried bread and fruit that they had from the day before and knew there would be plenty of water along their travels as the area was surrounded by many bountiful rivers and ponds.

Mr. Frog

he detective duo started out through a small hole in an old wooden fence that was barely standing. Strabismouse fit easily through the hole but it was a little bit of a squeeze for Patch Cat. They soon found a dirt road and they started to follow it as it wound through a tall field of grass. The blades of grass swayed in the gentle breeze that would come by every now and then. The sun was nice and warm and high in the sky. Soon they stumbled upon a small brook and they decided to walk down to get a quick drink.

As they got down to the brook they noticed a small frog lying by the side of the water watching the lily pads gliding

on the surface. "Good Day!" the frog exclaimed as he saw the two approach.

"And Good Day to you sir," Patch Cat replied. They quickly realized that the frog was wearing a pair of glasses and wondered if the frog could help them. "Mr. Frog," Patch Cat started, "I cannot help but notice that you are wearing glasses like myself, may I ask you why?"

"Certainly," Mr. Frog replied, "My right eye is more far-sighted than my left eye. The glasses help me see clearly. But since I was four years old before anyone realized I needed

glasses, I developed amblyopia. The eye that was more far-sighted did not develop as well as the eye that was not as farsighted. So, my Eye Doctor put a cloudy filter on my left eyeglass lens to help improve the vision in my right eye."

Upon hearing about Mr. Frog's filter both Patch Cat and Strabismouse became very interested. They were certain Mr. Frog could give them more information on treating amblyopia. "I have amblyopia too," Patch Cat said, "They gave me this patch to help my right eye. But I am curious, how does your filter work?"

"The filter works a lot like your patch Mr. Cat. It is a cloudy film they put on my eyeglass lens to blur the vision in my

good left eye in the hope that my brain will then choose to use my weak right eye. If my brain does use my right eye it should develop and some day see as well as my left eye."

"What is the difference between a patch and a filter?" asked Patch Cat.

"Wait... give me a second to catch up" Strabismouse exclaimed. He was taking notes as fast as he could.

"Well," Mr. Frog started, "A filter sticks to your lens so you don't have anything sticky, like an adhesive patch, on your face. I see you have a cloth patch that fits on your glasses, but some folks use adhesive patches that stick to their face. Filters are less noticeable, I bet you and your friend did not even notice mine until I told you about it. Also, the filter stays on my lens the entire time, where you take your patch off after a few hours. Also, you rarely need to replace filters, where adhesive patches have to be replaced every day or every couple of days."

"Does it work any better than a patch?"

"It pretty much works as well as a patch and gets similar results. Also, there are other things your Eye Doctor can do to your glasses to treat amblyopia."

"Like what?" asked Patch Cat as Strabismouse was quickly taking notes.

"Your Eye Doctor can give you glasses with the correct lens over the weak eye but a lens that is too strong over the good eye so it will blur the vision in that good eye."
"How does that work?"

"A strong lens makes everything look blurry for the good eye, and hopefully the brain will start using and developing the weak eye."

"That seems to make sense," Patch Cat answered. "But now I am curious, how do you know which is the best one to use?" "Well.." Mr. Frog replied, "...your Eye Doctor figures that out after examining you and discussing your eye condition with your parents."

"That makes sense Mr. Frog, but we still have one question. You mentioned that your glasses clear up the image in your right eye. So, with a clear image why does the right eye still not see as well as the left eye?"

"Hmmm..." Mr. Frog wondered, "That is a good question. To be honest I am not sure."

"Good enough, Mr. Frog," you have already been very helpful and we thank you. We will save that question for somebody else."

After saying goodbye and wishing Mr. Frog well, Patch Cat and Strabismouse gathered their things and once again started down the winding dirt road with the sun starting its downward trek across the sky.

Mr. Ant

hey did not make it far down the road until they stumbled upon an ant who was sitting beneath a small cherry blossom filled with beautiful white flowers. The ant was having a small snack of pine nuts and berries. "Well hello there," Mr. Ant said when he saw Patch Cat and Strabismouse approaching, "Would you like to join me for a snack?"

"We can do better than that..." Strabismouse replied, "We can add some dried bread and fruit and turn this snack into a feast." With that the three sat down and enjoyed a nice meal of pine nuts, dried bread and fruit. Patch Cat walked down to the brook and brought up some water in a

small leather pouch he brought with him. As they became quite full from their feast they began to relax and enjoy the breeze. They enjoyed the warmth of the sun while looking up at all the white flowers on the cherry tree. Strabismouse noticed something about Mr. Ant.

"Excuse me Mr. Ant. I do not mean to be rude. But it looks like your right pupil is much bigger than your left pupil. I only ask because as you can see my eyes are never straight. One of my eyes is always crossed in while the other is straight. As such I am very curious about the eyes. In fact, Patch Cat and I are actually on a mission this very day to try to learn as much about the eyes as we can. It appears that just maybe you could help us."

"I can certainly try," Mr. Ant replied. "I have amblyopia. My right eye sees better than my left eye. This happened because my right eye was always pointed at what my brain wanted to see, so my brain developed it well. But when I was born, my left eye crossed in and was not pointed at what my brain wanted to see, as a result my brain did not develop it as well."

"Your brain did not take turns using one eye and then the other?" Strabismouse asked.

"Unfortunately not," Mr. Ant replied, "if they had, both eyes would see fine and I would not need eye drops."

"Eye drops?"

"I put special eye drops in my good right eye which makes everything look blurry to my right eye when I look at things up close. Because of this my brain should choose to use the left eye when I am looking at things up close. Hopefully if my brain uses my left eye enough the vision in my left eye will improve. In addition to blurring the vision in my right eye it also increases the size of the pupil in my right eye as you noticed. There are various reasons why one pupil may be larger than the other pupil, for me, it is because of the

eye drops. If you have one pupil that is larger than the other and you are not on eye drops you can always go to your Eye Doctor for an exam, but it is not abnormal for your pupils to be slightly different in size."

"Will glasses help?"

"No. I do not need glasses. Glasses are for people who are nearsighted or farsighted. I am neither. My problem is that my left eye was crossed in for several years."

"But it looks straight now?"

"Yes, my Eye Doctor did surgery on my eye muscles. He weakened the muscle on the inside of my left eye that was pulling it in so now it does not pull in so much. This resulted in my eyes now being straight. I am very happy with that."

"But if your eyes are straight and you do not need glasses, why do you still need to use the eye drops?"

"It would be nice if I did not need the eye drops," Mr. Ant explained, "but while the left eye was crossed in the brain formed a habit of just developing the right eye and kind of

ignoring the left eye. The eye drop will hopefully break the brain of this habit and force the brain to develop the left eye. The brain will not just automatically start using my left eye again just because it is straight, because it did get into a habit of not paying attention to that eye for a long time."

"Force the brain?" Patch Cat asked curiously.

"Well you see, the brain wants all of the visual information in our world so it can gather information and make decisions. If we penalize the good eye by covering it or blurring it, the brain has two choices. It can continue to see blurry and not gather visual information clearly, or it can develop the weak eye so it will see better and will send the brain all of the visual information around us. Most often the brain chooses to develop the weak eye. That is why amblyopia treatment is so effective."

"Do you know if one treatment is more effective than another?" Strabismouse asked.

"It seems they are equally effective. Patching usually gets quicker results at first and then slows down, where blurring the good eye with eye drops seems to get more steady results, but after nine months or so the total improvement

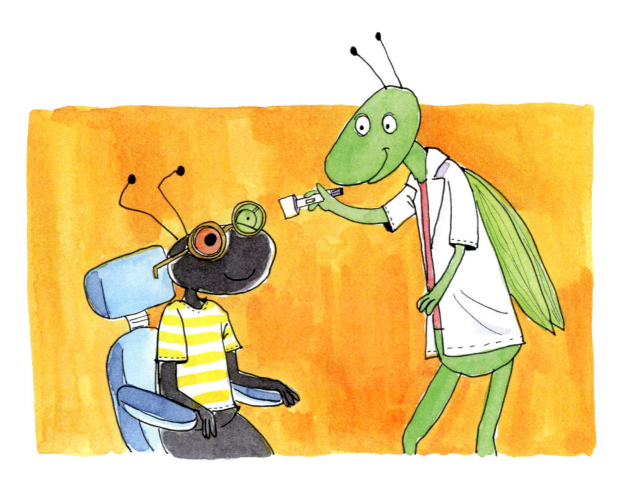

for each method is pretty much the same."

"If the results are pretty much the same why do they use different treatments, why not just have everyone use the patch?" asked Patch Cat.

"That is a great question," Mr. Ant replied, "You see, while the results are about the same, each method is only effective if people with amblyopia follow their Eye Doctor's instructions. Some people do not want to wear a patch so the Eye Doctor will try a filter. Some people do not want to wear a patch or filter so the Eye Doctor will use the eye drop.

Patches are nice because you know exactly how long the treatment is in place. Eye drops are nice because someone who resists amblyopia treatment cannot take an eye drop out like they can take a filter or patch off. So the different methods exist in order to find the one that is the best for each person. Plus, if the amblyopia is severe, meaning the vision in the weak eye is very poor, eye drops may not be effective. The brain may still prefer the eye with the drops over the weak eye. The key to amblyopia treatment is getting the brain to use the weaker eye in order to develop it."

"Wow!" Patch Cat exclaimed. "This is certainly some great information. We are really learning a lot about amblyopia and strabismus today." Strabismouse agreed as he was taking notes as fast as he could while listening to Mr. Ant.

"Now Mr. Ant, that just leaves one question. We have heard about the brain developing an eye after it has a clear image. If the eye has a clear image how does the brain not get that same image?"

"Well I must be honest with you Mr. Cat and Mr. Mouse, I am not sure."

"That is O.K. Maybe we will find the answer to that later,

you have been very helpful and we thank you."

"It was my pleasure. After all because of you I had a great feast today. You must come back some time so we can do it again."

"We will certainly do that," Patch Cat replied as he and Strabismouse lumbered back onto the dirt road and continued into the field. The sun was still warm but on its way down as was evident by the long narrow shadows that were cast on the ground.

Mr. Owl

atch cat and Strabismouse walked along the road as it dipped and turned through the field. The sun started to set as the day was coming to an end. They were starting to look for a place where they could curl up and sleep for the night when they noticed Wise Old Mr. Owl was just waking up from his nap on an old fence post. "Good day Mr. Owl," they both said.

"It was a fine day indeed" Mr. Owl replied, "and hopefully it will be even a better night."

Once again they noticed Mr. Owl was wearing glasses.

"Mr. Owl," Patch Cat started, "I see you have glasses like me. Would you mind if I ask why?"

"Not at all Mr. Cat. I have glasses because my eyes are not straight and I have double vision."

"You have strabismus?" interrupted Strabismouse.

"Ah, you know the proper name for it, why yes I do Mr. Mouse."

"I have strabismus too as you can see Mr. Owl. But what I do not understand is that my brain learned to ignore the second image so I do not see double, or two of things. Did your brain not learn to ignore the second image?"

"That is correct. The brain can learn quite easily to ignore a second image from strabismus when it occurs at a young age. It is called suppression. But after the brain has gotten into the habit of always using both eyes for years and then you develop strabismus later in life, like my brain did, you cannot easily ignore, or suppress, the second image. You end up seeing two of the same object, or have double vision."

"Is there anything that can be done for it?"

"Well the treatment is similar to the treatment you have for strabismus and amblyopia. I can wear a patch on one eye to block the second image. I can wear a filter on one eye to blur the second image so the second image does not bother me. Or, I may be able to get surgery on my eye muscles to try to straighten my eyes which would bring the two images together. There are advantages and disadvantages for every method. When you wear a patch or filter on your glasses it does get rid of your double vision, but you are not using your eyes together and that can affect your depth perception, or your ability to see in 3-D. If you get surgery, and it is successful, it does get rid of your double vision and then you can use both eyes together. The problem is sometimes your eyes are still not straight after the surgery and you may

still see double."

"How did you deal with your double vision?"

"I had a pair of glasses made that has a prism in it. Prisms shift light. So, if my eye is shifted, or crossed inward, the prism shifts the light outward so it puts those light rays back onto the part of my eye where they belong - the part of my eye the light would be on if my eye was straight. This way my brain is not even aware that my eye is crossed in and I see one single image. No more double vision. The best part is I am still using both eyes together."

"That sounds great! Why doesn't everyone with double vision use a prism?"

"Well, the prism will make your eyeglass lens a little thicker and things may look more blurry and some people do not like that. Also if you need a large prism it may be too much to put into an eyeglass lens. Sometimes the prisms do not work and you still have double vision. However, when they do work they are a great option."

"Wow!" Patch Cat said again. "We have learned so much today about the eyes. It was truly a very good day."

"Ask him your last question," Strabismouse whispered to Patch Cat.

"Do you think he will know?" Patch Cat responded.

"He is a Wise Old Owl, is he not?" Strabismouse answered.

"Ask me what?" Mr. Owl asked, now quite curious.

"Well," Patch Cat began, "we have learned so much about the eyes today, but one thing still puzzles us. We have asked everyone, but no one seems to know the answer."

"The answer to what?" Mr. Owl asked.

"We understand why if an eye needs glasses and does not have them, it will see blurry. And we understand if an eye is drifting why it may not see as well. But, if an eye is healthy, straight and wearing glasses so it is getting a good crisp clear image – how can it still not see well? What does it mean when someone says it has not developed well?"

"Ahhh, well done boys, you have finally gotten to the heart of the vision matter. You see, vision is actually a product of a few things. First, as you know, you do need an eye that is healthy, straight, and does not need glasses, or is wearing glasses if it needs them. This ensures the retina, which records the image and is located at the back of the eye, receives a crisp clear image. Now, in order for someone to clearly see something this recorded image must now be sent to the back of the brain where it can be interpreted. The pathway the image travels from the eye to the back of

the brain is called the visual pathway.

Think of the visual pathway as a bridge. All the parts of this bridge are present when you are born but they are not yet connected. As your brain begins to realize there is a clear image on the retina it starts to put the bridge together in order to get that image from the eye to the brain. The more of the bridge that gets built, the more ability it has to carry that image back to the brain. Now, under normal conditions the brain will build that bridge nicely and it will carry that image from the eye to the brain maintaining its original crisp clear form. However, when certain things occur the brain stops building that bridge. You have learned about some of those things today.

You know, if an eye is not pointed at what the brain wants to see because of strabismus the brain may stop building that bridge – it figures why should it build the bridge if it is only going to carry an image it does not want. If an eye has a blurry image because it needs glasses the brain may only build the bridge a little bit. This is because you would not need a complete bridge to carry a blurry image; a poorly built bridge would be capable of carrying a blurry image. So, amblyopia actually refers to a situation where something kept the brain from building a complete bridge. Or,

more accurately, a situation where the visual pathway did not develop to the point whcre it can keep an image fully intact while carrying it from the eye to the brain.

I'll give you one more example. Farmer Brown down the road takes a whole truckload of eggs to the market once a week. The market is about ten miles from his farm. The road is nice and smooth. When he gets to the market all of his eggs are in good shape. But, if he drove down a poorly developed or incomplete road that was bumpy and had many potholes, most of his eggs would be cracked by the time he gets to the market. The poor road would make it

impossible for him to carry his eggs to the market without breaking. In that same way, consider an image that is crisp and clear when the eye receives it. That same image may be blurry by the time it reaches the brain if it travels across a poorly developed visual pathway. I know that was a pretty long answer boys, but does that help at least a little?"

"That was fantastic!" said Patch Cat. "I understand it fully now! So when we patch, use an eye drop, or a filter over our good eye, we are trying to get the brain to start working harder to build the bridge, or develop the visual pathway, to the weak eye.

"Precisely!" Mr. Owl said.

"Wow!" Patch Cat said, "no one has ever been able to explain it to me like that before. I really feel I understand it now. You certainly are a Wise Old Owl."

"We cannot thank you enough" Strabismouse added.

"You are very welcome!" Mr. Owl replied, "I am happy I could help."

Satisfied that they had a very successful day and gathered

the information they needed they turned and headed back toward the road. Feeling very good about the day they decided to walk back home. The sky was clear and the moonlight shone brightly lighting their path. It was a good day.

The End.

Hey Kids

Take the Patch Cat and Strabismouse Pledge!

I Promise to follow the instructions of my Eye Doctor in the treatment of my lazy eye. I realize it may not always be fun but I understand with a little work now it will improve my eyesight and I will get to keep that improved vision for the rest of my life. I realize that the day will come when I will be very thankful that I did.

To The Parents:

Amblyopia treatment is only effective if there is a strong compliance to the treatment plan outlined by your Eye Doctor. As you know, sometimes as a parent you have to "pick your battles". There are few battles more important than your child's vision. Some children do not like the treatment methods for amblyopia and put up strong resistance to them. As many parents discover encouraging compliance can be difficult in some children. However, the alternative is a lifetime of reduced vision since amblyopia therapy is much less effective in older children. If your child is resistant to amblyopia therapy contact your Eye Doctor and ask him about things you can do to try to increase compliance.

A Message from Richmond Products

Your child's eye care professional will recommend the type of patch and a schedule for wearing the eye covering. Patches are available in four types and each has its advantages and disadvantages. You may start with one type and then need to change to another to accommodate the patching your child will tolerate. This needs to be discussed with your child's eye care professional.

Below are listed some of the available types:

Adhesive patches stick to the skin around the child's eye providing full coverage. This prevents any "peeking." Adhesive patches are a one-time use only patch.

Slip-Cover patches are designed for children that wear glasses. The patch attaches at the temple and nose piece of the frame.

Foils come in various grades to block the clarity of the dominant eye. They adhere to the child's glasses.

Traditional eye patches are are cupped to avoid contact with eye lashes.

You can order online at www.richmondproducts.com/shop then keyword "Patch" or by calling 505-275-2406.